Becoming an Organizational Scholar

T0329685

To Nina and Ana, my raisons d'être. (Tomislav)

To the girls in my life. Marisa, for being and smiling. Barbara, for loving and supporting me all the way. Marinka, for doing everything a mother can for her child. Sushi, for sitting at my feet in such a loyal manner when I was going through my academic odyssey. (Matej)

To academic givers who remained anonymous but have influenced our career paths tremendously.

Becoming an Organizational Scholar

Navigating the Academic Odyssey

Edited by

Tomislav Hernaus

University of Zagreb, Croatia

Matej Černe

University of Ljubljana, Slovenia

 Edward Elgar

PUBLISHING

Cheltenham, UK • Northampton, MA, USA

Published by
Edward Elgar Publishing Limited
The Lypiatts
15 Lansdown Road
Cheltenham
Glos GL50 2JA
UK

Edward Elgar Publishing, Inc.
William Pratt House
9 Dewey Court
Northampton
Massachusetts 01060
USA

Paperback edition 2022

A catalogue record for this book
is available from the British Library

Library of Congress Control Number: 2020950875

This book is available electronically in the **Elgar**online
Business subject collection
http://dx.doi.org/10.4337/9781839102073

ISBN 978 1 83910 206 6 (cased)
ISBN 978 1 83910 207 3 (eBook)
ISBN 978 1 80392 751 0 (paperback)

Printed and bound in Great Britain by T Books Limited, Padstow, Cornwall

Contents

Figures

Editors and contributors

EDITORS

Tomislav Hernaus is Associate Professor at the Faculty of Economics and Business (University of Zagreb, Croatia) and a Visiting Professor at the School of Economics and Business (University of Ljubljana, Slovenia). He has also been a Visiting Scholar at the Marshall School of Business (University of Southern California, USA). He holds the Certificate in Organization Design received from the Center for Effective Organizations, Los Angeles. His multi-level research interests include: organization design, business process management, human resources (HR) organization, work design and job interventions, innovative work behavior, and knowledge hiding. He is the author or co-author of four books, a dozen book chapters, and a significant number of scientific papers published in refereed journals such as the *Human Resource Management Journal, Human Resource Development Quarterly, Journal of Knowledge Management, Employee Relations, Expert Systems with Applications, Journal of Managerial Psychology* and *Business Process Management Journal*. He has received several awards and honors for his scientific contribution (e.g. the National Science Award of the Republic of Croatia, Highly Commended Award Winner at the Literati Network Awards for Excellence, EDAMBA top 10 dissertation awards, the Emerald/EMBRI Business Research Award for Emerging Researchers). He serves as co-editor of the *Dynamic Relationships Management Journal*, is an editorial board member of the *European Management Journal* and *Baltic Journal of Management*, and currently holds the position of AOM–HR Division ambassador for Croatia.

Matej Černe is Associate Professor at the School of Economics and Business (University of Ljubljana, Slovenia) and a Visiting Professor at the Faculty of Economics and Business (University of Zagreb, Croatia). He has served professionally as Head of the Open Innovation Systems Laboratory and Head of the Centre for Innovation Research, CERINNO, within the Centre of Excellence for Biosensors, Instrumentation, and Process Control (COBIK). At COBIK, he was active in the co-creation of disruptive solutions for hi-tech entrepreneurship and fostering innovation capacities at the individual, team, company and economy level in the Adriatic region within the PACINNO project. His research interests include non-technological innovations, creativity, organizational behavior and psychology, leadership and multi-level issues in management. He has received numerous awards for his research (e.g. Academy of Management Meetings best paper proceedings, CEEMAN Champions Award in the 'Research' category, EDAMBA top 10 dissertation awards) and his research has been published in top management and organizational behavior journals (e.g. *Academy of Management Journal, Human Resource Management, Journal of Organizational Behavior, European Journal of Work and Organizational Psychology, European Management Journal*). He also serves as an editorial board member for *The Leadership Quarterly, Human Resource Management Journal* and *Human Resource Management Review*, as Editor-in-Chief of the *Dynamic Relationships Management Journal* and as Section Editor of the *Economic and Business Review*.

CONTRIBUTORS

Eleanna Galanaki is Assistant Professor and Director of HRM Laboratory at the Athens University of Economics & Business, Greece. Her research work largely revolves around Strategic and International Human Resource Management. She is intrigued by the discourse on how the HRM practice links with performance at different levels of analysis and settings. She is a member of the editorial board of the *International Journal of Human Resource Management* and of the Editorial Advisory Board of *Employee Relations*. She also serves as a member of various bodies (OB SIG, Scientific Council, Executive Board) at the European Academy of Management (EURAM).

Ante Glavaš is Associate Professor of Organizational Behavior at the Grossman School of Business (University of Vermont [UVM], USA). He earned his PhD in Organizational Behavior from Case Western Reserve University, and joined UVM's Grossman School of Business in 2017. He has published numerous articles on corporate social responsibility, and was honored to receive the Emerald Citations award for his influential work in this area. Being a passionate teacher, he received The Outstanding Teaching Award for Management while working at the University of Notre Dame, as well as the Presidential Medal of Honor in Croatia.

Markus Hällgren is Professor of Management at Umeå School of Business and Economics (Umeå University, Sweden). He is the founder and leader of the international interdisciplinary research program "Extreme Environments – Everyday Decisions", and co-founder and organizer of the international network "Organising Extreme Contexts". Markus also co-founded the "Projects-as-Practice" approach. He has been a visiting researcher at Stanford

University (Scancor and Department of Sociology). His main research interests are sensemaking, extreme contexts and temporary organizations.

Spencer Harrison is an Associate Professor of Organizational Behavior at INSEAD (Paris, France). His area of expertise focuses on creating, coordinating and connecting. His research has been recognized through awards including the INFORMS Dissertation Award Finalist, the Academy of Management Journal Best Paper of the Year Award Finalist, and the Journal of Management Best Paper Award. His research has been published in top management journals including the *Academy of Management Journal, Organization Science, Journal of Applied Psychology* and the *Journal of Management*.

Amy Van Looy is currently an Associate Professor with the Faculty of Economics and Business Administration, Ghent University, Belgium, and is head of the research cluster "Process orientation" at the UGentMIS Management Information Systems research group. Her research interests include business process management and digital innovation. Her work has been published in highly-ranked academic journals and presented at top conferences worldwide. Previously, she worked as an IT consultant at CSC. Amy received the Masters degree in political sciences and the Ph.D. degree in applied economics. She is the recipient of the "Highest Award for Achievement" at the Dale Carnegie Consulting Program in 2007, the "Award for Best Contribution" at the OnTheMove Academy in 2010, as well as paper nominations (e.g., BPM2018) and paper rewards (e.g., BPM2019). Amy was nominated in the top 10 for "Young ICT Lady of the year 2014" by the Belgian magazine *DataNews*, and was recognized as a tech role model by the non-profit "InspiringFifty Belgium" in 2020 (i.e., for being one of Belgium's 50 most inspiring women in technology).

Jan Mendling is Professor with the Institute for Information Business (Vienna University of Economics and Business, Austria). His research interests include various topics in the area of business process management and information systems. He has published in *ACM Transactions on Software Engineering and Methodology, IEEE Transaction on Software Engineering, Information Systems, Data & Knowledge Engineering* and *Decision Support Systems*. His PhD thesis has won the Heinz-Zemanek-Award of the Austrian Computer Society and the German Targion-Award for dissertations in the area of strategic information management.

Hana Milanov is a Professor of International Entrepreneurship and Academic Director of the EMBA in Innovation and Business Creation at the Technical University of Munich (Germany), where she has also served as TUM's Senior Vice President for International Alliances and Alumni, and continues to serve as a Board Member at the Center for Digital Technology in Management. Her research has been published in journals such as the *Strategic Management Journal*, the *Journal of Business Venturing* and the *Academy of Management Perspectives* and her work was elected as a finalist in Strategic Management Society Best Paper and Heizer Doctoral Dissertation in Entrepreneurship awards. Hana finished her doctoral studies at Indiana University. Prior to TUM, she was an Entrepreneurship Professor at IE Business School (Madrid), where she still teaches as adjunct faculty.

Kristina Potočnik is Senior Lecturer in Human Resource Management and Head of the Organisation Studies Group at the University of Edinburgh Business School (United Kingdom). Her research mainly explores diverse factors that shape individual, team and organizational performance and resilience, looking particularly at the role of creative and innovative performance in different organizational settings. She has published her work in journals such as *Organization Science, Journal of Management, Journal of Occupational and Organizational Psychology*, and *European Journal of Work and Organizational Psychology*.

Alf Rehn is Head of Section and Professor of Innovation, Design and Management at the University of Southern Denmark (Denmark). He is an internationally active keynote speaker and strategic advisor from startups to Fortune 500 companies. His academic work focuses on issues of power, exclusion, creativity and innovation, and often builds on counterintuitive analyses of core assumptions within management thinking. His research has been published in journals like *Organization Studies, Journal of Business Research* and *European Journal of International Management*.

Sonja Rispens is Assistant Professor in Cooperative Organizational Behavior at the Human Performance Management Group (Eindhoven University of Technology, the Netherlands). Her research focuses on cooperation, conflict, and deviance in organizations, predominantly in the context of teams and work groups. Sonja has published in journals such as *Academy of Management Journal, European Journal of Work and Organizational Psychology, Negotiation and Conflict Management Research*, and others. She has received several awards for her academic work.

Joana Story is Associate Professor of Management at the São Paolo School of Business Administration (Fundação Getulio Vargas, Brazil). She has received several academic honors and awards. Her research interests are leadership and organizational behavior in organizations in global contexts. She has publications in prominent international journals such as *Journal of Management*,

Human Resource Management, Journal of Business Ethics and *Journal of Managerial Psychology.*

Karoline Strauss is Professor at ESSEC Business School (Paris, France). Her research focuses on individuals' relationship with the future and how an imagined future can impact careers and experiences at work, as well as how individuals attempt to influence proactively their own future, and the future of their organization. Karoline's work has been published in journals such as *Journal of Applied Psychology, Journal of Management, Journal of Organizational Behavior* and others.

Jelena Zikic is Associate Professor and Graduate Program Director at the School of Human Resource Management (York University, Canada). Her program of research and expertise centers on career transitions of diverse populations (e.g. unemployed, entrepreneurs, baby boomers, migrants), stress and coping. Her work has appeared in journals such as *Journal of Organizational Behavior, Human Relations, Human Resource Management Journal, Journal of Managerial Psychology* and *Journal of Occupational and Organizational Psychology,* among others.

'This book offers personal stories of rabbits beating wolves, jumping off mountains into the unknown, sharing advice and guidance to help grow one's career. It's incredibly useful; not least a copy would have helped dodge many trainwrecks learning the ropes. Have a read.'
Giles Hirst, Australian National University, Australia

'The editors were too modest in targeting this inspirational global collection of fascinating individual stories primarily for the rising cohort of doctoral candidates and early-career researchers. School leaders worldwide should encourage all their faculty members to read the book, reflect and jointly reinvent their respective institutions as exciting and synergetic archipelagos of the faculty individual Ithacas.'
Milenko Gudic, Founding and Managing Director of IMTA, Slovenia

'The novelty of this volume is exceptional. To have had such a resource at the start of my academic career would have helped me immensely to navigate many of the unexpected twists and turns along the way. The collection of insights from contributors globally, explaining their very personal experiences, makes the text both highly relatable and relevant!'
Elaine Farndale, The Pennsylvania State University, USA

'Working in academia is a wonderful privilege but it can also be a hugely uncertain and at times intimidating world to join and find one's place in. Becoming an Organizational Scholar: Navigating the Academic Odyssey provides a host of rich and very personal lessons from a diverse and inspiring group of international scholars based on their lived experiences of that world. The narrative style makes for a compelling read and it is the book I wish I had when I started on my journey. I highly recommend it.'
David Collings, Dublin City University, Ireland

'The academic career is fulfilling, but its passage is bumpy, especially in the early years. This unique book offers a roadmap via personal stories of a diverse group of mid-career management scholars who have mastered the journey. The stories are appealing, and offer much to learn. Their collection is compelling, making the book an essential resource for early-career organization scientists, program administrators, and academic consultants.'
Fariborz Damanpour, Rutgers University, USA

'This book provides a timely and wide-ranging series of international case studies of routes to becoming an academic, transitions from graduate student to academic status, balancing on the four-legged stool of academic practice (research, teaching, service and entrepreneurship), and developing an academic career. It is a lively and informative read for junior researchers planning for or in the early stages of academic careers.'
Stanley E. Taylor, Durham University, UK

PART I

Preparing for the voyage

1. An academic career: initiating the journey

Tomislav Hernaus and Matej Černe

Estimated reading time: **19 minutes and 35 seconds**.

CHAPTER HIGHLIGHTS

- Academia, with all its appeals related to pursuing your passions in an autonomous manner, represents a risky career journey that a very few manage to master successfully.
- Each scholar can and should develop his or her own *modus operandi*, a unique way of practicing scholarship that will eventually be effective within his or her specific academic environment.
- Higher education trends and ongoing reshaping of academic work impose a lot of imperatives for scholars, particularly young(er) ones.
- In this volume, instead of speaking about *the average* or *universal scholar*, we put upfront an idea of *a different* or *authentic scholar*.
- Our intention is to promote prosocial behavior, rejuvenate academic citizenship and give a new boost to academic discovery.

A journey of a thousand miles begins with a single step.
Lao Tzu

SCHOLAR(SHIP) AT THE CROSSROADS

A first step, whether made by a child or an apprentice, is characterized by a great human desire and is mostly driven by positive expectations. French people like to say: "Quand on veut, on peut [When we want, we can]!" However, we should not disregard a great amount of uncertainty present in decision-making, usually stemming from missing self-confidence, lack of knowledge and/or from not having experience. Both our goals and circumstances create the risk we have to take to prosper. Without taking the initiative in our lives, things will not happen by themselves, certainly not in a way we would like them to.

The world of academia is not so different from everyday life. Actually, it represents the real world to numerous scholars worldwide. Some of them are well-established university professors and research scientists with long and successful careers, others are young scholars or doctoral candidates that strive to enter and leave their mark within the field. While the former generally have secure job positions and already established routine practices, the latter are still trying to find their place under the sun. Most of them are aware of a very broad range of opportunities offered by academia, but they might struggle with a significant number of academic pitfalls and dead ends that could pop up along the way. Seductive as it is, academia represents a risky career journey that a very few manage to master successfully. It easily drags you in and shows you the beauty of the skies, but when you want to do something heavenly, it is anything but easy. Someone who has not tried it cannot know it.

Making a career in academia is not simple or predictable. Often you will be left on your own to make very important decisions. There will be no one to ask, or nothing to read about a particular topic of interest. You will not be able to find a solution easily or receive necessary advice about your research, primarily because there are no easy answers, or you are supposed to create one. However, besides being creative and producing a new science, an academic career is also strongly determined by the capability of handling ourselves and organizing our academic activities. Working within a knowledge-intensive occupation that provides you with a high level of autonomy, each scholar can and should develop his or her own *modus operandi*, a unique way of practicing scholarship that will eventually be effective within his or her specific academic environment.

Being original or even artistic in a sense is not easy, especially not today when scholarship is a hard game to play. Higher education trends and ongoing reshaping of academic work impose a lot of imperatives for scholars, particularly young(er) ones. The decline of budget funding and the emergence of "academic capitalism" (Slaughter & Leslie, 1997), together with increased competition and further globalization of the academic profession, have been detrimental to academic work in many respects during recent years (Ylijoki, 2005). Not only do (younger) faculty nowadays need to do "more" than their (experienced) forerunners in terms of teaching or research, but they also have uncertain promotion possibilities, circumscribed employment appointments, and are required to fulfill "inhuman" expectations placed by tenure committees. Obviously, the faculty work is changing – the research requirements, a teaching load, administrative and service demands, the diversity of appointments, the necessary skills and abilities (Austin & Wulff, 2004).

Aforementioned external threats make scholarly beginnings even harder to handle effectively. The increasing pressure on junior faculty to publish more and achieve distinction in their discipline (Schuster & Finkelstein, 2006) often leads to a burnout and makes professoriate a less attractive workplace. Those who manage to survive largely depict their work in very negative terms: "killing", "chaotic", "overloaded", "conflicting", "mad", and "disappointing" (Ylijoki, 2005). While some authors (e.g., Arnowitz, 2001, in Kalleberg, 2011) believe that the job of a university professor is becoming precarious, we are convinced that it is still "the best job in the world". You just need to know how to make "the right" moves.

THE ACADEMIC VALUE OF SHARING AND COLLABORATION

A common truth is that no person knows everything. Neither did Aristotle, Leonardo da Vinci, or Alexander von Humboldt. While they were undoubtedly the most knowledgeable people during their times, and have greatly entrusted our civilization with their knowledge, nowadays a highly-educated individual on average probably has more information than they had. The logic is clear – "if we want to see further, we need to stand on the shoulders of giants" (Newton, 1675, in Turnbull, 1959).

The same is applicable to reaching the master level in the academic profession. The need to better understand the faculty was explicitly recognized by 1942 when Logan Wilson published *The Academic Man* in an effort to systematize what was known of these professionals responsible for higher education (Schuster & Finkelstein, 2006). Since then, a traditional academic value of sharing has resulted in several very good and thought-provoking books of essays published about the academic life (for example, Andre & Frost, 1997; Deneef & Goodwin, 2007; Frost & Taylor, 1996; Hällgren, 2014). They are certainly a must-read literature for upcoming generations of scholars. Written by world-leading and well-accepted scholars, reflective essays offer deep insights into different aspects of the academic world. The notable knowledge base and long-career experience accumulated by hardened authors, translated into hints and advice, represent "a vitamin food" for each junior, and even for a large number of mid- and senior-career stage scholars.

However, we believe that things are not any more as they were. The world of academia is in constant flux, the academic work is adaptive and revolutionary, and the traditional understanding of the role of the professional academic has been strongly challenged (Fleck & Hess, 2014). The criteria of being a successful scholar, as well as pathways of becoming one are much different than 30–40 years ago. It is not that "the old school" professors no longer have legitimacy; yet senior scholars "need to stop setting a bad example" (see

Harley, 2019) in a world where traditional academic values are in conflict with processes of rationalization in business schools and universities. We thus entertain the possibility that young(er) scholars and academic apprentices could also hear something and learn a bit from the personal observations of their somewhat more experienced yet still mid-career colleagues.

This book is not intended to be yet another publication manual or a writing guide for doctoral students. It is not an academic survival handbook either. The aim of the book is to qualitatively analyze individuals' idiosyncratic lived experiences of academic careers. We do not want to be over-troubled with university and scholarly ratings, journal impact factors, citation rates, and similar quantitative bibliometric measures. While these numbers are definitely shaping perceptions of academic success and will be mentioned to a certain extent throughout the book, our intention is to apply a narrative approach. Instead of speaking about *the average* or *universal scholar*, we would like to put upfront an idea of *a different* or *authentic scholar*.

Each of us (volume contributors) is a *differentia specifica*. We have different goals, different backgrounds, different experiences, different skills and abilities, different work environments. On the other hand, we are not so very different at all. We definitely struggle with the same work challenges, study somewhat related organizational topics, and probably mostly share similar academic values. We are thoroughly immersed in our discipline and academic work. Our differences and similarities go hand in hand. By providing common ground that is supplemented with various flavors, we are looking forward to presenting readers with a well-informed, puzzling view of academic landscapes. This book does not aim to move the frontiers (i.e. to be a critical text) within the sociology of science, but its intention is to share personal stories about academic survival and scientific outreach.

THE MEMBERS OF THE CREW

Diversity is a mother of invention. However, too much diversity could be problematic. Thus, what we really need and expect for most of the time is a controlled diversity. This book certainly provides a diversity of success. A group of younger, mid-career researchers and still predominantly junior professors decided to share their thoughts, beliefs and gimmicks about how they do academic business – something that earlier sociological studies of science rarely focused on (Prpić, 2000). They offer a wide range of experience and expertise. Nevertheless, the diversifying academic profession (Teichler, 2010) and the paradigm of different academic worlds (Clark, 1987) led us to narrow the focus and to resonate our stories within the field of organization studies – a discipline that we are familiar with.

Our orchestra consists of the internationally composed group of younger scholars[1] who have already made a difference within academia. Even though historical analyses show that major scientific discoveries are the contribution of young people (Kuhn, 1962; Lehman, 1953; Musselin, 2007), by no means have we wanted to narcissistically think about ourselves as some kind of *übermensch* (superman *or* superwoman). Excellence among faculty members is certainly not unidimensional. The criteria of academic excellence have often been a topic of dispute. What really makes a great scholar is still non-consensual because it is almost impossible to find the dynamic equilibrium that will completely cover the diversity of academic work.

Subsequently, it should be clear that the choice of contributors for this volume was subjective. As editors, we decided to invite colleagues by profession, some of them whom we did not even know, but whose achievements were notable and admirable. Each author is a "high quality" scholar, in oversimplified terms, a person of exceptional competence and dedication to his or her academic tasks (Schuster & Finkelstein, 2006). The chosen ones are aspiring scholars (something that is evident from their curricula vitae [CVs]) who were brave enough to speak openly about and share their values and motives, positive and negative emotions, passions and fears, and first academic successes and failures. These 15 brave male and female musketeers decided yet again to take a risk and expose themselves in order to give. Certainly there are plenty more prolific scholars who would be interested to share their thoughts and do have something to say, but unfortunately the number of seats was limited.

The volume contributors' ages range between 32 and 47, with an average age of 40.[2] They represent an international group of scholars with different countries of origin (Austria, Belgium, Brazil, Croatia, Finland, Germany, Greece, Serbia, Slovenia, Sweden, United States) who mainly have assistant or associate professorship positions. Their academic experience[3] has been gained across 17 different European and North and South American countries (see Figure 1.1 for more details) and within 31 higher education institutions (for example, Boston University, Case Western Reserve University, IE Business School, Indiana University, INSEAD, London School of Economics, Nova School of Business and Economics, Royal Institute of Technology, Stanford University, Technical University of Munich, University of Edinburgh, University of Nebraska-Lincoln, University of Notre Dame, University of Toronto, Warwick Business School, WU Vienna, and others).

Each contributor is an independent and aspiring researcher with a respectable early-career track-record. In total, volume contributors have already published 48 books, 185 book chapters, 581 Web of Science (WoS) publications, some of which are in top-tier academic journals (*Academy of Management Journal, Journal of Management, Strategic Management Journal, Human Resource Management, The Leadership Quarterly, Human*

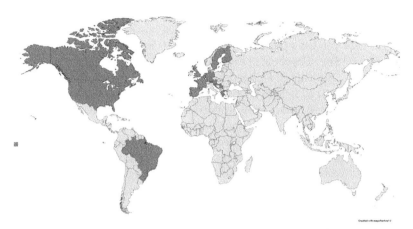

Note: Created with mapchart.net. The dark areas represent contributors' academic experience.

Figure 1.1   World map of contributors' academic experience

Resource Management Journal, Human Relations, Organization Science, Journal of Business Venturing, Journal of Applied Psychology, Journal of Organizational Behavior, Harvard Business Review, Organizational Behavior and Human Decision Processes, Project Management Journal, Journal of Business Research, and others). Their work has been largely cited (15 352 WoS citations and 54 643 Google Scholar citations on 16 November 2020),[4] and they have won numerous prestigious awards (e.g. PhD thesis awards, best paper awards, junior/emerging researcher awards, extraordinary teaching awards). Having a place on the journal editorial boards (*Academy of Management Journal, Academy of Management Discoveries, Human Resource Management Journal, Human Resource Management Review, The Leadership Quarterly, Journal of Applied Psychology, Journal of Management Studies, Journal of Business Venturing, Organization Studies, Journal of Occupational and Organizational Psychology, European Management Journal*) or playing important roles in professional associations (Academy of Management, European Academy of Management), as well as being visiting professors (for instance, Stanford University, UCLA, Aarhus University, HEC Montreal, University of Pennsylvania), grant holders and research project managers, they have confirmed their potential, passion, and responsibility for academic work. The contributing authors have been carefully chosen to cover working practices from different angles and perspectives. Thus, we believe the academic plate will be more presentable.

TO WHOM IT MAY CONCERN

The world of academia is a very crowded place in which to live and work. It is larger than you have probably ever imagined. In 2001 the National Center for Education Statistics counted about 1.11 million faculty members across the United States (Schuster & Finkelstein, 2006). Similar statistical data unfortunately do not exist at the global level, but we could assume there are certainly more than five million scholars worldwide. Although our autobiographical essays might be interesting to the whole academic population, we are modest enough not to think out loud that it could become an academic bestseller.

This volume is primarily targeted at doctoral candidates and early-career researchers. According to Meri (2007), just in Europe there are approximately 680 000 doctoral candidates (Ates et al., 2011). Similar numbers are applicable for the United States. That is a lot of young and ambitious people to write for. We were driven by Bailey's (1997) reflection that "reading about others struggling with similar issues, experiencing the highs and lows of the learning process, trying the same or similar kinds or techniques, and expressing the same kinds of values can be heartening". Something similar did not exist during our academic beginnings, so we wanted to make the academic life more understandable to newcomers.

The approaches and techniques explained throughout the book might inspire and help young scholars to become respectful members of the professoriate. Academic respectfulness should not be maintained through workaholism or by becoming the "hyper-productive publication machine". We do not support a ruthless "publish or perish" philosophy. In our view, the end does not justify the means. Higher university or department ratings are something very nice to have and to be proud of, but they do not represent a goal in itself. Instead of being constantly under pressure, exhausted and exploited, young scholars should have the opportunity to enjoy their scholarship. They need to find a work–life balance and the meaning of their work, because only in such circumstances can they contribute to their society.

We do hope that our specific writing style and personal reflections will have a positive effect on a potential cohort of readers. Our intention is to promote prosocial behavior, rejuvenate academic citizenship and give a new boost to academic discovery. As some might think, we do not have hidden self-promotion intentions. Instead, we would like to give what we have learnt from our experiences. Translated into the words of Harvard political scientist Robert Putnam: "We'll do this for you without expecting anything specific back from you, in the confident expectation that someone else will do something for us down the road" (Grant, 2013). Only such a way of reasoning can move us further afield towards a better and happier society.

DIE SPEISEKARTE OR THE BOOK MENU

The book is structured into six parts each approaching an academic career from a different perspective: (I) as preparing for a voyage; (II) as a journey; (III) through career transitions; (IV) as an act of balancing and role switching; (V) an arena to practice your personal style; and (VI) looking to the future and seizing the horizon. In total, we present three overviews and 15 autobiographical chapters.

To begin with and to prepare for the voyage, it is important to be clear about the full range and scope of work activities that most academics engage in. Therefore, *Tomislav Hernaus* and *Matej Černe* have written a chapter about academic work design. They address a four-legged stool approach that needs to ensure the balance among a diverse set of academic (i.e. research, teaching, service) and personal activities (i.e. family matters, growth and development).

The next three chapters describe an academic career as a unique journey. *Eleanna Galanaki* starts the adventure by comparing her academic career to Homer's epic poem, *Odyssey*. Career challenges, risks, and pitfalls, as well as rewards, opportunities, and benefits experienced in modern Greek academia are discussed in the light of the Ancient Greek text. She attempts to find analogies and antitheses between the original epos and the odyssey of her academic life. *Hana Milanov* continues by describing her unexpected country-hopping academic career path that took her from Croatia, through the United States and Spain, to Germany. In her chapter, she discusses similarities and differences between academic expectations, daily life, and work–life balance across countries and cultures. *Amy Van Looy* concludes this part of the book by putting upfront the idea of practice-oriented research. Specifically, her prior consultancy expertise and ongoing business practice experience strongly influence her academic behavior and performance, representing an inexhaustible source of research topics to pursue.

Academic career transition challenges, both approached from the historical and futuristic perspective, are well addressed in the following three chapters. *Jelena Zikic* describes herself as being a career nomad. Most of her career decision-making (i.e. international journey, migration, and work–family decisions) followed her career instinct, which certainly played a role at career intersections. Being a career researcher, she authoritatively talks about the benefits of continuous career reflection and reinvention. *Matej Černe* thoroughly explains the change in roles and responsibilities that accompany his career shifts triggered by several life-changing events. He builds the case of reaching a successful academic career by turning fortune into favor through practicing hard work, proactive behavior and being persistent. *Karoline Strauss* explores how our future work selves are shaped, questioned, abandoned, and reinvented throughout our academic careers, and how, despite a changing landscape in academia, they may provide a sense of purpose and direction. In a similar vein, she embraces the impact that each of us could have on others' future work selves as we advance into senior positions.

Academic balancing and role switching is certainly a challenge for the majority of contemporary academics. Therefore, we have included four chapters addressing this topic specifically. *Ante Glavaš* recounts how he followed a non-traditional path and eventually moved from being a corporate person to an academic position seeker. He reveals how his academic life was influenced by a single top-tier publication, and explains how it is still challenging to find meaning in the different roles that an academic plays. *Tomislav Hernaus* puts upfront the notion of constant struggle for survival between various types of academic activities. He recommends that junior scholars pay attention to the academic balance dynamics already present at the beginning of their journey by sticking to their personal philosophy, having sources of inspiration and support, and building ethics of responsibility. *Alf Rehn* discusses the many roles of the modern academic, and the manner in which this multitude establishes borders and border-crossings that challenge stable professional identities. His autobiographical case enquires into both the pitfalls and the positive aspects of switching between seemingly paradoxical positions, and suggests ways in which academics can overcome their anguish over playing multimodal roles. *Sonja Rispens* writes about the prevalence of collaborative relationships and conflicts that academic researchers face. Based on both personal experiences and scientific research, she clarifies the value of collaboration and at the same time describes the different types of conflicts we as academics may encounter while collaborating with other researchers.

Finally, the most extensive part of the book covers five chapters describing personal styles within academia. Indeed, each scholar experiences his or her own personal odyssey that might eventually be more or less successful. To increase the odds of the success, *Kristina Potočnik* takes the reader through her academic career, particularly highlighting the importance of serendipity and resilience for completing a PhD and persisting in academic circles. Drawing on self-experience, she presents a realistic picture of the often-mystified academic life by discussing some of the key challenges that an early-career researcher is likely to face. *Joana Story* uses the dance metaphor to present different career perspectives and personal experiences. Each dancing style introduced (fado, samba, capoeira, and choro) represents different career stage for which key success factors (or "dance lessons") for effective research have been offered. *Jan Mendling* explicates his case of growing up as an academic by emphasizing research collaborations as a great way of learning. From his standpoint, scientific teamwork represents the key factor of publication productivity, especially if you have a chance to collaborate with inspirational persons. *Markus*

Hällgren explores the opportunities to establish a research career by purposefully doing things differently. His chapter provides insights into the principles, tools, and methods that were used, and have continued to be used by the author in order to find and keep the passion alive. Last, but not least, *Spencer Harrison* takes a highly creative approach of reflecting upon academic work by asking what our children think about how we spend our time. His personal experiment yields some interesting insights on sacrifices we are expected to take while pursuing a productive and enriching academic career. Contributors' main messages to the new generation of scholars are concisely presented and briefly commented on by the editors in the ultimate chapter of this volume.

A BRIEF NOTE ON METHODS APPLIED TO EASE READABILITY

Unless you are an experienced academic, reading scholarly work is not always straightforward. This may be so because we (academics) mostly do not start writing from scratch; instead, we assume that readers are well enough informed about the topic to get engaged in the discussion at a certain level of understanding. Being aware of the problem, we (editors) have applied several "tricks" in order to make this volume more attractive to a wider (non-informed) audience. Specifically, what you can find useful to get motivated to read subsequent pages is as follows:

- Chapters follow a narrative approach to reflect on personal odysseys with a basic level of theorizing.
- Contributors were given freedom to craft their chapters as they prefer (content and substance, writing style, with or without referencing[5]), which ultimately resulted in a very disparate set of relevant academic career themes.
- The chapter length has been standardized (8 000 word count limit).
- Each contributor has received constructive editorial feedback from the perspective of an uninformed reader.
- Five key chapter takeaways have been recognized and highlighted by editors.
- An estimated reading time[6] is provided for each chapter.

Preparing this volume has involved much introspection and a search for reasons for the causes of our behaviors and approach to academic life. It shows "many roads that could be taken in an academic career" (Mello, 1997). Beyond literally opening the academic horizon, we also wanted to spread the idea about positive organizational scholarship and dare to hope that our book is maybe one such example. Eventually, we are not afraid to admit that we are hooked on being academics! Maybe you will feel the same after you read the book.

NOTES

1. Different ways of classifying faculty cohorts exist. For instance, according to Schuster and Finkelstein (2006), new entrants are faculty in the first seven years of full-time teaching, mid-career faculty are those who have between eight and 14 years of full-time teaching experience, and senior faculty have 15 or more years of full-time teaching experience. A more widespread approach is to see young researchers as those who have reached the age of 35 years or less (Prpić, 2000). Ates at al. (2011), under the term junior researcher, refer to all young researchers who have finished their doctorate and are working at the postdoctoral level within the academic/research sector. Within the United States, age level criteria seems to be somewhat higher, as they have the award "Top young professors under 40". Despite age differences, ranks of full professor and associate professor are considered to be senior academics, and assistant professor and lecturer ranks are usually considered to be junior academics (Aarrevaara & Dobson, 2013).
2. Although it should be noted that we were somewhat younger when the book project was initiated and the chapters had been written.
3. Here defined as previous and current work experience, scholarship visits longer than three months as well as formal enrollment in master of science or doctoral programs.
4. While these numbers are impressive, we should be fair and give a special credit to our "superstar" Jan Mendling who by himself has 5 600 WoS and 24 791 Google Scholar citations.
5. Most contributors decided to retain academic rigor and have cited other scholarly work to evidence and strengthen their argument. In total, 381 reference sources have been used in this volume.
6. We decided to follow a global trend (e.g., Amazon Kindle, McKinsey Digital, The Economist App) and recommended examples (e.g., Bailey, 2016; Messner & Wänke, 2011) to introduce an estimated reading time for each chapter. The Read-O-Meter online calculator has been used to calculate this time based on the 200 words per minute reading average.

REFERENCES

Aarrevaara, T., & Dobson, I. R. (2013). Movers and shakers: Do academics control their own work? In U. Teichler, & E. A. Hohle (eds.), *The Work Situation of the Academic Profession in Europe: Findings of a Survey in Twelve Countries* (pp. 159–181). Dordrecht: Springer.

Andre, R., & Frost, P. J. (eds.). (1997). *Researchers Hooked on Teaching: Noted Scholars Discuss the Synergies of Teaching and Research.* Thousand Oaks, CA: Sage Publications.

Ates, G., Hollander, K., Koltcheva, N., Krstić, S., & Parada, F. (2011). *Eurodoc Survey I: The First Eurodoc Survey on Doctoral Candidates in Twelve European Countries.* Brussels: Eurodoc – The European Council of Doctoral Candidates and Junior Researchers.

Austin, A. E., & Wulff, D. H. (2004). The challenge to prepare the next generation of faculty. In D. H. Wulff, A. E. Austin et al. (eds.), *Paths to the Professoriate: Strategies for Enriching the Preparation of Future Faculty* (pp. 3–16). San Francisco, CA: Jossey-Bass.

Bailey, C. (2016). *The Productivity Project: Proven Ways to Become More Awesome.* London, UK: Piatkus.

Bailey, D. (1997). The power of dialogue: Celebrating the praxis of teaching and research. In R. Andre, & P. J. Frost (eds.), *Researchers Hooked on Teaching: Noted Scholars Discuss the Synergies of Teaching and Research* (pp. 301–312). Thousand Oaks, CA: Sage Publications.

Clark, B. R. (1987). *The Academic Life: Small Worlds, Different Worlds.* Lawrenceville, NJ: Princeton University Press.

Deneef, A. L., & Goodwin, C. D. (eds.). (2007). *The Academic's Handbook.* Durham, NC: Duke University Press.

Fleck, C., & Hess, A. (2014). Introduction: Public sociology in the making. In C. Fleck, & A. Hess (eds.), *Knowledge for Whom? Public Sociology in the Making* (pp. 1–15). Farnham, UK: Ashgate.

Frost, P. J., & Taylor, M. S. (eds.). (1996). *Rhythms of Academic Life: Personal Accounts of Careers in Academia.* Thousand Oaks, CA: Sage Publications.

Grant, A. M. (2013). *Give and Take: A Revolutionary Approach to Success.* New York, NY: Viking.

Hällgren, M. (ed.). (2014). *Reflections on a Scientific Career – Behind the professor's CV.* Stockholm/Copenhagen: Liber/Copenhagen Business Press.

Harley, B. (2019). Confronting the crisis of confidence in management studies: Why senior scholars need to stop setting a bad example. *Academy of Management Learning & Education, 18*(2), 286–297.

Kalleberg, A. L. (2011). *Good Jobs, Bad Jobs: The Rise of Polarized and Precarious Employment Systems in the United States, 1970s to 2000s.* New York, NY: Russell Sage Foundation.

Kuhn, T. S. (1962). *The Structure of Scientific Revolutions.* Chicago, IL: University of Chicago Press.

Lehman, H. C. (1953). *Age and Achievement.* Princeton, NJ: Princeton University Press.

Mello, J. (1997). Teaching in the real world. In R. Andre, & P. J. Frost (eds.), *Researchers Hooked on Teaching: Noted Scholars Discuss the Synergies of Teaching and Research* (pp. 178–196). Thousand Oaks, CA: Sage Publications.

Meri, T. (2007). Doctorate holders. The beginning of their career. *Statistics in Focus, Science and Technology, 131*, 1–8.

Messner, C., & Wänke, M. (2011). Unconscious information processing reduces information overload and increases product satisfaction. *Journal of Consumer Psychology, 21*(1), 9–13.

Musselin, C. (2007). Transformation of academic work: Facts and analysis. In M. Kogan, & U. Teichler (eds.), *Key Challenges to the Academic Profession* (pp. 175–190). Kassel: UNESCO Forum on Higher Education.

Prpić, K. (2000). The publication productivity of young scientists: An empirical study. *Scientometrics, 49*(3), 453–490.

Schuster, J. H., & Finkelstein, M. J. (2006). *The American Faculty: The Restructuring of Academic Work and Careers.* Baltimore, MD: Johns Hopkins University Press.

Slaughter, S., & Leslie, L. (1997). *Academic Capitalism: Politics, Policies and the Entrepreneurial University.* Baltimore, MD: Johns Hopkins University Press.

Teichler, U. (2010). The diversifying academic profession? *European Review*, *18*(1), 157–179.

Turnbull, H. W. (ed.). (1959). *The Correspondence of Isaac Newton: Volume 1 (1661–1675)*. Cambridge, UK: Cambridge University Press.

Ylijoki, O.-H. (2005). Academic nostalgia: A narrative approach to academic work. *Human Relations*, *58*(5), 555–576.

2. Academic work design as a three- or four-legged stool

Tomislav Hernaus and Matej Černe

Estimated reading time: **20 minutes and 29 seconds**.

CHAPTER HIGHLIGHTS

- While you might view your academic appointment as a job (i.e. a means to an end) or a career (i.e. a pathway to achievement and prestige), only by understanding academic work as a calling (i.e. an identity integral to your life) will your efforts be meaningful, enjoyable, passionate and make a purposeful contribution to society.
- Three main pillars of academic work are teaching, research and service, portraying an academic's work as a three-legged stool (although we may want to add the fourth leg representing personal growth and development).
- Within set institutional expectations and boundaries, an academic work design decision is often made by an individual him- or herself.
- Generally, academics tend to have higher levels of job autonomy and task variety, but lower levels of task interdependence than knowledge workers from business organizations.
- Different performance dimensions of academic work (teaching, research and service [citizenship]) should not be evaluated separately, but integratively.

Having an academic career is a privileged position but one that has obligations as well as responsibilities.
Stewart R. Clegg

INTRODUCTION

Being a university professor is a noble and honorable occupation in society. It is also a very attractive and prestigious profession that gives you a lot of autonomy and freedom, offers you a position of power and increases your social status. Teaching predominantly young(er) people allows you to be in touch with the energy of youth; consulting provides you with the opportunity to have an impact within the business world and learn from it at the same time; while studying and investigating emerging research issues makes your efforts meaningful and intellectually challenging.

However, we should not forget that academics also have very demanding and time-consuming jobs. Although most scholars do not have a strictly defined working time, they often find themselves working on weekends, holidays, or until late hours of the night. In addition, the diversity and complexity of academic tasks create a lot of strain and pressure, something that some academics cannot cope with. Therefore, in order to avoid personal disappointments and institutional failures, we need to better understand the meaning and content of academic work. What does it really mean to be a scholar and what does it look like to work at a university or some other higher education institution? By providing an overview of scholarly tasks and roles, as well as academic responsibilities and requirements, we would like you to be well-informed about the world of academia in which we are living.

WORK ORIENTATION AND THE MEANING OF ACADEMIC WORK

Each employee goes through his or her work-related ups and downs. It is a normal occurrence within the workplace that we cannot escape from. There will always be some tasks we do not prefer (i.e. either see them boring and routine, or overcomplex and highly demanding), roles that we would like not to have (e.g. being a messenger of bad news), or time periods when it would be better to be somewhere else (e.g. in the middle of a very teaching-intensive semester). However, beyond such individually-based positive or negative moments, we also conduct more general evaluations of our jobs. Specifically, theoretical assertions from sociology and psychology provide us with the concept of *work orientation*, meaning that people can subjectively experience the work they do in one of three distinct ways: as a job, a career, or a calling (Baumeister, 1991; Bellah et al., 1985). These three categories guide individuals' basic goals for working (see Glavaš, Chapter 9, this volume), capture beliefs about the role of work in life and are reflected in work-related feelings and behaviors (Wrzesniewski, 2011).

While you might view your academic appointment as a job (i.e. a means to an end) or a career (i.e. a pathway to achievement and prestige; Berg et al., 2010), only by understanding academic work as a calling (i.e. an identity integral to your life) will your efforts be meaningful, enjoyable, passionate and make a purposeful contribution to society (Dik & Duffy, 2009). Individuals with callings are self-confident, and have a stronger identification and engagement with their work (Bunderson & Thompson, 2009); they are likewise highly motivated by the content of the activity itself and thus perform better with higher levels of life and job satisfaction (Wrzesniewski et al., 1997).

A sense of calling can grow or diminish as a result of the work context (Wrzesniewski, 2011). In other words, we agree with Linda Darling-Hammond (2006) who described the belief that "good teachers are born and not made" as one of education's myths. Such a viewpoint has further been supported by research conducted by Gallup on a representative sample of more than 8 000 American workers. By studying people who love their work, it became clear that "almost none initially landed the jobs they loved; rather, they landed ordinary jobs and turned them into extraordinary ones" (Lopez, 2013).

BALANCING ACADEMIC ROLES AND EXPECTATIONS

The modern business professor is supposed to wear many hats. While the Humboldtian ideal[1] of "unity of research and teaching" is still relevant, some additional roles exist and are broadly subsumed under the category of service. This familiar academic triumvirate of teaching, research, and service delineates what we do as scholars. Although we could explain academic duties somewhat differently, for example through four kinds of scholarship responsibilities (i.e. discovery, integration, application, and teaching; see Boyer, 1990), a more traditional view is followed describing three main pillars of scholarly work.

Teaching came first. Representing the act of convincing an audience to consider a point of view (if not agree with it) and to learn a certain set of facts and/ or ideas, it was qualified by Aristotle as "the highest form of understanding" (Boyer, 1990). Today, teaching is often viewed as a routine function.

For many centuries, scholars practiced service that was inseparable from teaching. However, at the beginning of the twentieth century, as universities became larger and more bureaucratized, and professional societies were established, service activities started to be acknowledged as a separate academic role. Nowadays, *service* is an academic duty that embraces a wide range of public obligations: outreach to community groups, service to industry and practitioners of the professions, and participation in efforts to make the academic community relevant to important state or regional constituencies (Kennedy, 2003). Despite the importance it has, a vast majority of scholars see time spent on administration (being the major part of service) as wasted, often not even regarded as a legitimate demand (see Clark, 1987).

In contrast, *research* serves as the primary basis for prestige in academia. Not surprisingly, many academics have lost the taste for pluralism (Ghoshal, 2005) and focus on their identities as researchers (Milanov, Rehn, this volume; Ruth, 2008), mainly because this part of the scholarly effort is mostly appreciated and explicitly rewarded. You cannot advance and receive a tenured position without meeting at least the minimum criteria set for promotion (in other words, you have to publish, no matter whether you have something to say or not; see Billsberry et al., 2019), where a track record of published research usually has the highest relative importance. Relatedly, not a small amount of higher education institutions practice opening singular posts which are either teaching or research oriented (Musselin, 2007), no longer requiring all-in-one scholars.

Each pillar of the academic work requires time and resources. As roles and responsibilities are becoming more demanding, tensions inescapably occur between these different aspects of academic life. Some of us (academics) prefer research more than teaching, others put their bets on teaching, a few might take service as their call of duty, and some still try to balance efforts across different academic roles (see Hernaus, this volume). While there is no right or wrong answer (it is person- and context-dependent), we like the idea behind a basic law of the universe: "harmony is variety in unity" (see Bartunek & Rynes, 2014). As multiple roles are necessarily interconnected (McDaniels, 2010) and not mutually exclusive (Lucas & Murry, 2011), a well-developed academic should engage in a multiplicity of activities addressing different domains of academic work.

An academic work design decision is often made by an individual him- or herself. Although certain expectations exist (and might vary) by institutional work arrangements (Musselin, 2007), each scholar has control over personal destiny, and should plan career development idiosyncratically by maintaining his or her sense of identity (Mello, 1997). One should, however, be aware of a continuous, temporal flow of an academic life. Different roles are usually more or less addressed in different career stages, supporting Lee Knefelkamp's (1990) metaphor of "seasons", presuming changes of interests and focus in different phases. While it certainly helps to create and keep the pipeline filled at each stage of development (Darley et al., 2007), we should acknowledge that there is no rhythm that fits every single person (Boyer, 1990). Balance will eventually emerge from movement (that is, role and task switching).

ACADEMIC TASKS AND PROCESSES

The main academic roles need to be unbundled to gain further understanding of the academic profession. To date, surprisingly little is to be found in the academic literature about the specific nature of scholarly responsibilities. Yet, the components of academic work are constantly multiplied and differentiated, increasing the scope of expected activities. Both task-based and process-based views help us to conceptualize what are we expected to do. The former sheds a light on the increasing diversification of the academic task portfolio (that is consisted of numerous teaching-, research-, and service-oriented activities); the latter targets underlying ongoing mechanisms that generate outputs of our work (i.e. thinking, reading, writing, learning).

Teaching- and Student-related Activities

Typically, teaching is narrowly defined as interacting directly with students in face-to-face or online classrooms (Wulff et al., 2004). However, the *front-office activities* such as time spent in class, office and contact hours (advising, coaching, and mentoring) represent only the tip of the iceberg. Other, by no means less important, *back-office activities* also exist and require our time and span of attention. For instance, curriculum innovations and program development, class (material) preparation, student assessment and grading, classroom research, finding internships for students, writing letters of recommendation, online learning material maintenance, and so on. Some of these activities are not merely the execution of routine tasks but rather an opportunity to experiment and practice creativity (Robey, 2014).

Research- and Writing-oriented Activities

Research – the systematic investigation into and study of materials and sources in order to establish facts and reach new conclusions (Lexico, 2019) – encompasses a spectrum of explorative and exploitative activities. *Search for new knowledge* is mostly project-based, either formally or informally organized. It includes planning activities (e.g. writing research proposals and research project fundraising, research group development, research design), organizing activities (e.g. supervising a research team, managing research budgets/contracts), and execution activities (e.g. literature review, data collection, data analysis, result write-up). These search-based activities are supposed to be followed by *dissemination-based activities* (e.g. writing academic papers, presenting scholarly conference papers, authoring or editing books, publishing journal papers), which should eventually enable knowledge transfer and offer sound theoretical and practical contributions. Ultimately, according to great British experimental scientist Michael Faraday: "The secret is comprised in three words – Work, Finish, Publish" (in Gladstone, 1874).

Service- and Administration-oriented Activities

The service role is diverse and includes multiple subroles and responsibilities to the institution, the discipline, and/or society in general. *Institutional subroles* are mostly unavoidable and often time-consuming, usually present at multiple levels, i.e. departmental, school, or college, and campus-wide (Lucas & Murry, 2011). For instance, the majority of academics at least to some extent serve as members of scientific committees and task forces; they might be also responsible for administrative work, serve as faculty advisors to student organizations, and some of them are supposed to take on academic leadership positions (e.g. dean, vice-dean, department chairs). *Professional subroles* are mostly voluntary yet career value-adding activities. Gatekeeping activities such as journal editorships, reviewing scholarly papers or evaluating grant proposals are often supplemented with activities such as chairing a scholarly conference session, organizing a scientific conference/roundtable, serving on a scholarly association, keynote addresses or service on an accrediting team. Finally, *community subroles* include political engagement (for instance, government or party involvement, being a member of social movements or a participant in local community development), participation in public discourses with scholarly knowledge (e.g. media appearances, blogging and podcasting, writing newspaper columns, taking a part in popularization of science activities, publishing professional papers), and consulting services (e.g. providing expertise and practical solutions to corporate or community clients, serving on corporate boards and/or steering committees).

Personal- and Development-oriented Activities

Teaching, research and service compose a "three-legged stool" model of academic work (see Figure 2.1). Such a view may be further enriched by an additional leg framed *personal- and development-oriented activities*. For instance, nowadays ongoing time and effort is required by academics to practice personal branding and maintain online profiles (e.g. ResearchGate, Academia. edu, LinkedIn, official web page, personal web page), acquire new knowledge, learn new tools, and master research methods (e.g. attending professional workshops and research/method seminars, participate in Coursera or similar online education courses). No less important is a continuous search for a holy grail, that is, trying to reach a work–life balance. Such a state of equilibrium is more a myth than reality (Gambles et al., 2006). On one hand, being a thinker,

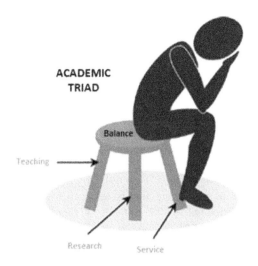

Figure 2.1   Academic roles as a three-legged stool model

reader, writer and learner mean that we are constantly processing ideas, data, and information, which certainly requires extra effort. Time needed for these ongoing activities is often taken from your significant other – being a partner, parent, and friend. Rather than trying to achieve the impossible, we should made a shift towards work–life integration and blend what we do personally and professionally in order to make both work (Schawbel, 2014).

WORK CHARACTERISTICS OF ACADEMIC JOBS

(Academic) work design reflects the content and organization of scholars' work tasks, activities, relationships, and responsibilities (Parker, 2014). It not only shows how tasks and roles are structured, enacted and modified (Grant & Parker, 2009), but explains how particular bundles of work characteristics (i.e. objective and relatively stable job attributes; Morgeson & Campion, 2003) shape work behavior. Although work design differences certainly exist across academic positions, a universal overview of an academic profession[2] provided by the Occupational Information Network (O*NET) states the following:

- Job incumbents have a lot of freedom to make decisions (85%) and to determine tasks, priorities and goals (71%).
- Multiple tasks have to be handled (19 core and six supplemental tasks).
- A total of 52% of job incumbents contact with others most of the time, an additional 30% have constant contact with others.

- Getting information (86%) and interpreting the meaning of information for others (77%) are very important job activities.
- Thinking creatively is quite important (74%).
- Coordinating the work and activities with others is less required (43%).

Our own research, conducted on the sample of 181 scholars (see Hernaus et al., 2019) and compared to the results obtained from 139 managers and 373 professionals (see Hernaus & Mikulic, 2014), showed that university professors, on average, have higher work autonomy (M = 4.03, SD = 0.87) than knowledge workers from business organizations (M = 3.67, SD = 0.76). Likewise, task variety is higher in academic (M = 4.30, SD = 0.71) than observed business occupations (M = 4.16, SD = 0.69). However, it seems that academic job positions are more standalone, that is, academics experience lower levels of task interdependence (M = 3.19, SD = 0.73) than corresponding business people (M = 3.54, SD = 0.63).

Such findings are not surprising. The academic profession is indeed a very free profession. Scholars allocate their time according to their preferences (Hohle & Teichler, 2013), and feel free to decide how much time they devote to specific roles. However, the autonomy of an academic researcher is not unconditional. Rather, there are obligations to abide by university rules, follow professional norms, and fulfill social expectations. One cannot "go at it alone" and expect to look back on a fulfilling career (Robey, 2014).

A high level of task variety means that a lot of multitasking happens within an ordinary academic working week. Even in the course of a day's work, scholars are expected to switch between different tasks and to partition their activities to meet the conflicting role demands (Bonesso et al., 2014). For instance, we prefer to squeeze a meeting or administrative work in between teaching classes, or like to have an early morning start for writing and research. Such a transitioning *modus operandi* creates "continuous partial attention" (Shao & Shao, 2012), it is effortful, and it eventually influences the level of academic creativity and subsequent productivity.

A somewhat lower level of task interdependence (in comparison to the business practice) does not mean that academics operate in isolation. They may deliver their courses independently (although co-teaching does also apply, especially in the case of executive education), but when it comes to research, it is all about teamwork. Research collaboration, also referred to as "team science", involves the cooperative work of researchers to achieve a common goal of producing new scientific knowledge (Cummings & Kiesler, 2014). Joining forces and achieving complementarities across different knowledge and methodological backgrounds may qualify a certain research group to be competitive in reaching top-tier publication targets.

In terms of time pressure and academic workload, it is interesting to note that almost no one outside academia knows how heavy the workload really is (Kennedy, 2003). The uninformed majority believe that scholars have extensive summer and winter holidays; do not need to go to work on a daily basis; and usually do not work as much as they should (i.e. less than eight hours per day). The truth is quite opposite. Professoriate work today is not a leisurely occupation (Cummings & Kiesler, 2014). A lack of time and living constantly under time pressure characterize the everyday academic reality (Ylijoki & Mäntylä, 2003).

Evidence shows that scholars are facing an *overloaded plate* (Rice et al., 2000) with an average of 49 working hours per week (Huisman et al., 2002). Specifically, more than one-third of research university faculty reported 55+ working hours weekly (Schuster & Finkelstein, 2006). While 50- and 60-hour workweeks are not uncommon among members of the professoriate (Lucas & Murry, 2011), the amount of workload is similar to managerial time allocation, as chief executive officers (CEOs) report working on average 55 hours a week (Bandiera et al., 2012).

From our own quarter of a century's experience in academia, we (the editors) know how easy it is to commit to things, that is, more reading, more writing, to take on an extra project, to keep loading yourself up. Eventually, you end up overloaded (Kearns & Gardiner, 2008)! The problem is that much of academic work is unstructured and poorly defined, so we lack having a consensual "workload model" (Ates et al., 2011). Despite a widely assumed decomposition of academic work (academics in Europe are expected to spend about 40% of their time on teaching, 40% on research, and the remaining 20% on service and administration; see Kwiek & Antonowicz, 2013), a field survey showed that they spend more time on research than on teaching during the year (see Hohle & Teichler, 2013). Yet, teaching load is what makes a significant difference.[3] In many European universities professors feel they are overburdened with administrative and teaching responsibilities and find it difficult to remain competitive in their own research (Scholz et al., 2009). What you can do is to *make* time and practice scheduled writing (Strannegård, 2014).

ACADEMIC PERFORMANCE

What we do as academics does not mean much if we do not know how well we perform in the multiple roles that we have. Each role has somewhat different goals and criteria for success. While most professors achieve academic status through their research and publication track record (Boyer, 1990), we should not neglect excellence in teaching or service performance. A single focus on pushing publications for the sake of publications thus takes a bit of the soul out of what scholars are there for (Hällgren, 2014).

Research Performance

Research ability is, no doubt, the primary reputational currency (Kennedy, 2003). The maxim "Publish or perish" dominates the lives of academics. It favors the culture of productivity (Courpasson, 2013) and puts increasing pressure on academics to publish scholarly work in order to succeed. This is certainly not an easy game to play; a lot of players (scholars) are "fighting" for a very limited space (top-tier publication outlets). Studies on research production have shown that about 10% of university professors publish almost half the total number of academic publications written by university professors (Teichler, 2010). Very easily you may fall into a trap of expanding the amount of research beyond what is either morally (e.g. salami publication, PhD factories) or physically possible (increasing the risk of burnout). Instead, why not publish less but better and more relevant "stuff" (Courpasson, 2013). Various options are at hand (publishing single- or co-authored papers; publishing empirical, theoretical, or review papers; choosing publication targets; deciding to pursue book projects, etc.). Although some would not agree, how often one's work is cited is a measure of scholarly "influence". Impact factors, h-indexes and other scientometric indicators (for an extensive review see Vinkler, 2010) have been used extensively in appointment, promotion, pay, and funding decisions. The marginal dollar value of a single citation to articles in top-tier journals has even been estimated (Judge et al., 2007). Thereby, with no surprise, analytical tools such as Publish or Perish software (Harzing, 2010) are developed to measure the efficiency of faculty publications through author/journal impact.

Teaching Performance

Teaching is now receiving substantially greater weight in the tenure-granting process in most research universities, as it should (Kennedy, 2003). This is not surprising, because great teachers create a common ground of intellectual commitment (Boyer, 1990). What is more and more relevant is not meeting the minimum course requirements; instead, what really matters is enriching student experience to make a lasting contribution in their lives (Grant, 2008). Nowadays, metrics and methodologies for measuring teaching quality in higher education have already been thoroughly developed (e.g. the Teaching Excellence Framework; see Gunn, 2018). Besides widely accepted student evaluations, some of the most common performance indicators are peer evaluations, class attendance, the percentage of students passing exams, or teacher value-added (TVA) calculations. What certainly helps to boost classroom learning are teaching awards to honor outstanding teachers and celebrate teaching excellence.

Service (Citizenship) Performance

Scholars have a responsibility towards society that is not best served through publications or classroom teaching alone. They should also be good citizens and make their mark by going an extra mile (that is, beyond what they are formally expected to deliver). Outstanding citizenship performance will not make up for inferior task performance. However, if a person's task performance is good, substantial citizenship behavior makes the person much more valuable, and that value may make a difference in a difficult tenure or promotion decision (Darley et al., 2007). An important part of academic citizenship is engagement with practice. For instance, John Austin suggested to us that "the value of the academic is often less in the actual research and more in helping practitioners improve their critical thinking so that they can better distinguish between good and bad data (regardless of whether the data were generated in the academic world)" (Bartunek & Rynes, 2014). Indeed, when academic researchers take the perspectives of practitioners, they may succeed in conducting research that practitioners will judge as more useful (Mohrman et al., 2001).

Different performance dimensions of academic work should not be evaluated separately yet integratively. In the last decade, an increasing number of universities started to focus on and have adopted the academic portfolio concept for evaluating faculty performance and making personnel decisions. In a nutshell, an academic portfolio is a reflective, evidence-based collection of materials that documents teaching, research, and service performance. It brings together, in one place, information about a professor's most significant professional accomplishments (Seldin & Miller, 2009) and could be efficiently organized by using reference manager software (see Bhargava et al., 2014). This might be necessary and well-received to get insights about the faculty's profile and improvements made in different academic performance domains. What might be particularly appreciated is achieving role alignment. Recent research has shown that academic alignment plays a crucial mediating role when predicting scholars' productivity and well-being (Pereyra-Rojas et al., 2017).

Ultimately, what we should strive for is not career success *per se*, but for career fulfillment, i.e. a more subjective assessment of worth that is not commensurable across scholars (Robey, 2014). In other words, what really counts is our self-reported level of job and life satisfaction, and the sense of love and passion for academic work (Ruth, 2008). We are not saying that an instrumental and mostly quantitative approach to academic excellence should be discarded (in many cases it is a good proxy for resource allocation, promotion decisions or a basis for academic reputation; e.g. Söderholm, 2014); it just needs to be supplemented with the more personal experience of our academic career to stand the test of time of the "So what?" question as a career assessment tool.

NOTES

1. This emerged in the early nineteenth century, dating back to Wilhelm von Humboldt, who at the time of the Prussian reforms relied on a growing educated middle-class and thereby promoted the claim on general education.
2. We referenced the position of a business teacher.
3. A high teaching load is defined as nine or more weekly hours; a low teaching load is defined as six hours or less (Schuster & Finkelstein, 2006).

REFERENCES

Ates, G., Hollander, K., Koltcheva, N., Krstić, S., & Parada, F. (2011). *Eurodoc Survey I: The First Eurodoc Survey on Doctoral Candidates in Twelve European Countries*. Brussels: Eurodoc – The European Council of Doctoral Candidates and Junior Researchers.

Bandiera, O., Prat, A., Sadun, R., & Wulf, J. (2012). *Span of Control and Span of Activity*. Working paper 12–053. Boston, MA: Harvard Business School.

Bartunek, J. M., & Rynes, S. L. (2014). Academics and practitioners alike and unlike: The paradoxes of academic–practitioner relationships. *Journal of Management*, *40*(5), 1181–1201.

Baumeister, R. F. (1991). *Meanings of Life*. New York, NY: Guilford Press.

Bellah, R. N., Madsen, R., Sullivan, W. M., Swidler, A., & Tipton, S. M. (1985). *Habits of the Heart: Individualism and Commitment in American Life*. New York, NY: Harper and Row.

Berg, J. M., Wrzesniewski, A., & Dutton, J. E. (2010). Perceiving and responding to challenges in job crafting at different ranks: When proactivity requires adaptivity. *Journal of Organizational Behavior*, *31*(2–3), 158–186.

Bhargava, P., Patel, V. B., Iyer, R. S., Moshiri, M., Robinson, T. J., Lall, C., & Heller, M. T. (2014). Academic portfolio in the digital era: Organizing and maintaining a portfolio using reference managers. *Journal of Digital Imaging*, *28*(1), 10–17.

Billsberry, J., Köhler, T., Stratton, M., Cohen, M., & Taylor, M. S. (2019). From the Editors: Introduction to the Special Issue on Rhythms of Academic Life. *Academy of Management Learning & Education*, *18*(2), 119–127.

Bonesso, S., Gerli, F., & Scapolan, A. (2014). The individual side of ambidexterity: Do individuals' perceptions match actual behaviors in reconciling the exploration and exploitation trade-off? *European Management Journal*, *32*(3), 392–405.

Boyer, E. L. (1990). *Scholarship Reconsidered: Priorities of the Professoriate*. Stanford, CA: The Carnegie Foundation for the Advancement of Teaching.

Bunderson, S., & Thompson, J. A. (2009). The call of the wild: Zookeepers, callings, and the double-edged sword of deeply meaningful work. *Administrative Science Quarterly*, *54*(1), 32–57.

Clark, B. R. (1987). *The Academic Life: Small Worlds, Different Worlds*. Lawrenceville, NJ: Princeton University Press.

Courpasson, D. (2013). On the erosion of 'passionate scholarship'. *Organization Studies*, *34*(9), 1243–1249.

Cummings, J., & Kiesler, S. (2014). Organization theory and the changing nature of science. *Journal of Organization Design*, *3*(3), 1–16.

Darley, J. M., Zanna, M. P., & Roediger III, H. L. (2007). *The Compleat Academic: A Career Guide*. Washington, DC: American Psychological Association.

Darling-Hammond, L. (2006). *Powerful Teacher Education*. San Francisco, CA: Jossey-Bass.

Dik, B. J., & Duffy, R. D. (2009). Calling and vocation at work: Definitions and prospects for research and practice. *The Counseling Psychologist*, *37*, 424–450.

Gambles, R., Lewis, S., & Rapoport, R. (2006). *The Myth of Work–Life Balance: The Challenge of our Time for Men, Women and Societies*. Chichester, NJ: John Wiley.

Ghoshal, S. (2005). Bad management theories are destroying good management practices. *Academy of Management Learning & Education*, *4*(1), 75–91.

Gladstone, J. H. (1874). *Michael Faraday*. London, UK: MacMillan and Co.

Grant, A. M. (2008). Employees without a cause: The motivational effects of prosocial impact in public service. *International Public Management Journal*, *11*(1), 48–66.

Grant, A. M., & Parker, S. K. (2009). Redesigning work design theories: The rise of relational and proactive perspectives. *The Academy of Management Annals*, *3*(1), 317–375.

Gunn, A. (2018). Metrics and methodologies for measuring teaching quality in higher education: Developing the Teaching Excellence Framework (TEF). *Educational Review*, *70*(2), 129–148.

Hällgren, M. (2014). Scholars' experiences. In M. Hällgren (ed.), *Reflections on a Scientific Career – Behind the professor's CV* (pp. 7–16). Stockholm/Copenhagen: Liber/Copenhagen Business Press.

Harzing, A.-W. (2010). *The Publish or Perish Book: Your Guide to Effective and Responsible Citation Analysis*. Melbourne: Tarma Software Research.

Hernaus, T. (this volume). Walking the line: In search of academic balance.

Hernaus, T., & Mikulic, J. (2014). Work characteristics and work performance of knowledge workers. *EuroMed Journal of Business*, *9*(3), 268–292.

Hernaus, T., Černe, M., Connelly, C., Poloski Vokic, N., & Škerlavaj, M. (2019). Evasive knowledge hiding in academia: When competitive individuals are asked to collaborate. *Journal of Knowledge Management*, *23*(4), 597–618.

Hohle, E. A., & Teichler, U. (2013). The teaching function of the academic profession. In U. Teichler, & E. A. Hohle (eds.), *The Work Situation of the Academic Profession in Europe: Findings of a Survey in Twelve Countries* (pp. 79–108). Dordrecht: Springer.

Huisman, J., de Weert, E., & Bartelse, J. (2002). Academic careers from a European perspective: The declining desirability of the faculty position. *The Journal of Higher Education*, *73*(1), 141–160.

Judge, T. A., Cable, D. M., Colbert, A. E., & Rynes, S. L. (2007). What causes a management article to be cited – article, author, or journal? *Academy of Management Journal*, *50*(3), 491–506.

Kearns, H., & Gardiner, M. (2008). *The Balanced Researcher: Strategies for Busy Researchers*. Cambridge, MA: Vitae.

Kennedy, D. (2003). *Academic Duty*. Cambridge, MA: Harvard University Press.

Knefelkamp, L. L. (1990). Seasons of academic life. *Liberal Education*, *76*(3), 4–12.

Kwiek, M., & Antonowicz, D. (2013). Academic work, working conditions and job satisfaction. In U. Teichler, & E. A. Hohle (eds.), *The Work Situation of the Academic Profession in Europe: Findings of a Survey in Twelve Countries* (pp. 37–53). Dordrecht: Springer.

Lexico (2019). English dictionary, thesaurus, & grammar help. *Lexico Dictionary*. Retrieved December 13, 2019 from http://www.lexico.com.

Lopez, S. J. (2013, May 26). Hone the job you have into one you love. *The New York Times*. Retrieved October 17, 2019 from https://www.nytimes.com/2013/05/26/jobs/honing-the-job-you-have-into-one-you-love.html

Lucas, C. J., & Murry, J. W., Jr. (2011). *New Faculty: A Practical Guide for Academic Beginners*. New York, NY: Palgrave Macmillan.

McDaniels, M. (2010). Doctoral student socialization for teaching roles. In S. K. Gardner, & P. Mendoza (eds.), *On Becoming a Scholar: Socialization and Development in Doctoral Education* (pp. 29–44). Sterling, VA: Stylus.

Mello, J. (1997). Teaching in the real world. In R. Andre, & P. J. Frost (eds.), *Researchers Hooked on Teaching: Noted Scholars Discuss the Synergies of Teaching and Research* (pp. 178–196). Thousand Oaks, CA: Sage Publications.

Milanov, H. (this volume). Reflections of a traveling academic: The good, the bad … often not anticipated.

Mohrman, S. A., Gibson, C. B., & Mohrman, A. M. (2001). Doing research that is useful to practice: A model and empirical exploration. *Academy of Management Journal*, *44*(2), 357–375.

Morgeson, F. P., & Campion, M. A. (2003). Work design. In W. C. Borman, D. R. Ilgen, & R. J. Klimoski (eds.), *Handbook of Psychology: Industrial and Organizational Psychology* (Vol. 12, pp. 423–452). Hoboken, NJ: Wiley.

Musselin, C. (2007). Transformation of Academic Work: Facts and Analysis. In M. Kogan, & U. Teichler (eds.), *Key Challenges to the Academic Profession* (pp. 175–190). Kassel: UNESCO Forum on Higher Education.

Parker, S. K. (2014). Beyond motivation: Job and work design for development, health, ambidexterity, and more. *Annual Review of Psychology*, *65*(15), 661–691.

Pereyra-Rojas, M., Mu, E., Gaskin, J., & Lingham, T. (2017). The higher-ed organizational–scholar tension: how scholarship compatibility and the alignment of organizational and faculty skills, values and support affects scholar's performance and well-being. *Frontiers in Psychology*, *8*, 450.

Rehn, A. (this volume). Dissociative identities in academia: Notes on paradox and multimodal role-play.

Rice, R. E., Sorcinelli, M., & Austin, A. (2000). *Heeding New Voices: Academic Careers for a New Generation*. Washington, DC: American Association for Higher Education.

Robey, D. (2014). Career fulfilment: The journey to tenure and beyond. In M. Hällgren (ed.), *Reflections on a Scientific Career – Behind the professor's CV* (pp. 109–124). Stockholm/Copenhagen: Liber/Copenhagen Business Press.

Ruth, D. (2008). Being an academic: Authorship, authenticity and authority. *London Review of Education*, *6*(2), 99–109.

Schawbel, D. (2014, January 21). Work life integration: The new norm. *Forbes*. Retrieved June 3, 2019 from https://www.forbes.com/sites/danschawbel/2014/01/21/work-life-integration-the-new-norm/#29fb4f2f2911.

Scholz, B., Vuorio, E., Matuschek, S., & Cameron, I. (2009). *Research Careers in Europe Landscape and Horizons*. Strasbourg: European Science Foundation.

Schuster, J. H., & Finkelstein, M. J. (2006). *The American Faculty: The Restructuring of Academic Work and Careers*. Baltimore, MD: The Johns Hopkins University Press.

Seldin, P., & Miller, J. E. (2009). *The Academic Portfolio: A Practical Guide to Documenting Teaching, Research, and Service*. San Francisco, CA: Jossey Bass.

Shao, D. H., & Shao, L. P. (2012). The effects of multitasking on individual's task performance. *International Journal of Business Strategy, 12*(1), 51–53.

Söderholm, A. (2014). Building academic success through fun and relevance. In M. Hällgren (ed.), *Reflections on a Scientific Career: Behind the Professor's CV* (pp. 43–54). Copenhagen: Copenhagen Business School Press.

Strannegård, L. (2014). Read, write and get it right. In M. Hällgren (ed.), *Reflections on a Scientific Career – Behind the Professor's CV* (pp. 33–42). Stockholm/ Copenhagen: Liber/Copenhagen Business Press.

Teichler, U. (2010). The diversifying academic profession? *European Review, 18*(1), 157–179.

Vinkler, P. (2010). *The Evaluation of Research by Scientometric Indicators*. Oxford, UK: Chandos Publishing.

Wrzesniewski, A. (2011). Callings. In K. Cameron, & G. M. Spreitzer (eds.), *Handbook of Positive Organizational Scholarship* (pp. 45–55). Oxford, MA: Oxford University Press.

Wrzesniewski, A., McCauiey, C., Rozin, P., & Schwartz, B. (1997). Jobs, careers, and callings: People's relations to their work. *Journal of Research in Personality, 31*(1), 21–33.

Wulff, D. H., Austin, A. E., Nyquist, J. D., & Sprague, J. (2004). The development of graduate students as teaching scholars: A four-year longitudinal study. In D. H. Wulff, & A. E. Austin (eds.), *Paths to the Professoriate: Strategies for Enriching the Preparation of Future Faculty* (pp. 46–73). San Francisco, CA: Jossey Bass.

Ylijoki, O.-H., & Mäntylä, H. (2003). Conflicting time perspectives in academic work. *Time & Society, 12*(1), 55–78.

PART II

Academic career as a journey

3. Academic career as an Odyssey: allegories from the work of Homer and personal experiences in modern Greece

Eleanna Galanaki

Estimated reading time: **19 minutes and 27 seconds**.

CHAPTER HIGHLIGHTS

- Academic career is a non-linear process where everything takes much longer than initially planned; one needs to persevere and be resilient.
- Target wisely (your publication chances are much higher when the journal outlet has already published similar articles, i.e. showed interest in your topic of research).
- The success of academics is not a one-man-show (find companions and allies).
- What goes around comes around – helping and citizenship behavior will open channels of collaboration.
- Our career is a constant and never-ending learning experience that evolves and develops continuously.

A man who has been through bitter experiences and travelled far enjoys even his sufferings after a time.
Homer, *The Odyssey*

THE LEGACY OF HOMER

The definition of *odyssey* (Merriam Webster, 2019b) is:

1: a long wandering or voyage usually marked by many changes of fortune (e.g.,
    "his odyssey from rural South to urban North, from poverty to affluence, from
    Afro-American folk culture to a Eurocentric world of books")
2: an intellectual or spiritual wandering or quest (e.g., "an odyssey of
    self-discovery", "a spiritual odyssey from disbelief to faith").

The Odyssey is one of the two major Ancient Greek epic poems attributed to
Homer. It is, in part, a sequel to the *Iliad*, the other work ascribed to Homer.
The poem mainly focuses on the Greek hero Odysseus (known as Ulysses in
Roman myths), king of Ithaca, and his journey home after the fall of Troy.
It takes Odysseus another ten years to reach Ithaca after the ten-year Trojan
War. During his absence, it is assumed that Odysseus has died, and his wife
Penelope and son Telemachus must deal with a group of unruly suitors (the
Suitors, also known as Mnesteres or Proci), who compete for Penelope's
hand in marriage. Meanwhile, Odysseus is wandering around the Aegean Sea
and further down to Italy and the "land of the dead". He is chased after by
Poseidon, god of the sea, who seeks revenge because Odysseus blinded his
son, the Cyclops Polyphemus.

In this chapter, I am inspired by Homer's *Odyssey* and attempt to find analogies and antitheses between the original epos and the odyssey of academic life,
as I experienced it myself, in Greek academia. I should let the reader know that
I am currently in the middle of my career (14 years after my PhD) and hold
a tenured post of Assistant Professor in Organizational Behavior at Athens
University of Economics and Business. I am also happily married and a mother
of three wonderful kids and I am convinced that my family is both my anchor
and sails in my journey, for which I am grateful.

OBSTACLES AND ENABLERS

The Unknown and Unpredictable

All the events in the *Odyssey* are unknown and unpredictable. Odysseus
himself is found in so many unknown places and has many different encounters in ways he could not have predicted (Ismaros, the land of the Cicones, the
Lotus-Eaters, the Cyclops Polyphemus, Aeolus with his winds, the cannibal-
istic Laestrygonians, the witch-goddess Circe, the land of the dead, the Sirens,
Calypso's island, the six-headed monster Scylla and the whirlpool Charybdis
are the most characteristic ones). None of them was expected or according
to schedule. In an academic career, a junior academic expects that her or his
career will be a well-planned course, following specific milestones: doctoral
research, writing of a thesis, defense, presentations at conferences, the writing
of papers and submission to journals (aiming first at those with higher rankings

and, if that is not feasible, contending with lower-ranking ones), acquiring teaching experience, filing for a job, pursuing tenure and development, and so on.

My personal experience does not agree with this linear, milestone-related development. A list of indicative unexpected events (both positive and negative) follows:

- Delays in data collection: I hardly know of any social researcher who has not experienced any delay in data collection. For me the most telling example was the collection of questionnaires for my PhD research. I had to collect 100 questionnaires, which, given the nature of the data, had to be completed through interview (either by phone or, in most cases, face-to-face, at the interviewee's office). The respondents were the most senior person in the Human Resources Management (HRM) department of each organization contacted, so reaching an agreement for a visit or phone interview was already an expected challenge. What was a surprise to me was the high ratio of annulments and the need to reschedule meetings, when all my days were already committed. Almost half of the originally scheduled interviews were eventually rescheduled. I still remember vividly the sense of accomplishment that I felt on the days that I managed to complete two on-site interviews (my personal record was four interviews in a day). I had predicted that data collection would last up to six months. Finally, I managed to complete the process in almost a year … It was frustrating and time-consuming. At the same time, it was one of the most valuable experiences in my studies: I visited so many companies and discussed my topic with so many experienced HR professionals from different industry sectors that I still use examples in my HRM classes. Plus, working in a small country and market, I still meet and have contacts with some of the interviewees and I am more able to speak their language[1] when I collaborate with practitioners during a consulting project or on other occasions.
- Delays in the review process. I know *no one* who has not experienced unexpected (and undesired) delays during the review process of their work. It is common, even with the highest ranked journals, which usually have a quick turnaround time. My latest such experiences have proved that this is usually related to the lack of reviewers. An editor who does not desk reject immediately but delays assigning reviewers is interested in your work and he/she may take longer than expected to find adequate reviewers. My current publishing strategy is to always cite all the relevant papers that have been published in the targeted journal, not only because this is necessary for a comprehensive literature review, but also to ease the work of the editor who will be searching for relevant reviewers. I must admit that, despite my strategy, I still get delays in the review process.

- Unavailability of examiners: I have experienced this every time that I needed to finalize the date for a formal examination/evaluation (for the PhD defense, for applications in every post I have filed for and during development evaluations). The larger the committee, the most difficulty in arranging for them to meet. Applications like Doodle have considerably eased the process in comparison to ten years earlier, but even in my latest evaluation for development, in 2018, when a committee of a dozen professors needed to reach a quorum, it was quite a challenge to find the right date. Practically this is a task that – at least in my country – the applicants bear, because they have an interest in speeding up the process.

- Invitation to submit papers and chapters: At some point in one's career, you start being invited to submit your work. This is obviously an honor. It is also an opportunity to update and present work that you do not consider fit for the highest ranked journals. For me, such invitations allow me to foster my networks, to increase the visibility of my work and sometimes even to come back and utilize works that I considered complete. Pay attention to invitations from publications that charge fees or editing expenses. Usually they do not have any academic merit. I only reply to invitations from academics whom I know and respect. This safeguards the quality of the produced overall output of which my work will form part.

Obstacles that Become Enablers: Calypso/Ogygia

Homer's *Odyssey* book 5 describes how Odysseus finds shelter at the island of Ogygia, where the nymph Calypso lives. He stays with her for seven years as a prisoner, because she wants to keep him on her island to make him her immortal husband. Odysseus can no longer bear being separated from his wife Penelope and his patron goddess Athena asks Zeus to order Calypso to release Odysseus from the island, so eventually Calypso concedes, sending Odysseus on his way after providing him with wine, bread and the materials for a raft. She also gives him useful tips on the route and on how he should sail, on the dangers that he should avoid and so on. This is a recurring theme in Homer's *Odyssey*: former obstacles or enemies often become enablers or allies and vice-versa. In an academic career, it is also common for past obstacles to become enablers. I will give an example.

"Someone conducting research similar to mine": It sounds like the typical nightmare for a researcher. You completed your paper, and when you are ready to submit it for publication to your targeted journal, a paper with similar hypotheses, data and methodology is published. Where will you publish, and what will be your paper's contribution? This is indeed an unpredictable situation which might occur from time to time. There is a wonderful aspect to this, though: your topic is currently popular and papers similar to yours do get published in the journal of your choice. The key message here is to continue working on the paper and to turn this to an opportunity.[2] You will need to devote considerable effort in changing (in order of importance) the conceptualization (1), the research questions (2), and the methods (3) of your work in such a way that it adds to the already published work. Your chances of acceptance to the journal are much higher when it has published similar articles, thus showing interest for your topic of research.

Companions and Critical Allies

Odysseus, throughout his adventures and wandering, almost always has characters who support and help him. This is true for almost everything one accomplishes. Even if we tend to believe that the academic life is a very lonely one, the success of academics is not a solo performance. To begin with, by definition, research and teaching, the main pillars of academic function, are based on knowledge that previous researchers have developed. Therefore, in a very broad sense, academics have as companions and allies the older academics who have advanced our knowledge in a way that makes our current research meaningful. As Isaac Newton put it in his famous quote mentioned by the editors in Chapter 1 of this volume: "if we want to see further, we need to stand on the shoulders of giants" (Newton, 1675, in Turnbull, 1959). Apart from the theoretical allies, however, there are numerous people who will become your allies and companions in your academic life.

Athena – mentor
In the *Odyssey* epos, the most critical ally for Odysseus is Athena, the wisdom goddess who repeatedly protects Odysseus and helps him return home. The most telling example of Athena's intervention is when, during Odysseus' absence, she takes on the appearance of *Mentes* (Mentor), a friend of Odysseus and she meets Telemachus, Odysseus' son in order to advise him how to deal with the suitors. In fact, this is the provenance of the term "mentoring", i.e. the act of giving advice and helping younger people to develop their potential and succeed.[3] I mention the story of Mentor, because the most valuable allies that any academic has are her/his mentors. The first and obvious mentor is usually the doctoral supervisor. There may be other mentors and role models in one's career, but the doctoral supervisor is the most critical. I was blessed to have Professor Nancy Papalexandris (I hope that she does not mind my mentioning her name here) as my supervisor. She was a very good mentor, not only because as a professor, when I first collaborated with her, she was very successful and renowned for her research on HRM and organizational behavior (OB) in Greece. What really made her a great supervisor was her drive to improve things and accomplish even more achievements (even after

her retirement she is one of the most active academics I know), her willingness to develop people around her and leave them room to cultivate their skills and maximize their potential, her honest concern at a personal level for people, as well as her clear judgment and composure, rooted in long-term experience in academia and a steady code of ethics. These "soft skills" of my supervisor were crucial for my development, even more than her scientific and technical knowledge. I am convinced that the choice of the supervisor is one of the first but also the most critical career choice in academia. As with mentoring in general, the key to good supervision is for the supervisor to honestly want the growth and development of the young researcher.

I still recall a joke that we used to share with my colleagues at the Hellenic Association of Doctoral Researchers, a group that we founded in 2003 with other Greek doctoral candidates and which unfortunately, to the best of my knowledge, is not active anymore. Allow me to share the joke here, as it underlines the role of the supervisor/mentor in academic research:

> In the middle of the forest, on a sunny day, the Wolf meets the Rabbit. The Rabbit has gathered loads of papers in front of him on a rock and writes incessantly. At the question of the Wolf on what he is writing with such diligence, the Rabbit answers: "My doctoral thesis". The Wolf asks what's the topic of the thesis and the Rabbit answers: "The superiority of herbivores over carnivores". At the mocking laughter of the Wolf over the ridiculousness of the topic, the Rabbit challenges him to prove it and invites the Wolf to escort him to a nearby cave. In a few minutes the Wolf is seen running away, wounded and full of scratches. The same scenario is repeated with almost all carnivore animals that pass by the Rabbit: they get beaten up when they question the validity of his hypothesis. Later, we see the Rabbit exiting the cave, escorted by the Lion, who is saying: "As I was telling you, Rabbit; in a doctorate, the key success factor is the supervisor, not the topic."

I recall with fond memories the laughs that we shared with my fellow doctoral candidates at the impotency of carnivores to defend their conviction/base hypothesis in the face of the potent supervisor of the Rabbit.

I was lucky to have good mentors in my career even after the completion of my PhD. In general, I sought to collaborate with people from whom I had something important to learn. Obviously, you learn something from everyone you collaborate with. I am convinced that I learn a lot from my students, for example. However, there are people in everyone's field who can become mentors and it is a joy to collaborate with them in many ways. The question is whether and how we show gratitude for their unselfish giving. Very often we are not able to do so. Recently, with colleagues, also Professor Nancy Papalexandris' mentees, we have found a way to express our indebtedness: we have decided to co-edit a collective honorary volume of papers published in recognition of her contribution to the area of HRM, OB and general management, throughout her academic career (Galanaki et al., 2020).

Phaecians (Nafsika, Arete, Alcinoos)

Odysseus was not only assisted by gods. He received help from many different individuals, the majority of whom he had never met before. A characteristic example is the reception by the Phaecians, at his last stop on his way to Ithaca. As a castaway he gets washed up on the coast of the island of the Phaecians, where he meets the princess Nafsika, and she takes him to the palace, where he is hosted by her parents, king Alcinoos and queen Arete. They provide him with flawless hospitality and when they learn who he is and his story, they arrange for one of their ships to take him to Ithaca. The behavior of the Phaecians is indicative of how Homer introduces allies to assist his main hero. The help from them is unexpected, but it is Odysseus who welcomes and asks for it. Odysseus is a character who is open to people around him: he trusts others (taking calculated risks), asks them for help, and makes them participants in the drama. We may call it an "Odyssey" after the name of the main character, but there are many allies who produce the outcome, i.e. the return to Ithaca.

One of the career strategies that I have been quite consistent in following (mostly because it is in accordance with my personality) is being open to other people, trusting, and offering collaboration and help when possible. Generally, this opens a channel of trust and, when in need, I am also able to ask for assistance, advice, information, etc. Since the beginning of my career I have been involved in several extra and voluntary activities. I have done this without other motivation or a hidden agenda, only for the sake of each activity's cause. Now, looking back at them, I realize that each of these activities has allowed me to develop some network, ability or competence that I had not foreseen. For example, my involvement in the Hellenic Doctoral Researchers' Association, for which I was the first president, allowed me to develop a large network in Greek academia and cross-disciplinary thinking, as well as the confidence to pursue representation positions.

At the time we were members of the European Doctoral Federation, Eurodoc, where I also served on the Executive Board for one year. I think that this developed my ability to cooperate with people from different countries. In both organizations I contributed as much as I could because I believed in their cause and wanted to contribute. I did not expect more than the cause itself at the time.

Years later, when I was asked to run as Greek representative at the European Academy of Management (EURAM official web page: http://euram-online .org/), I was happy to take this up and run for the position. It was after the EURAM Conference in Istanbul (2013), where there was a record number of Greek participants in comparison to previous years, that a position at EURAM's Executive Board was open to Greece. I had participated in previous EURAM conferences and had appreciated the format and scope of the Academy, so I was willing to contribute to its mission.

Right now, I fear that I have taken up too many responsibilities in EURAM, because in addition to the Greek representative position, I have also taken on the chairing of the General OB track (95 submissions in total in 2019, one of the largest tracks of the conference) and this is a lot of work and responsibility. However, I have come to consider that work that you do for your academic field pays off. I am not able to count the outcomes of my EURAM involvement, but I believe that several of the latest opportunities in my career (guest editing positions, invited speeches and chapters in contributed volumes) are to a large extent related to this. To sum up, the ancient odyssey and my career experience agree in this respect: voluntary, extra work and citizenship behavior open channels of collaboration and allow others to reach out to you and possibly assist you when needed.

DESTINATION AND JOURNEY

The work of Homer has inspired several modern thinkers, authors and poets. My favorite work is the poem "Ithaca" from a Greek poet Cavafy (1975). Allow me to share it with you:

Ithaca

As you set out for Ithaca
hope your road is a long one,
full of adventure, full of discovery.
Laistrygonians, Cyclops,
angry Poseidon—don't be afraid of them:
you'll never find things like that on your way
as long as you keep your thoughts raised high,
as long as a rare excitement
stirs your spirit and your body.
Laistrygonians, Cyclops,
wild Poseidon—you won't encounter them
unless you bring them along inside your soul,
unless your soul sets them up in front of you.

Hope your road is a long one.
May there be many summer mornings when,
with what pleasure, what joy,
you enter harbors you're seeing for the first time;
may you stop at Phoenician trading stations
to buy fine things,
mother of pearl and coral, amber and ebony,
sensual perfume of every kind—
as many sensual perfumes as you can;

and may you visit many Egyptian cities
to learn and go on learning from their scholars.

Keep Ithaca always in your mind.
Arriving there is what you're destined for.
But don't hurry the journey at all.
Better if it lasts for years,
so you're old by the time you reach the island,
wealthy with all you've gained on the way,
not expecting Ithaca to make you rich.

Ithaca gave you the marvelous journey.
Without her you wouldn't have set out.
She has nothing left to give you now.

And if you find her poor, Ithaca won't have fooled you.
Wise as you will have become, so full of experience,
you'll have understood by then what these Ithacas mean.

I set this work apart because it expresses in the best possible way the feeling that in odyssey the most important aspect is the journey itself rather than the destination. The journey is a learning process that evolves and develops constantly. Homer does not seem to care much about describing Ithaca or the years that Odysseus spent with his family after his return home. As in all fiction, the journey is far more interesting than the outcome of or the final destiny of the main character.

In a similar vein, in an academic career, one's CV is dominated by achievements and learning opportunities that have enabled one to develop Knowledge, Skill, Ability, and Other personal characteristics (KSAOs). Obviously, good posts and tenure in well-known universities are an intended destination for most junior academics. However, alternative career outcomes may also define the success of the journey. I have met so many business researchers who, after completing their doctoral studies, decided that an academic career would not be ideal for them. Working for industry, in managerial or consulting positions, can be a success for many of us who efficiently utilize their KSAOs in business-led contexts. And, actually, these people are best equipped to address the long sought-for calls for a more evidence-based management in action (Reay et al., 2009), as they have largely developed KSAOs in running research and evaluating research outcomes during their early academic experience. I also know of academics, mothers and fathers, who have developed great parenting potential as a result of long experience of learning and teaching. In their case, the journey has allowed them to develop skills that can be utilized effectively in their family life.

On the other hand, people in academia share a common benefit: our career is a constant and never-ending learning experience. Learning is our core business and, as described in Cavafy's "Ithaca", learning, trying and experimenting, *per se*, constitute a self-satisfying process. We have the benefit of constantly satisfying our self-actualization needs (according to Maslow's [1943] hierarchy of needs) through our work. Further, more basic needs (such as self-esteem, and physiological and safety needs) are also satisfied to a large extent with our work, regardless of our career outcome (post, promotion, and so on). Few professions can convincingly claim the same. The only human need that an academic career seems to fail to meet is that of love and belonging. Even if academic teachers constantly interact with their students during teaching, our journey can be a very lonely one. Relations with other people are finite in time, depending on the duration of a course (students), a research project (fellow academics) or a consulting project (business clients). Moreover, most of our work is conducted in isolation, for example, writing, performing analyses, making notes and preparing course materials, and studying. It is a lonely road, but very worthwhile and rewarding.

NOTES

1. More than before, because the communication of academics with practitioners is, by definition, difficult and I fear I am not an exception.
2. This has happened to me a few times, but I cannot describe them all, as some involve other people who may not agree with my mentioning our story. I can share the example of my latest paper "Effects of employee benefits on affective and continuance commitment during times of crisis", though, recently published at the *International Journal of Manpower*. During the literature review for this project, I had missed a 2010 article by Benjamin Artz, named "Fringe benefits and job satisfaction", in the same journal. When I later identified it, I had already written my first draft, which, at the time, had both organizational commitment and job satisfaction as dependent variables. I had to rework the paper in a way that it would contribute to the open discussion that Artz had started, so a lot of work rewriting it. But the discussion was already there, open for my paper to participate in it.
3. Specifically, the definition of *mentor* (Merriam Webster, 2019a) is:
    1 [capitalized]: a friend of Odysseus entrusted with the education of Odysseus' son Telemachus
    a trusted counselor or guide
    tutor, coach".

REFERENCES

Cavafy, C. P. (1975). *Collected Poems*. Princeton, NJ: Princeton University Press.

Galanaki, E., Nikandrou, I., & Panayotopoulou, L., eds. (2020). *Collective Volume in Honour of Professor Nancy Papalexandris*. Athens: Editions Benos.

Maslow, A. H. (1943). A theory of human motivation. *Psychological Review, 50*(4), 370–396.

Merriam Webster (2019a). Mentor. *Merriam Webster Dictionary*. Retrieved February 10, 2019 from https://www.merriam-webster.com/dictionary/mentor.

Merriam Webster (2019b). Odyssey. *Merriam Webster Dictionary*. Retrieved February 10, 2019 from https://www.merriam-webster.com/dictionary/odyssey.

Reay, T., Berta, W., & Kohn, M. K. (2009). What's the evidence on evidence-based management? *Academy of Management Perspectives, 23*(4), 5–18.

Turnbull, H. W. (ed.). (1959). *The Correspondence of Isaac Newton: Volume 1 (1661–1675)*. Cambridge, UK: Cambridge University Press.

4. Reflections of a traveling academic: the good, the bad… often not anticipated

Hana Milanov

Estimated reading time: **24 minutes and 25 seconds**.

> ### CHAPTER HIGHLIGHTS
>
> - Have a research question you care for and find meaning in what you do.
> - Be pragmatic; the best dissertation is a done dissertation.
> - When you move, be aware of six months to a year of adaptation "costs" which will have implications for the research productivity.
> - Adapt the teaching material to your own strengths and preferences (enjoy creating your own material).
> - The academic leadership position allows so much perspective and provides opportunities to connect initiatives, resources, and people.

One doesn't discover new lands without consenting to lose sight,
for a very long time, of the shore.
Andre Gide, Nobel Prize winner

THE ACCIDENTAL ACADEMIC

Just a few days before starting to write these pages, it was 15 years since I left my hometown of Zagreb to set off on the most unexpected path that took me to where I am today. How to distill something that might be helpful? I did not want to zoom in so much as to write a bullet point list of tips for "how to get tenure", "how to publish", and so on, yet anything else felt as if it may become too broad, and therefore remain on the surface.

As I reflected, I realized that one way to think about the last 15 years is to conceive them as a series of choices (although not all were of the planned, intended kind, as hinted in this title). A correlate of making big choices, at least in my life, was accompanied with the keyword "transitions". Many an academic's CV portrays a nomadic journey, so transitions should not be unexpected. It is just that I did not expect to be an academic to begin with. Almost none of this was really *planned*. Getting a doctorate. Leaving home. Changing three countries. Becoming a Senior Vice President (SVP) of one of Europe's best technical universities before even growing a proper gray hair. Yet, somehow, looking back, I take pleasure that many of the dots connect.

STUMBLING INTO ACADEMIA

If one were to ask my parents, I should have been an actress (father), or lawyer (mother), or perhaps a doctor (both). Apparently, I pretended well and argued superbly, and was generally thought to be a high potential child. To my parents' amazement, I went to study economics. I knew it then, and I am even surer of it now: I did not opt for this choice because I was passionate or even intellectually curious about it (following high school, I had little of both, it turns out). It was because high school chatter convinced me that this might be the best way to *postpone* the decision of "what I want to become when I grow up".

Being an all-round A student all my life, I have excelled in taking exams, obeying the rules, understanding what pleased the teachers and performing to expectations. A poster child for many envious parents, and a perfect case of creativity killed, according to Sir Ken Robinson (Robinson, 2006). The schooling system did little to help me understand what I wanted to become. I watched with envy (a few of) my friends who with conviction went to study architecture and medicine – it was their calling, they said.

Fast-forward four years. As I was completing my undergraduate studies, it was in a moment of serendipity, that getting out of a tram en route to the university I ran into a family acquaintance. Upon learning of my excellent grades, he asked me if I would consider applying for a research assistant position at the Institute of Economics, Zagreb, just across the university building. To be honest, I had no idea what a research assistant does. I was polite and said, "That is a very nice idea". He quickly mentioned how this in part means continuing with studies, and I recall thinking, "Well, this would be convenient, doing something I already know how to do". This was Croatia, 2002. Jobs were not exactly flying off the shelves, and students' ambitions were lost somewhere between being told by parents it is best to get a "stable job with a state owned enterprise" and that same state going through a rough ride with privatization of many of those jobs. I applied and got the position.

ON PROTEIN BARS, FAKE IDs, A LIBRARY THAT CLOSES SIX HOURS IN A YEAR AND A TINY QUESTION OF RESEARCH IDENTITY

A few months into my days at the Institute of Economics, Zagreb, a delegation from Kelley School of Business came to look for a cooperation partner in delivering a small-scale MBA program based on a development grant received from the US government. The director of the institute was wise enough to "craft a deal" for the partnership, one that would allow his scientists to go and advance their work in a top research environment in the US. They looked around the institute for the first candidates – I spoke good English, wasn't married or with a family, and hadn't started a master's yet. Target identified. I did the TOEFL (Test of English as a Foreign Language), GRE (Graduate Record Examinations), and was told I'd been accepted. *Into what?* I share below a few anecdotes that turned out to be defining lessons for the PhD (and much of my career going forward).

As shown in the abundant research in biology, business and, yes, even studies of academics in sociology, malleable PhD students are very imprintable targets (a popular example of imprinting is a chick hatching from an egg, and upon seeing a cat, thinking for the rest of its life that the cat is its mother). A description of imprinting as discussed in management research suggests that characteristics of an entity shaped during a sensitive moment of its existence can persist for decades, in spite of subsequent environmental changes (Simsek et al., 2015). In these sensitive early academic years, when we are still being defined as scholars (and in my case, age-wise, as people) we are ready targets for absorbing not only what we do but also *how it's to be done.*

I arrived in the US on 15 August 2013. The first months were full of impressions. For example, I learned that the fact that public transport exists in a town the size of Bloomington, Indiana is considered quite advanced, so no one made a big deal about the fact that this same public transport did not operate on weekends. Now, in Bloomington you could not hail a taxi on the street, you had to use your cell phone to call one. But you couldn't get a cell phone contract without a credit history. And you could not get a credit history without a credit card. Bottom line, I had to get a credit card to start accumulating credit history or basically face the prospect of staying at home on the weekends for the next four years. Similarly, I realized it was considered normal to jog in the middle of the night in the deep snow, but considered profoundly strange to carry one's groceries by foot in the middle of a sunny day (in their defense, a random stranger offered me a ride to alleviate my "suffering" while carrying groceries from the store five minutes back to my home).

On the professional side, I was shocked to learn that a lunch commonly consists of protein bars or a quick sandwich (my parents' nest in Zagreb served lunches with a soup and a main course every day). A lunch break – if taken – is best used to talk about papers, or run on the treadmill reading them. On campus orientation day, upon touring the library, the librarian profoundly apologized to us because the library (otherwise open 24/7) is closed for six hours on the night of Christmas Eve. This set the stage for expectations on how hard doctoral students should work, which I probably took too literally, also seeking to compensate for being the youngest kid on the block. During my PhD, I gained almost 10 kilograms, had three different categories of skin problems at once during proposal defense time, and probably set the stage for the disc hernia I suffered years later. There should be a more balanced way to do this, and I wish I was more proactive about learning from others about how to manage the PhD process. Here are a few tips, at least from my experience:

- **Having a research question you care for:**"What is the research question that keeps you up at night?" was one of the first questions we were asked on orientation day. Listening to my peers (all older than me, and far less "accidental" in pursuing their PhD) answering this question by sharing their puzzles and dilemmas, I realized quickly that *this* will be the question that keeps me up at night. Why was I the only one without a research question that keeps me up at night? Was I doomed to be unsuccessful due to lacking one? It turns out, having a healthy dose of curiosity, paired with discipline and rigor can still allow for questions others find interesting, and helps you to establish a publishing record. However, if you can pair what academics find interesting with something you personally care for, it will make an often-hard journey that much more rewarding.
- **Have your PhD serve you, do not be a servant to your PhD**: I looked to get a great grade in all my courses and please the teachers in every class discussion and exam (rings a bell, early education?). Instead, I should have thought how any of these courses could help advance *my research,* and prioritize accordingly. You have to protect your time and be very picky about what you read and write.[1]
- **"The best dissertation is a done dissertation"**: We heard this on average once a week, and there is a reason. It is so easy to get side-tracked, and you will learn quickly that the dreaded "ABD" (all but dissertation) is a category associated with failure in the US system.

(I should clarify that I am saying this with another imprinted bias in mind, which is that anyone doing a doctorate aims to do research in top-tier schools, which implies minimizing your teaching and publishing in top journals in hunting for a tenure.[2] This, of course, does not have to be *your goal.* It might be that you have completely different reasons for doing a doctorate, and that the pressure of "publish or perish" doesn't apply to you.)

What is the ultimate take-away here? My PhD choice was "accidental". I stumbled into academia, and I did not pick where I would do my PhD (which is really quite unusual in the US system). So I write this for those who have not chosen their PhD program yet. You have a chance of choosing the environment that will imprint you. Conquering the mountain of successfully finishing the PhD is of course a great accomplishment in itself, and one should feel proud. However, during my PhD, it was made clear to us that the only criterion of *real* success is to end up in a highly ranked, research-oriented school with a tenure track position. Indeed, our advisors were informally evaluated on the good "placement" of their students in the job market. Your way may be different, of course, but it is good to ask yourself some questions first, and be mindful about choosing both the advisor and the school accordingly. Upon entering the tenure race, the criteria of "excellence" are not as simple as finishing a PhD or landing *a* job. Your work is to be judged by and evaluated against the outputs of a much broader community. In research, this community is literally global, competing for the top journals and research funds. And then there's teaching. And service/administration. If you want to become a faculty member, that is. Here is what that transition looked like.

ON SIESTA, BEING THE YOUNGEST PERSON IN CLASS, AND GETTING MY FIRST TENURE

I became an associate professor at IE Business School in Madrid, Spain, on 1 May 2007 (labor day, ironically), at the age of 26. If you consider that the average age of my MBA students at the time was 28, you can appreciate how grateful I was that someone would take a bet on me, although I was primarily judged on my research potential. To put this into perspective, some rough calculations would say that two million euros looked at me walking into the classroom (the students knew their math, too, some literally making comments about the value of each class session, and the return on investment expected from it). This pressure alone resulted in the convenient side-effect of losing all those extra kilos gained during the PhD journey. It also meant that, in addition to landing in a new country, where I did not speak the language, had zero social capital (though adored everything about Madrid and the IE Business School otherwise), I had to find a way to both maintain my research and build an identity as a teacher. Having moved by now three times across languages, systems, and countries (Croatia to US, US to Spain, and Spain to Germany), I estimate six months to a year of adaptation "costs", which naturally also has its implications for the research productivity. So I will write about those two transitions: finding my feet in a new context, and becoming a teacher.

As opposed to the US, where one can literally set up a life over a weekend and there's a 1-800 number or website for everything, moving to Spain meant that just opening a bank account took multiple visits to the bank, exchanging "besos" (kisses) with the personal banker, and explaining why I am not comfortable with signing a contract on which they wrote "Hana Hrvatsko Milanov" (Hana Croatian Milanov) as my name, given that it did not compute in their mind that I do not have a middle name, so they added the nationality from my passport instead. Following this and similar other experiences, I graciously accepted the IE's offer to provide private language lessons. Result: I was almost fluent in Spanish in my first year there and this helped a lot in feeling at home, finding friends and allies, and generally getting rid of much of the daily stress that comes with navigating the world when you don't speak the language. Side-effect: I spent four to six hours a week with my Spanish teacher, and at least that much more recovering from the intensity of each lesson. If you add to that those two million euros of expectations waiting for me in the classroom several times a week (and the temptations of a girl facing the glories of Madrid after four years surrounded by cornfields), you quickly realize that the day doesn't have enough hours. So I ended up not sleeping enough – again.

I estimate that in that first year, I spent on average two days preparing for one class (IE was predominantly teaching the case method at the time). As a private business school, it was only natural for the teacher to care about student evaluations, and I was dreading the day of receiving mine. As expected, the first round was far from something I would hang on a wall. It can be devastating reading students' comments after all that hard work, and it is hard not to take them personally. It took many conversations with dear colleagues and some time to process the emotions and gain the clarity of mind that allows one to soberly reflect on the experience, learn from the many mistakes, and do it again – hopefully better. And it did get not only progressively easier, but also even very enjoyable with time.

While in my first round I inherited another colleague's syllabus, I learned how to adapt the teaching material to my own strengths and preferences. Actually, with time, I took a lot of pleasure in creating my own material – exercises, workshops, and entire courses. I also learned to be more open, transparent about my age and background, trust the students, and be less controlling and dominating in how I led class discussions.

Ironically, one of the big lessons in entrepreneurship we try to teach our students is to work with their own means given how futile it can be to control the uncontrollable (see Sarasvathy's [2001] work on effectuation). I was doing exactly the opposite in my first teaching round, and only later learned to embrace the lesson in my own teaching. I learned teachers do not necessarily have to have all the answers, but that we can help our students structure their thinking in a dialogue with us.

Ironically again, it took a great student to illuminate the #1 challenge question most entrepreneurship faculty face when entering a classroom – whether "entrepreneurship can be taught". Rather than waiting for students to ask that question and be put in a position to "defend my job" when addressing it, I chose to start my classes by asking the question from the start. In one of my early classes, one student responded: "Professor, I think you are asking the wrong question – shouldn't it be about whether one can learn entrepreneurship?" There, in that one minute interaction, I not only got validation of opening up debates as a pedagogical tool, but also learned to trust students more, and leverage the biggest strength we get from our research training: having conversations that challenge assumptions, open minds, and ask the right questions. I remain eternally grateful to that student for opening my eyes, and have embraced the philosophy ever since. Of course, teaching preparation still takes time, yet I have learned to enjoy the slight uncertainty of teaching a case for the first time, and allowing difficult questions to be kernels of good debates, rather than seeing them as personal attacks.

"YOU CHOSE TO MOVE BACK TO EUROPE?"

Becoming a young faculty member also meant I was often invited to doctoral workshops, where in those days age-wise I still felt closer to the students in the class than to some of my faculty peers. In one of these workshops, the topic was about the academic job market, and there were two discussants: one who finished his PhD in Europe and got a job in the US, and me – the US graduate with a job in Europe. I was quite surprised when I realized that, in some ways, I was positioned to be the "odd duck" in the room. For who would leave the well-oiled engine of research in the US only to venture into a new language and face the prospects of a delayed tenure? In my frustration, I realized that in some ways, they were right (echo: imprint of research excellence).

The US has many advantages for playing the tenure game. It is easier to maintain one's network there, there are ongoing paper workshops, presentations, a more homogeneous research environment, and certainly no language barriers. At the same time, I recalled having the prospect of getting a job in another small US college town (where many of the greatest research schools are to be found and admired), with protein bars for lunch, without public transport, without opportunity to travel back home for a couple of days, and quickly concluded that – for me at least – there was more to life than a route-to-tenure. Being able to *walk* the vibrant streets of Madrid home, grabbing a *late* dinner with a friend, enjoying dance performances on the weekend, and being close to all other wonderful aspects of Spain and Europe meant a more fulfilling life. While it did come with a price of adjusting, learning the language, and more effort to keep the research productivity – the price of not being the elite researcher was offset by the value of life outside of it.

Did I mention my fiancé was in Germany all this time?

ON MUESLI FOR LUNCH AND BECOMING A SENIOR VICE PRESIDENT

My last country hop, ironically in the year of getting tenured in Madrid, took me to Munich. I was sad to leave Madrid – in many ways, the IE Business School and the incredible people I met there, and the city itself got under my skin. I built my identity as a professor there, and enjoyed all the perks of adult life with a proper salary (following very humble lifestyle of a PhD student). At the same time, at the age of 32, the depleting inner energy reserves of flying between Spain and Germany on a bi-weekly or monthly basis for five years were sending a strong message. While the academic job market in Germany was portrayed to me as rigid and unwelcoming of younger talent, a great opportunity presented itself when I ran into a colleague I knew from conferences who told me about Technical University of Munich (TUM) pioneering a tenure track system modeled on the US one. This meant a chance to reunite in one place my personal and professional selves. As sad as I was to leave Madrid, I was excited about this chance for unity. New language: Take #2. New academic system: Take #3.

Moving to Germany was a completely different experience. I was somewhat experienced and more rigid in my ways. I also wasn't moving alone like the last two times, but coming to a "safe base" moving in with my fiancé, now husband. This ironically had its counter effect in being much slower in building up my social circle, both at work and outside it, which is something I would do differently if I started again. Life was now differently set up: while at IE, the job *was* my life; all of a sudden there was a more clear separation between socializing and work, as well as this additional challenge of not being able to work nights whenever the job called for it, as I started finding a balance between publishing and trying to reserve weekends for family life. Germany brought more structure to my life, along with other modifications in schedule. Moving from Madrid to Munich meant everything started two hours earlier. Being used to 2 pm Spanish lunches, I was the black sheep of the department, eating muesli for lunch (this of course changed some months in, and my entire biorhythm changed, but this is again an illustration of those "hidden costs" of changing countries).

The other usual costs of changing systems were there, too. For example, German professors are direct "employers" of their PhD students, which brings completely different responsibilities, dynamics, and processes to the table, compared to the US system where students have dedicated programs and only later start working with a faculty *advisor*. At the same time, faculty in Germany has much more freedom in what and how they teach. While freedom of course opens wonderful opportunities for creativity and self-expression, the learning curve of how to navigate the system was steep for me. I did ask many questions, but as I was the only newcomer to the German system in the department, it felt inappropriate to continuously be "catching up" given my career stage. In this regard, the experience of changing systems and countries twice, which should have worked to my advantage from the learning perspective, strangely backfired.

Instead of being more understanding of the difficulty of moving, I was very impatient with the process and with myself, perhaps counting on the "international move experience" to make things somehow faster this time around. To this day, I am not sure I can offer more concrete advice apart from suggesting giving yourself time and a kind word every now and then. Second move, again time lost in adaptation. My imprinted expectation of research excellence was haunting me again. And just as I was finding my feet in the new set-up, I was invited to consider applying for a position of a SVP of International Alliances and Alumni for the University.

THE "BACK STAGE" OF ACADEME

It was a difficult decision. Coming from the US, every professor would tell you that admin is any researcher's worst nightmare. To give your time to anything but research is borderline sinning in scholarly terms. Weighing out the pros and cons (and the list was long on both sides), what finally prevailed was not the objective argument, but much like with other decisions so far – the feeling. As much as I felt Madrid was a better place for me than a top school in a small college town, and as much as I felt I needed to unite my personal and professional selves despite just getting tenured in Spain, the feeling of wanting to discover myself in a new role outweighed the rational concerns of seriously undermining my research output and missing the joys of teaching by dedicating time to a demanding administrative role. But I have never been anything but a student or professor all my life. Could I do something else – well? My academic brother jokingly told me: "I have worked in industry many years. Your worst enemy is your expectations of your impact. Sometimes the greatest managers just need to *not mess up* something. You will do fine."

You guessed it – I agreed, applied, interviewed, and was elected as the SVP. If I was the youngest in my PhD, then in the classroom, I was again the youngest – in the boardroom. Moreover, I was the only non-German (non-German speaking and non-German academic), only non-engineer or natural scientist, and soon the only female in the boardroom, too. This profile was something I had to learn how to occupy, but also made for some interesting situations in meetings with national and international delegations (e.g. the wonderful colleague I worked with most closely in this role, who technically reported to me, was male and older than me, which often meant that I was taken to be his subordinate, and he, instead, the SVP). Taking this role provided incredible learning opportunities – both about how universities work (as a faculty member, one does not appreciate the complexity behind the scenes), and how *I work*.

I have never been a manager and, all of a sudden, many of the wonderful theories of organizations, management, and leadership we stretch and test in our research came to life in a whole new way. What is an organization? How to structure work? What is competition and how to compete by collaborating? How to navigate relationships with national and international alliances? How to make a great leader in a setting where traditional means like "carrot and stick" do not apply (in public universities, salaries are largely set by the Ministry, and positions are equally rigid, without many opportunities for promotion or for demotion for that matter). I had to learn how to delegate, read briefings, and deal with other people taking control of my calendar. In essence, this meant that all the training of seeking mastery of the topic and depth in research was replaced by the need to grow the skills to navigate an often-turbulent surface. There wasn't a day when I wasn't jealous of an average MBA student who had the luxury of learning through multiple cases and exercises how to grow their communication, decision-making, negotiation, and leadership skills. Management professors are not trained to manage (or lead) – at least not commonly so. Isn't it ironic?

At the same time, I had the pleasure of working with and knowing many dedicated and selfless people who poured their heart into making universities work, and who are the unsung heroes of many initiatives. In this role, I discovered the pleasure of shining a light on their work, and creating bridges to enable their energy to make its way to the goal. In general, as a scholar who studied networks, I found another component of my identity develop – that of a "tertius iungens", or the "third one who connects".

The position of a board member allows so much perspective and provides opportunities to connect initiatives, resources, and people – something that wasn't obvious to me when I started. I also loved representing the university – it turns out, having listened to hundreds of pitches in my life (and coached students how to do it) helped in crafting good stories that captured people's attention. And TUM had great stories to tell. I loved flying around the world, and learning about other universities and meeting their leadership. It again makes one humble, meeting these academic giants, many of whom are also quite inspiring leaders.

At the same time, one of the best things this position gave me is an appreciation of how much I love my professor job. I missed working with students, I missed the classroom, I missed reading in depth and thinking. Having said that, if each international move meant losing up to a year of academic productivity, having spent three years as an SVP international means that I am doing a lot of catching up as I type these lines. My imprinted self judges me for agreeing to write this chapter, and claims I should have rather spent time writing a "proper" academic paper. However, there is more and more research showing that imprinting is not all there is to it. Changing imprints, breaking out of old ones and occasionally adopting new ones is possible and – more importantly – interesting to do. So 15 years in, I am finally trying to be a bit more patient and forgiving to myself for the lack of accomplished academic excellence in return for engaging with great talent and paying it forward. I may have accidentally stumbled into this journey, but there are still many rewards to be enjoyed ahead.

"Luck is where preparation meets opportunity" we often tell our students. Prepare well, but keep your eyes open – I will.

NOTES

1. This is a habit that will prove to be even more important in a professorial career when everyone is wanting to take a piece of that precious research time.
2. I should explain that it took me a good semester to catch onto all the jargon of academe, from its many abbreviations ("I got a second R&R in JBV after a desk reject in AMJ" really didn't mean much in the beginning!) and semi-told rules of tenure track. A strong network is the best way to navigate this fuzzy space.

REFERENCES

Robinson, K. (2006). Do schools kill creativity? TED2006 talk. Retrieved October 9, 2019 from https://www.ted.com/talks/sir_ken_robinson_do_schools_kill_creativity/discussion?ref=animaker.

Sarasvathy, S. D. (2001). Causation and effectuation: Toward a theoretical shift from economic inevitability to entrepreneurial contingency. *Academy of Management Review*, 26(2), 243–263.

Simsek, Z., Jansen, J. J. P., Minichilli, A., & Escriba-Esteve, A. (2015). Strategic leadership and leaders in entrepreneurial contexts: A nexus for innovation and impact missed? *Journal of Management Studies*, 52(4), 463–478.

5. How I keep myself motivated: dancing between consultancy and academia

Amy Van Looy

Estimated reading time: **25 minutes and 5 seconds**.

CHAPTER HIGHLIGHTS

- Academic research is not only about theorizing but also about creating novel artifacts that are of direct use for real-life business practices.
- Work hard in order to reach a goal (it implies some sacrifices).
- Try to find constructive feedback as early as possible from peers; distill the right comments among the sometimes-opposing opinions.
- The majority of papers need multiple revision rounds or consecutive submissions to different journals.
- Take your job seriously but not yourself.

When you change the way you look at things, the things you look at change.
Max Planck

INTRODUCTION

I am writing this chapter during the pregnancy leave of my second daughter (Spring 2017), which seems like an ideal moment to reflect on my career and to take a more philosophical lens. Let us start by introducing myself. I am currently an Assistant Professor at Ghent University (Belgium). Being part of the UGent Management Information Systems (MIS) Research Group, I coordinate the research cluster called "Process Orientation" (which is a new task in my professorial role). I am also affiliated to the School for Social Profit and Public Management at the same university. The latter is a business school, which implies that I regularly give courses to business people.

As an Assistant Professor, I am following a five-year tenure track to become a tenured (Associate) Professor. Being in my fourth year, I have reached almost all objectives for next year's assessment, which gives me more space to let creativity prevail. At first, I was indeed impressed by the strict goals set for publication outlets, project grants and PhD assistance. The scientific objectives hardly consider that most of my time is actually dedicated to teaching assignments. This is especially true during the first years when starting up new courses, but also later on due to program reforms.

Nonetheless, I experienced that those goals are reachable when making appropriate efforts, and I can start anticipating (to some extent) the goals that come next. In particular, becoming a Full Professor will take about another ten years at our university (i.e. with one intermediate round, thus five plus five years), and this with even more challenging objectives. Hence, having such expectations in mind, I can honestly say that my PhD period (with all its ups and downs) remains the most fascinating time of my academic career because my main focus was on doing research.

Nowadays, a typical day at the office is largely filled with teaching, meetings and reviews, whereas my own research comes next (and rather during evenings or weekends). On the one hand, I wish I had more focus on research because I regularly feel guilty that my own research projects (consequently) take more time. On the other hand, I also get the opportunity to experience new roles, such as being a manager (e.g. for our faculty, audits or program reforms) and a coordinator or facilitator (e.g. for regular students and PhD students), which also contribute to my self-development and to moving out of my comfort zone.

What follows is the story of my personal journey in academia, including the key turning points:

- **First career steps (outside academia)**: exploring new horizons and a life-changing meeting.
- **First PhD year**: curiosity and creativity result in a first top publication.
- **Second PhD year**: the struggle between perfectionism and pragmatism.
- **Third and final PhD year**: finishing unfinished business.
- **Tenure track**: new hopes and aspirations.

FIRST CAREER STEPS (OUTSIDE ACADEMIA): EXPLORING NEW HORIZONS AND A LIFE-CHANGING MEETING

Although I am currently a professor in information systems and business administration, I actually hold a master's degree in political sciences. When I was 18 years old, I had no specific job in mind and my interests were wide. For instance, during secondary school, I specialized myself in both mathematics and languages because I had always wanted to become a teacher of those courses. Once the decision for a university program had to be made, I also informed myself about courses on history, law and psychology. I eventually subscribed myself for political sciences, which I saw as a mix of the previous topics, at the University of Antwerp (Belgium). For my master's years, I chose a specialization in public administration and I wrote my master thesis about the role of an electronic identity card for e-government (which was still a digital innovation by that time; comparable to the smart city trend nowadays). Once I graduated, I was soon contacted by an international information technology (IT) consultancy firm, called CSC,[1] which was looking for young potential in their Belgian e-government projects. CSC was especially interested in profiles with expertise in the governmental business context, and it offered internal training courses to obtain the required IT analysis skills and project management knowledge.

Simultaneously, I was offered a PhD position by the faculty of communication sciences at another university (KU Leuven, Belgium). Doing a PhD had always been on my mind given the fact that I graduated as the best student in class (i.e. bachelor's degree with "Magna Cum Laude" and master's degree with "Summa Cum Laude"), my teaching aspirations, and that I love to read and write. Nonetheless, my academic degrees also taught me to work hard in order to reach a goal, which implies some sacrifices. Therefore, I decided to explore the (for me unknown) business world instead of staying within the familiar university walls. I especially wanted to experience how organizations operate in reality (instead of reading about this in books), and how it feels to better differentiate work/study from my spare time at home.

During my three-year career as an IT consultant, I got many opportunities to orient myself towards business informatics and to go outside my comfort zone. I also had the pleasure of working with a bunch of dynamic and enthusiastic colleagues and friends. Although tasting how businesses think was such a boost to my confidence, this enrichment was also accompanied by mandatory training moments, several (consultancy and social) events and assignments outside business hours. The latter might be particularly true for consultancy, in which you work for diverse projects/clients as well as for your consultancy firm (for example, teambuilding, knowledge sharing, networking, proposal writing).

Hence, after almost two years, it felt more like working long hours for a client or a boss instead of contributing to my self-development, and I started thinking of a career switch (e.g. to become a history teacher at my local secondary school). By that time, I also followed a workshop on Business Process Management (BPM) during which a KU Leuven professor in business informatics was present. We started talking during dinner and, after a few weeks, I asked her whether she could help me obtain a PhD grant. Although our combined research proposal was eventually not accepted, she told me that her colleagues in Ghent were still looking for PhD students, and that is how

I became connected to Ghent University with the KU Leuven professor being part of my doctoral advisory committee.

FIRST PhD YEAR: CURIOSITY AND CREATIVITY RESULT IN A FIRST TOP PUBLICATION

My story continues with a three-year journey as a teaching assistant at the University College of Ghent, and simultaneously as a PhD student and associate researcher at Ghent University. This rather complex situation explains the reason why I had two promotors – one in each institution.

Although a teaching assistant at our faculty is expected to contribute his/her time to 50% teaching assignments and 50% research, the former was initially relatively limited (e.g. some practical sessions and guidance of dissertations and internships) since program reforms would only start in the following PhD years. Given this context, I had the chance to spend more time on my research topic from early on and to quickly dig deeper into the domain of BPM in general (Weske, 2010) and business process maturity in particular.

My initial idea was to develop and validate a maturity model for cross-organizational business processes, because many maturity models already exist for business processes and BPM (Paulk, 2004; Sheard, 2001). The choice of working with maturity models was also driven by prior business practices, in which I experienced that organizations are open to tools that help them advance and to practice benchmarking. This initial idea, however, frequently changed in direction as the PhD progressed, and eventually my three required PhD papers coped with analyzing and synthesizing the existing process-centric maturity models. Each study approximately covered a full PhD year, namely:

- a literature review study to define the main concepts concerning business process maturity and the related maturity models, since this turned out to be a point of discussion in the existing body of knowledge;
- a classification study to build and test a theoretical framework covering the diverse capability areas in the many process maturity models; and
- a design-science study to build and test a decision tool to select one process maturity model out of the many existing models based on predefined selection criteria that help find a fit with an organization's needs and to better respond to business practice.

While the first PhD months were mainly dedicated to learning more about the BPM discipline in general, I soon started to narrow down my focus by searching for existing maturity models in academic and non-academic literature. This effort resulted in a comprehensive sample of 69 models, which was only possible since I already had a certain research topic in mind as from the beginning. Otherwise, teaching assistants are normally expected to explore the discipline during the first year in order to find a research topic to work on from their second year onwards.

At that time, I did not know the acquired sample of maturity models would become the thread of my PhD because I still wanted to develop a cross-organizational process maturity model. Nonetheless, when reading more about my research topic and the sampled maturity models, I experienced some burdens in terminology, scope and design of those models. These three gaps were the inputs for my first literature review study, which was accepted by a top academic journal after a few months. By researching a topic that is not yet well established in academia, I identified the gaps with which I first struggled myself, but which also provided me with unique publication opportunities. Additionally, I believe this first article was not possible without the required doctoral training courses that we had to follow, one of which was related to advanced academic writing skills.

Regarding the compulsory doctoral training program,[2] Ghent University has established doctoral schools per discipline. For instance, I was part of the doctoral school for social and behavioral sciences, and had to follow three specialist or in-depth courses.[3] Given my prior work experience, I was granted an exemption for courses on transferable skills, which typically deal with topics such as communication skills, career management or leadership and personal management. Still, I voluntarily followed a course on academic writing in English, as mentioned above.

Another element worth mentioning is the need for early feedback in academic conferences and doctoral consortia. The latter mostly precedes an actual conference and it is characterized by smaller and closed groups of PhD students receiving constructive experts' feedback. The emphasis of a doctoral consortium is also more on a research proposal than on research conducted. For this purpose, I strongly advise submissions to doctoral consortia from the first year onwards. Particularly, at our faculty, each PhD student typically tries to attend one conference or doctoral consortium per year, taking into account the budget constraints. In my case, I attended two doctoral consortia (i.e. one when my first year had just finished[4] and another one at the end of my second year[5]) as well as two conferences (i.e. one abroad and one in Belgium) during my third year.[6]

In sum, I experienced this first PhD year as the most creative and fun period in my career because everything was new to me and nothing was really expected. During that year, I also did not feel demands imposed by my supervisors, who gave me the freedom to explore my own ideas. Since my performance is better when I am not under pressure (e.g. one top publication and one doctoral consortium publication after the first PhD year), my story also illustrates that universities are not necessarily benefiting from formulating too high expectations for their academic staff in an attempt to quantify their qualitative output (e.g. which is usually the case during a tenure track). Hence, for the sake of creativity and for encouraging novel ideas, I hope universities and governments worldwide will trust and believe in the ambitions of their staff.

SECOND PhD YEAR: THE STRUGGLE BETWEEN PERFECTIONISM AND PRAGMATISM

During my second PhD year, my teaching assignments were extended and I also contributed to the start-up of a BPM course. Regarding research, I remember this year as being full of question marks on the specific topic and hurdles to find the right methodology and analysis techniques.

Regarding the classification study, I experienced difficulties to find the right statistical tests to classify the sampled process maturity models. I therefore read many statistical books and even contacted the professors with whom I followed statistical courses. Based on the statistical information I found, it was clear that I would never be able to classify all characteristics of a process maturity model at once, since too many characteristics exist and they also have different measurement levels.

After trial and error, and consequently many frustrations, I woke up one day with the idea of narrowing down the classification study to one specific set of characteristics, namely the capability areas. Once I obtained this pragmatic insight, I was able to finish the work relatively fast and to submit the study to a top academic journal. Although the acceptance of this second journal publication went relatively well (i.e. given the fact that most papers need multiple months and years to get accepted; see Recker, 2013), it would take a few extra years before it was actually available in print. Nevertheless, once the acceptance was received, my supervisors started talking about the possibility of finishing my PhD when a third study was completed.

Hence, during this second PhD year, I also started the design-science study for which I first had to find an international expert panel to identify the selection criteria, and then to develop the decision tool in my third year. Although this would be my final PhD study, it felt quite challenging because I expected limitations in my network to finding subject matter experts from different continents, and in my programming skills to doing the actual coding work. To my surprise, the international experts were more responsive to my invitation than I had hoped. Some of them still remembered me from a conference that we both attended, or they were genuinely interested in my work. In addition, the programming issue could be solved by doing the coding together with a senior developer, which I was used to doing as a former business analyst and functional analyst.

Thus, the second PhD year was definitely a mix of dark clouds with several moments when I really wanted to give up, and other moments of sunshine and new hope.

THIRD AND FINAL PhD YEAR: FINISHING UNFINISHED BUSINESS

During my last PhD year, my teaching assignments were again extended and I became responsible for developing a novel course on social media management from the perspective of business students. Since social media were still on the rise (e.g. most students did not know about Twitter at that time) and most books were limited to either a technical or a marketing perspective, this additional course took much of my time. By relying on guest lectures from business people during this start-up year, I was still able to finish my PhD that year. Once the PhD was finished, I would have more time left to advance the social media course for the coming years and to write the findings in a Springer textbook (Van Looy, 2016). Hence, again a pragmatic approach was required to finish on time, albeit with a more ambitious plan in mind for later on.

Regarding research, I spent the rest of my time developing and validating the decision tool, and wrapping up what was in my mind. Again, I profited from my business network to identify case organizations that were willing to test and use the decision tool. The tool was also renamed, with "BPMM Smart-Selector" being a more appealing name. While the tool is free to use,[7] a database records every usage and requests organizations to fill out an evaluation form. By gathering such data, follow-up research may be facilitated to improve the tool at a later stage and to gain insight into the decision process of organizations. Hence, this third study illustrates that academic research is not only about theorizing but also about creating novel artifacts that are of direct use for real-life business practices, with the first two studies being the more theoretical prerequisites.

A typical PhD at our faculty consists of three "publishable" studies bundled in a book. By the time of my PhD defense, my first study was published, my second study was published online but the printed version was forthcoming, and my third study was under review in a top academic journal. Thus, for the PhD book, I still had to write an introduction (i.e. with gaps and research questions) and a conclusion (i.e. with discussions related to the research questions and suggestions for future work), which were published afterwards in a Springer book (Van Looy, 2014).

In Belgium, a PhD is defended in multiple stages, which is valuable for addressing constructive feedback and for allowing in-depth brainstorming. First, the supervisors and other members of the doctoral advisory committee have to agree, and additional (international) jury members need to be contacted, all of which should be approved by the faculty board. Then, a pre-defense with all committee members follows behind closed doors, during which the PhD student presents his/her work and responds to the committee's questions. Afterwards, the PhD student is expected to adapt the work based on the comments received. For minor feedback (i.e. when comments can be handled within – let us say – two to four weeks), the public defense will take place as planned. Otherwise, the public defense will be postponed. During the public defense, the talk should also be more focused to reach a wider audience and thus aims at research communication from a more practical point of view. Also good to mention is that a PhD defense at our university (and in Belgium in general) is quite binary: either you successfully defend your PhD and obtain the doctor's degree, or you don't. In other words: successfully defended PhDs do not get a ranking nor are they provided with additional honors.

I must admit that the day of my PhD defense felt awkward, especially because I do not enjoy standing in the spotlight. Therefore, I had only invited my parents, some family members and a few friends. The event and talk were also in English, and most of my invitees did not feel comfortable with the language and research jargon. When looking back at the event, I am glad that this memorable day is over. Hence, from my point of view, the PhD journey was more important than the destination.

TENURE TRACK: NEW HOPES AND ASPIRATIONS

In less than one year after my PhD defense, I got the opportunity to become an Assistant Professor at Ghent University due to the integration of some educational programs at the University College of Ghent and Ghent University.[8] In other words: our faculties at both institutions had merged into one, and I was ready for the position in an open vacancy. Although I do not wish to under- or overestimate my own abilities, I still feel the envy of some thinking that my promotion was too easy. By this, I mean that other people with a similar profile might also deserve such a position, while they have to wait multiple years as a post-doc and, possibly, leave university. Probably it is also about being the right person, in the right place, at the right time. In the end, a lot of competition exists in academia.

Talking about the tenure track expectations directly brings me to my first pregnancy and pregnancy leave. I was pregnant when entering my new position as an Assistant Professor. Because the transitional measures (i.e. following the integration of two faculties into one combined faculty, mentioned above) were still under discussion at a higher management level, they remained unclear until the first tenure track year. Unfortunately, I received them during my pregnancy leave with a deadline of only a few days to discuss and accept them. Because of general confusion after the faculties' integration, the retrospective character of the defined objectives and the bad timing, I was taken by surprise. For instance, a lot of emphasis was put on obtaining (external) research grants, while most project calls for that academic year were already closed when receiving the defined objectives.

In addition, being an Assistant Professor coming from the University College of Ghent, I would not be able to act as a main PhD supervisor (only as a co-supervisor) nor to submit research proposals without another promoter of the faculty, creating a strong dependency on the goodwill of others. Luckily, most of these restrictions will disappear in the coming years when fully entering the academic staff of Ghent University.

Furthermore, the faculty agreed that the load of the tenure track expectations would be reduced by six months per pregnancy leave to facilitate a work–life balance. In Belgium, a pregnancy leave takes about 15 weeks. I consider this length of time sufficient to recover physically and to get used to my new role. Additionally, if your first newborn baby sleeps a lot, you might find some time to regularly check your work mailbox, hold Skype sessions with your PhD students and research collaborators, perform teaching preparations and even conduct some research. Now that I have a second baby girl and a toddler running around the house, my second pregnancy leave is inevitably less productive and I will be happy when I find some time to do the follow-up on mails and ongoing assignments. Although I confess to being a workaholic with a smartphone addiction (which might not necessarily be a good thing), becoming a parent is the most wonderful and grateful period that exists. Luckily, kids know how to grab the attention from early on. Moreover, we can rely on the support of grandparents.

Let us return to the work-related changes after my PhD:

- The **teaching assignments** have been extended with additional courses. For instance, this academic year, I was involved in six courses, for most of which I had a responsible function. Additionally, I coordinated multiple internships and (bachelor's and master's) theses.
- Regarding the **research activities**, I became the responsible coordinator of the "Process Orientation" research cluster within the UGent Management Information Systems (MIS) Research Group[9] in 2015. The "Process Orientation" research pillar investigates the organizational and managerial aspects of business processes and BPM. As such, it concerns a multidisci-plinary pillar, aiming at creating synergies between the domains of business informatics and organization theory (for example, human resource management, strategic management, performance management, innovation management) in order to enhance business (process) performance. This pillar also helps organizations reorganize properly and take advantage of digital transformation by investigating best practices to become more

process-oriented, and this by considering a fit with an organization's business context.

- Currently, I am also **co-supervisor** of two ongoing PhD research projects at UGent. What I have learned from guiding dissertations is the importance of empowerment; the student is in the driver's seat, and the supervisor can only act as a facilitator. For instance, a first PhD student under my supervision decided to stop doing research and became a software engineer after one and a half years. Although I felt as if I had failed in my job, I cannot blame myself for not giving the required support. People's interests may differ, and PhD studies are not evident for everyone. The sooner you recognize your personal dreams and aspirations, the better.
- Another new duty is **writing proposals** for research projects. In the future, acquiring external funding will further increase in importance due to the expected budget savings. Although I do not lack novel research ideas, the fact that I am recently appointed continues to be my disadvantage. In particular, lower budgets and more proposal submissions inevitably result in even lower acceptance rates, with preference given to senior profiles already experienced in project grants, top publications and PhD supervision to reduce the project risks.
- Other **service-related activities** concern, among others, being a member qualified to vote on the faculty board and examination committee, being a reviewer or (senior) editor for several conferences and academic journals, and providing training to business people.

CLOSING NOTES

One PhD, two pregnancies and almost a tenure position later, I feel it is time to share my story and inspire PhD students and other young faculty members. What follows are a few dos and don'ts of our profession.

- Try to seek **constructive feedback** as early as possible from peers (e.g. your supervisors, other established researchers or during conferences and doctoral consortia). However, keep your eye focused on your research purpose to distill the right comments among the sometimes-opposing opinions, and to discuss these in a timely fashion with your supervisors or doctoral advisory committee.
- Try to find a way to cope with **criticism**. For instance, a top academic journal submission may provide you with multiple sheets of reviewers' comments requiring a revision, although you have worked hard to get the paper submitted. Instead of being angry or sad or immediately correcting

the manuscript, give yourself a few days to take a distance and to understand what the reviewers are actually telling and advising you.

- Try not to be (too) disappointed when you receive a **rejection for a paper** submitted to a conference or journal. The majority of papers need multiple revision rounds or consecutive submissions to different journals. Once accepted, you will be proud that the result will be an improvement on the initial submission.

- Try not to be (too) disappointed when you receive a **rejection for a research grant**, because (too) many research proposals are submitted and budgets are (too) limited.

- Try to build your **personal business network**, including experts from academia and business (e.g. to collaborate with, to let your work be validated, or to keep up-to-date about essential business problems). Do not be afraid of talking to experts; they are also just ordinary people like you and me. You might also want to create professional accounts of social media and a personal website for people to get acquainted with your interests and work.[10]

- Try to write a **structured paper** by starting from a clear problem formulation with gaps and related research questions, and answer these questions throughout the remainder of the paper. In order to have a better overview of the paper's structure, you might start a draft with bullet points instead of full sentences, and possibly use figures and/or tables to better summarize your thoughts.

- Try to identify your **most productive moments** in a day. For instance, if you typically start your day at a slower pace, you can start doing some routine work or checking your mailbox first, and keep the most challenging jobs for later that day (or vice versa). Alternatively, you can tactically start with the most annoying tasks so that your day can move on and end with things that are more positive (or vice versa).

- Try to apply **mail management** if you are distracted too easily when emails arrive. For instance, decide on a limited number of times for checking your mailbox (e.g. only at three fixed times per day, let us say at 9 am in the morning, at noon, and at 6 pm in the evening).

- Try to define what **motivates** you and makes you happy, including a good **work–life** balance. Sometimes you will get the most creative ideas while doing something completely different (e.g. lying in bed, being on holiday or playing with your children).

- Finally, try to **take your job seriously but not yourself**. Nobody is perfect. We should all have a private life beyond work, no matter how much we love what we do.

Regarding my personal avenues, I expect to be promoted from an Assistant Professor to an Associate Professor next year. Afterwards, becoming a Full Professor would fulfill my career expectations in the longer term. I also intend to continue with my BPM classes for professionals, probably write a practical handbook about that course, and collaborate with the business world but mainly for research purposes. Although I love doing consultancy projects too, each day only has 24 hours and so decisions have to be made. In the end, I like doing research more, though under the condition that it has relevant practical contributions to letting businesses and people evolve. I also hope to inspire my bachelor's and master's students, and help my PhD students take some important steps in their lives.

Given today's importance of acquiring external funding, I aspire to further sharpening my proposal writing skills in order to obtain the financial resources needed to realize many more of my ideas. Ideally, we need one additional PhD student each year in order to have PhD tracks in different stages and to fulfill the high number of defenses required. This inevitably means that my role as a researcher will rather turn into an idea generator and facilitator, while I also love conducting research myself. For the same purpose, I also pursue more international collaborations in the future in order to strengthen the research projects and to learn from each other. And, last but not least, I wish to ensure a more comfortable work–life balance by frequently working from home and deciding on my own flexible working moments (e.g. with periods of long working hours alternating with periods of more feasible hours, or sometimes ending a working day early but restarting work during evenings or weekends).

Working in academia can either be seen as a dream job or as a burden with high expectations, harsh comments of peers and an imperfect work–life balance. The same is true for doing a PhD, which is a rollercoaster full of question marks (e.g. not only about your research topic and your methodology, but also your determination). Nevertheless, for me, it is definitely worth the pain. Hence, instead of staying in an ivory tower or living in the clouds, I will keep dancing between consultancy and academia.

NOTES

1. Computer Sciences Corporation (https://en.wikipedia.org/wiki/Computer _Sciences_Corporation; currently called DXC Technology: http://www.dxc .technology/ [accessed May 27, 2017]).
2. See https://www.ugent.be/doctoralschools/en/doctoraltraining/programme/ structure.htm (accessed May 27, 2017).
3. I followed one specialist course on Management Information Systems and two advanced statistical courses.
4. See http://otm.academy/ (accessed May 27, 2017).
5. See https://bpm-conference.org/BpmConference/ (accessed May 27, 2017).

6. In the field of Information Systems, I strongly encourage PhD students to attend conferences like ICIS, ECIS, HICSS, Caise, BPM, DESRIST, etc. Please consult your supervisor to find an appropriate conference track.
7. See http://smart-selector.amyvanlooy.eu/ (accessed May 27, 2017).
8. Through the integration of the academic courses of the partner university colleges into the universities, Ghent University has added over 6 500 students and 500 extra staff members. This also strengthens Ghent University with several campuses, including Campus Kortrijk.
9. See http://www.mis.ugent.be/ (accessed May 27, 2017).
10. See http://www.amyvanlooy.eu/ (accessed May 27, 2017).

REFERENCES

Paulk, M. C. (2004). Surviving the quagmire of process models, integrated models, and standards. In *Proceedings of the American Society for Quality Annual Quality Conference*, 24–27 May, Toronto, Canada.

Recker, J. (2013). *Scientific Research in Information Systems: A Beginner's Guide*. Berlin–Heidelberg: Springer.

Sheard, S. A. (2001). Evolution of the frameworks quagmire. *IEEE Computer, 34*(7), 96–98.

Van Looy, A. (2014). *Business Process Maturity: A Comparative Study on a Sample of Business Process Maturity Models*. Berlin–Heidelberg: Springer.

Van Looy, A. (2016). *Social Media Management: Technologies and Strategies for Creating Business Value*. Cham: Springer.

Weske, M. (2010). *Business Process Management: Concepts, Languages and Architectures*. Berlin–Heidelberg: Springer.

PART III

Academic career transitions

6.   Career nomad: from career instinct to action?

Jelena Zikic

Estimated reading time: **25 minutes and 5 seconds**.

CHAPTER HIGHLIGHTS

- Most significant personal learning comes from lots of trial-and-error, extremely hard work and long hours.
- Use the best career compass that you have – your "career instinct".
- Self-discipline and passion for a specific research topic will help you through endless days and nights of work.
- Success is a subjective category; it can be measured by more than a classic chase for tenure at an Ivy League school.
- Be aware of the importance of reinventing how we do things in order to reconnect with what keeps one energized and engaged.

The one who does not turn things topsy-turvy,
who is unhappy at work,
who does not risk certainty for uncertainty,
to thus follow a dream,
those who do not forego sound advice at least once in their lives,
die slowly.

Muere lentamente quien no cambia de vida cuando está insatisfecho con
*   su trabajo o su amor,*
Quien no arriesga lo seguro por lo incierto
para ir detrás de un sueño,
quien no se permite al menos una vez en la vida huir de los consejos sensatos ...

Martha Medeiros, "Die Slowly" (2018).

This, and other extracts from this poem in this chapter, are used by permission, from Martha Medeiros, *Non-Stop*, p. 126. © first published (2018) by Austin Macauley Publishers Ltd™ (www.austinmacauley.com).

INTRODUCTION

Careers research is my home. Reflecting on my own career journey is a unique opportunity to indulge in some true career self-exploration. Not the least, my dissertation was also on the same topic (Zikic, 2005). It is a privilege to be the subject matter of my own study and offer some lessons learned to those taking the same road.

One paradigm that helps me reflect and organize my thinking about my career journey, as well as one used in some of my research, is the intelligent career framework and the three ways of knowing (Arthur et al., 1995). While it introduces "order" in the midst of career chaos, it also allows me to reflect around three main areas of career building that I find useful for any careerist to consider. It portrays careers as a combination of our motivation and identity or *knowing-why*, complemented by our skills and abilities or *knowing-how* and, finally, it would not be a career without the presence of others/relationships or *knowing-whom*.

FROM MIGRATION TO EARLY INTERNATIONAL CAREER: THE ROLE OF CAREER INSTINCT

I was a teenager when my parents decided to leave our home country, Serbia (then Yugoslavia) in search of new career opportunities and a new life. As the only child at the time, the move also meant enriching my options and future education. It was definitely a risky and uncertain decision, but one that also brought new adventures to our lives. As a teenager, this also meant a tough new beginning, leaving everything and everyone I knew and starting over again. The migration experience had an impact on the rest of my career and to this day continues to shape my identity. Little did I know that I was about to embark on a full-blown international and a very much nomadic career.

In a new country, a new world – Canada – my early career experiences were characterized by independent decision making; following my own "career instincts" and making decisions without any local mentors around. With the enormous trust my parents had in me, I experienced total independence in my career decision making and ended up also following the path of "passion". During my studies, I chose courses that seemed relevant to what I enjoyed and what I knew about myself at the time, never considering where this may take me eventually or how these decisions might shape my career options in the future. I chose social studies, art history, and languages, among other subjects. Unlike my peers, more native to the new country I was living in, I never considered the value of taking core sciences (physics, chemistry, various math subjects) for future career choices. In fact, I was surprised that in the North American school system students could choose their subjects, even at the high school level; this was contrary to the European system where I came from and where many of the subjects were pre-determined so early in one's education.

While in high school in Toronto I was already discovering my passion, nothing to do with management, business, or sciences, but rather it was learning a new language in Canada (Italian!). Based on my passion and progress in the language, I was given a unique opportunity to engage in my first study experience abroad, and to study in a classic European high school for some time while I lived with an Italian family. There was no need to think twice: what could have been more fitting than going back to Europe and learning a language I so much enjoyed. Going to Italy as a teenager from a Canadian high school was my first of many self-discovery journeys.

At the end of high school, and following a migration experience and a student exchange, still as a teen, I felt grown up! As the time to choose university came around, I continually had high concern for my career and felt I needed to take control of my career, i.e. a prime example of the 'Careers as Action' metaphor (Inkson, 2004) and career construction theory (Savickas, 2005), perhaps even more so than the local students. Given my lack of local mentors or any local advice (other than frequently going to guidance counselors at my high school!), I constantly felt like a newcomer. Instead, I used the best career compass I had at the time, my "career instinct". I chose what I enjoyed and what I was curious to learn more about: psychology and languages, a logical career combination! Based on my good grades, I was also accepted to study these subjects in one of the best universities in the country and a prestigious college within this university, University of Toronto and Victoria College.

CAREER INTERSECTION #1

While I was majoring in Psychology and in the Italian language in parallel and equally nurturing both of these passions, my career decision making was becoming more difficult. Throughout my university years I was continually seeking new career opportunities, led by my curiosity and constant need to be proactive about my future. I worked as a research assistant alongside developmental psychologists and gained my first insight into the world of research. Those moments certainly enhanced my understanding of who I was and my 'knowing-why' became even more defined in the direction of psychology. Yet, my relentless passion for languages and culture continued in parallel while at the University of Toronto. Driven by my desire for new cross-cultural experiences, I found an opportunity to spend my third year abroad. Back in Italy, like a fish back in the water, I was studying in the well-known University of Padova. Later, I was awarded a prestigious scholarship to study in Siena, Italy; at the end of my five-year-long undergraduate degree I even had the opportunity to enter Harvard School and continue my study of languages there! You can just imagine how I felt being at such a prestigious Ivy League research university.

While all seemed to be going well, my first major "career intersection" awaited me. Little did I know that with my five-year bachelor's degree in my hands I was going to become neither a "psychologist" nor a teacher of the Italian language. At the same time, I also had this strong feeling that I was not done studying. I longed for more learning, more contact with academia, but was far from knowing that I was heading for an academic career myself.

At this point I experienced what many of us encounter routinely, that is a combination of luck and careful career planning, one's persistence leading to a unique career opportunity. This is well described in career studies as "planned happenstance" (Mitchell et al., 1999). Due to a set of circumstances, in my case helping my boyfriend at the time apply for a master's degree at London School of Economics (LSE), about which I knew virtually nothing, I decided to send my documents too! This led to an unplanned opportunity to pursue an MSc (master of science) degree in Social and Organizational Psychology at LSE as a continuation of my academic path. At the same time, my conscious career planning efforts were to combine my talent in languages with my equally intriguing passion for the field of psychology and pursue further studies in the field of speech pathology; however, this wasn't panning out as planned! Here begins a new chapter of my career. My decision to go to London also meant an end to my academic study of languages. It was instead the beginning of language learning becoming hobby and something I continue to pursue to this day. Instead, my time at LSE meant the beginning of a lifelong journey into work psychology and organizations.

BEYOND CAREER INSTINCT: CAREER ACTION AND REPUTATION MATTERS!

My master's degree was time for further career exploration and reflection. I took my first class in Human Resource Management, became aware of my interest in applying psychology to the workplace, and solidified my newly acquired passion towards the field of organizational psychology/behavior. It was through my MSc degree thesis that I confirmed how much I enjoyed the research aspect of my studies. I had a chance to conduct my own study from beginning to end focused on examining Karasek's work demand/control model (1979) by using a sample of bank employees in London. At this time,

I became cognizant of the challenges posed by occupational stress and in general became concerned with well-being at work. I also discovered concepts such as organizational identity (Albert & Whetten, 1985) and identification, and our ability to identify with such entities where we work, or study for that matter. These topics continued to occupy me in my early PhD years, but they also continue to be part of my research agenda to this day.

In London I found myself appreciating how much the environment where we work and live has an impact on us. First, I learned that I thrive in institutions and groups where I can connect to diverse individuals (i.e. in terms of cultural background as well as knowledge base), and where unique cultural experiences were on my fingertips; living in London and studying at LSE was just that. Second, I also learned about my "knowing-how" or rather how I enjoy learning and developing myself further in a complete autonomy and with a flexible schedule; these will in fact become key characteristics of my academic lifestyle. Thus, not only was my MSc experience formative in terms of quietly discovering my ideal work environment and what kind of work rhythm seems to suit me, but it also equipped me with topics that I wanted to research and explore further.

CAREER INTERSECTION #2

The second major "career intersection" I had to navigate was: What to do after graduating from LSE? Whether to pursue a job in consulting industry, as that seemed to be one opportunity I could embark on or to perhaps continue studying. At this intersection, I was again guided by my curiosity, career concern, and desire to explore all my options; fully exemplifying career construction theory (Savickas, 2005), but again not without some happenstance (Mitchell et al., 1999).

While visiting Toronto during the holidays, still in the course of my MSc degree, I ventured back to my *alma mater* to learn about a PhD program that somehow corresponded to my study interests at LSE. This visit out of curiosity and concern for what is next for me, led to an unexpected "information interview" with a PhD program director at University of Toronto, Rotman School of Management. At this time, I learned that the reputation of the institution where I was studying meant a lot! LSE happened to be recognized internationally and my unexpected interview (sometimes the best things in life just happen unplanned) was rather an invitation to apply to Rotman School's PhD program for the following fall. I will never forget the words of the program director, a well-known academic in human resources: "If the correlation between what you told me today about yourself/background and your application documents is 1.0, you are accepted."

Contrary to much of the career planning narrative, my career decision to pursue a doctorate came as a combination of happenstance, curiosity and also hard work. By hard work I am referring to my dedication to continuous learning, to being accepted into LSE and an endless desire to take career "action" and find out what is next for me. I believe that the type of life experiences we live, such as migration in my case, can trigger career action and dictate how we choose to pursue our careers. Whether I wanted to or not, I have become a "fighter" who had to put in effort to find my place beneath the sun.

I could probably write this whole chapter just about those four and a half years in the PhD program, but it would not provide a complete understanding of all complexities that make up one's career. These four years were a mix of persistence, hard work, and self-discipline, three key ingredients that allowed me to successfully complete the program. Like many of us, I also struggled, especially in Year 1, and of course even wanted to quit the program. What kept me in the program, in addition to my own persistence, was one faculty member who believed in me. While as PhD students, and due to the nature of the process, we typically do not get much positive feedback, especially early in the process; the trust of one faculty member, that I was in the right place, helped me continue.

Another reason why I persisted was the ability to meet other scholars in my discipline, thus expanding my "knowing-whom", while I was attending two major conferences early in the PhD program. One was closely related to organizational identity and reputation, what seemed to occupy me in my writing at the time, and the other was our yearly Academy of Management (AOM) meeting that only that year happened to be in Toronto! What better way to reassure me that I was on the right path than meeting other scholars who had equally intriguing ideas and were willing to chat with a curious PhD student! Lastly, I also persisted in this academic self-discovery due to encountering my passion for a specific research topic. It was the start of my adventure into career studies and, of course, my ability to find a supervisor who was an expert in the topic and was willing to take me on.

While my supervisor assisted me in completing my dissertation in record time, despite it being a multi-method longitudinal study, I realize that it was also my self-discipline and passion for the topic area that helped me through endless days and nights at the computer and in my university cubicle. This part of my journey would not be complete without acknowledging another integral part of "knowing-whom" in my life, that is significant people around me and outside the PhD program, from family to friends, who believed in me and granted me time, space, and endless support.

To conclude, my PhD dissertation led the way to my first academic job at a top ranked international business school. I had no doubts it was time to return to my European roots, undertake study of another language and immerse myself in the new culture. Thus, I took the more unusual route, I welcomed a new challenge. I was not afraid, despite being trained in the North American Ivy League type school, to spread my wings and fly away to a different academic world and a different continent.

> He who does not travel,
> who does not read,
> Who does not listen to the sounds of life,
> Who does not find grace in himself, dies slowly.

> *Muere lentamente quien no viaja,*
> *quien no lee, quien no escucha música,*
> *quien no halla encanto en si mismo.*
>   Martha Medeiros, "Die Slowly" (2018).

WHEN CAREER MEETS OTHER IDENTITIES

Our academic journey also offers a unique ability to integrate work and other life domains in a coherent whole while also allowing for constant reinvention. In my case being an academic allowed me to engage with my other salient identities, to develop an international career corresponding fully to my multicultural identity (i.e. starting from the migration experience and study abroad periods to this reaching its climax in my desire and ability to search for my first academic job internationally). I continued to rely on my career instinct that it was the right time to go back to Europe, to my native continent. As a result, I only searched for tenure track positions in the European academic market. It took a fair bit of research and exploration to understand my options abroad, different education systems and international networks as I was moving from the North American academic system to a European one. At this stage, in addition to my curiosity, I was driven by my career confidence that I would be well positioned back in Europe. Again, my career actions are fully reflected in the metaphor "Career as Action" (Inkson, 2004).

The search for the first academic position, much like any job search effort (i.e. the topic of my dissertation too), is an especially trying time in our careers and having a clear vision of your future academic identity is of utmost importance. My vision was driven by my desire to immerse myself back in the old continent and reconnect with my roots. I felt I had a lot to contribute as an international scholar in a European business school setting. After having interviewed at several schools across Europe, and contemplated a few offers, I decided to join IE Business School in Madrid, one of the top international European business schools. Interestingly, during my interview/job talk process, the Dean at the time immediately connected to the fact that I studied at LSE, his *alma mater* as well (I am not saying that this was a decisive coincidence for me to be employed, but sometimes such things might matter). Obtaining this tenure track position was certainly a big achievement for me as well as the completion of my PhD program back at the Rotman School of Management.

This first academic work experience very much shaped who I was to become as an academic. Not only did I have a chance to teach and research what I was trained to do, but I also needed to learn a new language and immerse myself in a new cultural experience. This was an equally enriching part of my academic journey. Again, I was integrating active language learning (daily private lessons offered by the school, which was very much appreciated from my side) into my daily research and teaching routine. I was adapting to the new society, international colleagues and student body. This for me was the type of challenge I enjoyed. My multicultural identity and passion for languages was fully in synch with where I chose to work and start my academic career. The international business school environment also allowed me to further develop as a scholar and elevated my teaching expertise while I continued to build an active research agenda.

After several years in Spain, there came a time for the next career transition, not necessarily intersection: I chose to cross the ocean yet one more time! Few of us make these bold moves back and forth between very different institutions and cultures; I decided it was the right time and the right choice for me. I joined my family back in Canada and soon after obtained a tenure position at York University in Toronto. While choices around work and family/non-work domains made me move back to Canada, I realized the salience of these other identities for me: the fact that I valued my life outside of work and that "success" for me was measured by more than a classic chase for success and tenure at an Ivy League school, for example. My career at York University continues to be a perfect balance between my freedom to conduct the type of research that I am passionate about and allowing me to fully integrate work, family and my other interests, while still pursuing an active research agenda and continuing to engage in many international opportunities.

In fact, by moving back to Canada (i.e. one of the most multicultural societies) I was even more committed to nurturing culture and diversity as part of my work, both in my research and life in general. For example, I created a unique study abroad program at York University allowing me to transfer the importance of cross-cultural experiences to my students. I have created an extensive network of collaborators in other countries and regularly visit and present my work internationally. For example, I am one of the founding members of a large cross-cultural careers project (the 5C project) and continue to nurture multiple international partnerships. Most recently I was chosen to Chair the International Committee of the OB (Organizational Behavior) Division in the Academy of Management and enjoyed developing this group and its important activities. These engagements and partnerships allow me to continuously develop and reinvent my work and my cultural understanding. As a result, many of my publications include samples and collaborations that span international boundaries.

CAREER–LIFE INTEGRATION: FROM BELLY DANCING TO PARENTING

Very early in my academic career I understood that to be a successful academic I must develop and nurture myself outside of academia. This idea of integrating other life domains to enhance my ability to be productive and satisfied at work started early in my PhD career. I was driven by this instinctive feeling that I had additional "space and time" beyond my academic life that I must engage with. It translated into finding dance classes and somewhat related to my early life dedication to modern dance. At the University of Toronto where I was pursuing my PhD it was easy to find this opportunity in what is known as the "Heart House" of the university (center for arts/culture/well-being of students). In dance I also wanted to explore a new territory and chose belly dancing: it had a connection to music and cultures that I enjoyed and wanted to know more about. I often joke that writing my dissertation and belly dancing complemented each other really well! Thus, dancing played a major role in providing a much-needed escape from the academic world and letting me explore beyond research.

Over the years I continued to integrate different interests into my academic world. However, the climax of this strategy was the birth of my two boys who are the best possible 'integration' beyond academia one could ever imagine. Having children has been an instrumental and transformational part of who I am. My children taught me how to quickly switch between integrating life domains and successfully segmenting them when needed. Their presence has improved my ability to prioritize, making me realize that certain parts of my day as well as times of the year are reserved for my family only. For example, the month of July, commonly known in my family as 'Holy July', is reserved for completely switching off; being fairly consistent in allowing myself to indulge in life outside work. Family travel, exploration, and life in nature becomes my priority during those weeks.

It has not always been easy to maintain an active academic agenda with other life domains, but endless support from my close family has been a constant part of my life, allowing me to remain a committed scholar. I also believe that the autonomous nature of our career assists in finding more creative ways to integrate various life domains. Finally, after having children, parenting also became part of my research agenda. Parenting was such a powerful part of my life that I realized how I was changing my identity in relation to how I did my work. Specifically, I started writing about how being a parent made me a better person and a better academic. On this topic I have written several short articles (e.g., Zikic, 2016) and run some workshops too. What other profession allows one to work on questions that are so integral to your everyday life and identity?

More recently, as my children have become more independent, I have realized that again I have that special "space and time" that calls for engagement with a completely different interest, so I started acting. Acting allowed me to connect with the audience at a different level and yet also to express who I was in more creative ways. Finally, after a few years of that type of integration, I am now using yoga and meditation as an important part of life outside of academia.

> He who becomes the slave of habit,
> who follows the same routes every day,
> who never changes pace,
> who does not risk and change the color of his clothes,
> who does not speak and does not experience,
> dies slowly.

> *Muere lentamente quien se transforma en esclavo del habito,*
> *repitiendo todos los días los mismos senderos,*
> *quien no cambia de rutina,*
> *no se arriesga a vestir un nuevo color*
> *o no conversa con desconocidos.*
> Martha Medeiros, "Die Slowly" (2018).

CAREER REFLECTION AND REINVENTION

As one's program of research develops and that magic academic milestone – tenure – has been reached, what is next? I found this period of my career most satisfying. It was the right time for spontaneous reflection and reinvention in terms of topics, ways to conduct research, as well as colleagues with whom I was collaborating. This profession offers us the opportunity to work on questions that are of relevance to the broader society but also questions that somehow respond to our own concerns and passion towards certain issues/ phenomena. It was at this stage of my career that I started to study a population that has always been part of my journey – skilled migrants and migration experience as a career transition. This is a phenomenon close to my heart, and one I continue to explore in relation to migrant resilience, for example: how it is built and what experiences may further strengthen and/or weaken it. What can we learn about these major career and life transitions as scholars of management and how do these findings inform our society?

This type of career reflection led me to actively seek funding to study these questions. What this also meant was learning a new craft, the "knowing-how" of grant writing. Thus, while still focusing on studying career transitions,

I have ventured into studying several related topics such as cross-cultural mentoring relationships. I have also continued my ongoing passion for understanding professional identity processes, now in the context of skilled migrants and identity under struggle.

Reflection and reinvention also brought about new challenges. In my case this was many new opportunities for local and international collaboration which now I had to manage at an increased pace. I had to learn when to say "no" and how, by renouncing some opportunities, I was allowing my reinvention to flourish, rather than becoming a slave to too many projects I could not handle successfully. I realized the importance of being selective in regard to career opportunities that come my way and also that not all collaborations and relationships with colleagues will energize me in the same way. Clearly this career lesson also came with a cost, whereby some projects took much longer to finish and had to be completed despite my desire to move on to new ideas.

This part of knowing-how continues to this day. I continue to explore somewhat new perspectives and topic areas as well as new ways to do my work. In my research, I continue to engage in new international collaborations, as an ongoing pillar of my career. For example, I find creating professional development workshops with colleagues from abroad is a vehicle to engage in further collaborations and share expertise with other often more junior scholars. This volume is certainly an example of such strivings.

Moreover, in my teaching I have also reinvented the way I engage with my graduate students in particular. It is at this stage of my career that I realize how much I have learned so far in my own journey and how much I enjoy sharing this knowledge with my keen and hard-working PhD students: the joy of seeing my students develop into scholars, who surpass their supervisor and who teach me a lot. While I may be very much a "hands on" type of supervisor, I take pride in coaching my students not only in their dissertation tasks but also in what it means to become an active scholar and contribute invaluable knowledge to the academy and society overall. Perhaps I also teach them to take risks, as I did, and to explore beyond what is familiar, both in their research and in their future job opportunities.

As I reflect now, I consider myself in "mid-career" to be an expert on career transitions of diverse populations. What makes me push forward is my new passion for developing junior scholars, sharing my knowledge, and giving back to academia. Writing this chapter also made me realize the importance of reinventing how we do things in order to reconnect with what keeps one energized and engaged. What is unique about our career, in this respect, is the independent nature of this reflection. While you may share these experiences and contemplations with colleagues, mentors and others, it is often in-depth self-reflection and trial-and-error that allows us to adjust, shift, and move on. Finally, while one's academic path may be a long journey, one of persistence and resilience, there are several key characteristics of this career that are equally unique and almost impossible to find in other occupations. First is a fair bit of freedom to choose the topics we wish to study, and which may engage us for years and decades on end. Second is the autonomy not only in the type of work we do, but also in the type of collaborations and relationships we wish to build with other academics and other audiences. Finally, we have the freedom to work in a variety of spaces and places.

REFERENCES

Albert, S., & Whetten, D. A. (1985). Organizational identity. In B. M. Staw, & L. L. Cummings (eds.), *Research in Organizational Behavior* (pp. 263–295). Greenwich, CT: JAI Press.

Arthur, M. B., Claman, P. H., & DeFillippi, R. J. (1995). Intelligent enterprise, intelligent careers. *Academy of Management Executive, 9*(4), 7–22.

Inkson, K. (2004). Images of career: Nine Kew metaphors. *Journal of Vocational Behavior, 65*(1), 96–111.

Karasek, R. A. (1979). Job demands, job decision latitude and mental strain: Implications for job redesign. *Administrative Science Quarterly, 24*(2), 285–308.

Medeiros, M. (2018). *Non-Stop.* London: Austin Macauley Publishers.

Mitchell, K. E., Levin, S. A., & Krumblotz, J. D. (1999). Planned happenstance: Constructing unexpected career opportunities. *Journal of Counseling & Development, 77*(2), 115–124.

Savickas, M. L. (2005). The theory and practice of career construction. In S. D. Brown, & R. W. Lent (eds.), *Career Development and Counseling: Putting Theory and Research to Work* (pp. 42–70). New York, NY: John Wiley & Sons.

Zikic, J. (2005). *Job Loss as Career Growth: Predictors and Outcomes of Career Exploration and Job Search during Involuntary Career Transition.* Unpublished PhD thesis. Toronto: University of Toronto.

Zikic, J. (2016, May 9). Being a parent made me a better manager, and vice versa. *Harvard Business Review Digital Articles.* Retrieved February 3, 2019 from https://hbr.org/2016/05/being-a-parent-made-me-a-better-manager-and-vice-versa.

7. My academic life: a series of fortunate events[1]

Matej Černe

Estimated reading time: **31 minutes and 21 seconds**.

CHAPTER HIGHLIGHTS

- Choose a topic that you are really passionate about.
- One of the best things about being in academia is being internationally connected.
- When you learn something on your own rather than asking someone for every little piece of advice, you not only really learn it for the long run, but also build up your self-efficacy beliefs.
- We can determine the outcomes with our efforts, or at least influence the probability of succeeding to a significant extent.
- If you work really hard and invest a lot of time and effort into something, good things are bound to happen, sooner or later.

> *There are times to stay put, and what you want will come to you,*
> *and there are times to go out into the world*
> *and find such a thing for yourself.*
> Lemony Snicket, *Horseradish*

INTRODUCTION AND EARLY DAYS

The writing of the first part of this chapter (I started writing it in 2013–14) coincides with the offer to fill the shoes of my virtually first real *boss*, Professor Marko Jaklič, and to take over as the Head of the Laboratory for Open Innovation Systems (LOIS) at the Centre of Excellence for Biosensors, Instrumentation and Process Control – COBIK.[2] COBIK was my first real employer that kick-started me into the research world approximately ten years ago. Thinking about this, I cannot avoid reflecting on what a long way I have come from being extremely silent and not really knowing what is going on or how I could contribute during some of the first LOIS sessions, "dominated" by prominent professors and researchers, to enrolling into a PhD program at the Faculty of Economics of the University of Ljubljana (FELU – now School of Economics and Business), getting some first positive research outcomes (i.e. publications), and later on starting to contribute actively to the research community. But let us start at the beginning. And I really mean the beginning.

I showed signs of wanting to become a doctor of philosophy quite early. After all, this was the "occupation tag" that I wrote for myself when we were acting as adults and reporting on our readings in the third grade of primary school, and everyone had to choose an occupation for themselves to make it more interesting (of course, before or after that, I also wanted to become a waiter, a CEO, or a potter). I always used to read *a lot*. During my teen years, I set out to read or at least browse through all the books in the Novo mesto[3] library, which is not a small library at all. After reading through the psychology, sociology and business sections, I encountered law and taxes sections, and my ambitious plan stopped right there. My mentor and PhD supervisor Miha Škerlavaj, who I will write about a bit later, once said that it was good that this had happened so that I was able to focus my attention and energy on something more productive. I had never liked studying, at least, not until the second part of my bachelor studies at FELU. Selective reading, playing video games, hanging out with my friends and playing basketball was much more important for me than school and learning.

I enrolled into the bachelor studies at FELU, the management track, not by accident, but as a result of a tremendous series of events. During my high school years, I got to know myself, my drivers and interests, and I was mostly thinking about studying either law or languages (English and Spanish). I also liked psychology a lot, but I knew that I would need to study really hard and push for good grades in the baccalaureate[4] in order to get accepted for psychology studies. I also linked this psychology liking to management, so I was pretty much sure what to search for.

As I wanted to make an analytically-driven decision, a couple of us friends went to information days at some of the schools within the University of Ljubljana in which we were interested in enrolling for the next year. I checked out the Faculty of Arts and the Faculty of Social Sciences, the Faculty of Economics' next-door neighbor, but mostly went there to accompany a friend. By the time we were to go back, I had no idea where and what I wanted to study. However, I ended up studying at FELU because of a coincidence – by receiving a very positive evaluation from a friend's aunt, who was just finishing her master's studies there – without ever being at their information day or inside their building.

FIRST CONTACT: HOW I STARTED WITH RESEARCH AND THE ACADEMIC WORLD

I was first acquainted with scientific research by my bachelor's thesis mentor Sandra Penger. I basically chose her because of the topic (authentic leadership and positive psychology) and because I had a good impression of her from some of the management courses. She directed my writing of the bachelor's thesis as if it was a scientific paper, and thus I got the first sense of its common structure and writing style as well as research methods.

I became better acquainted with the academic life when I first started off as a course assistant right after finishing my bachelor's thesis,[5] in 2008. Robert Kaše, a prominent scholar whom I am now sharing my office at FELU with, was then an assistant professor and a Human Resource Management (HRM) course coordinator, and he published a call on the FELU website looking for course assistants. I was selected, and I embarked on a new journey as a teacher, and I am still running those workshops within the HRM course. The best piece of advice that Robert gave us was that "students are just people and you should be talking to them the way you do to other people – once you realize this, it's easy".

When discussing my bachelor's and master's studies, I definitely have to mention the wonderful group of students that I was a part of. Working with them on just about any group assignment provided me with a great sense of teamwork and it was actually my first experience of working together with others on something. The named group of students presented a great support system both in relation to my work and my personal life, and that is something I have strived for ever since.

COBIK: MY BIG OPPORTUNITY

When I was finishing my master's studies I started thinking about my potential job. I always used to carry a notebook where I listed ideas for my own business, what I have to read/look into, what I need to do (not the everyday things, such as to-do lists, but much broader, e.g. learn neurolinguistic programming). I decided not to constrain myself and instead to try as many things as possible, and because I was fortunate in not needing to work to support myself, I actually could do this. For example, I spent half a year helping and feeding the homeless at a day shelter in the Ljubljana center, and thus learned a lot about human psychology and that, if I could talk to those people, I could talk to anyone. Plus, through volunteering (apart from a "selfish" reason to better myself and my skills, and boost my CV), I got a sense of belonging to the community and the power of helping. Then, as I was approaching the end of the second year, and was thinking about what to do next and whether to perhaps embark on doctoral studies, a great opportunity came along.

I met my future PhD mentor Miha Škerlavaj while I was taking an advanced management course, where he delivered a lecture on social network analysis. A couple of weeks later, I was at the promotion of the book *Authentic Leadership* (Dimovski et al., 2009). In the book, the authors actually cited some of my work from my bachelor's thesis. Miha was also in the crowd, so we got to talk a bit about the topic, about leadership, and so on. It was nothing special, but about a month later I got a call from him informing me that there was a great opportunity to get employment at COBIK.[6] The job included doing research mostly related to my PhD, writing, publishing and disseminating academic papers, doing dissertation work, collaborating in Miha's (and other) research initiatives, and being involved in some COBIK projects, predominantly in writing applications for new research projects and new funding opportunities.

I remember that Miha told me: "If I were in your shoes, I would take this opportunity hands-on!" And I did as I was told. I had taken the opportunity to do just research (of course, later on I also worked on numerous projects, project applications, and was also teaching at FELU as a teaching assistant – every year going well beyond the limit of 100 teaching hours). I also had quite a lot of discretion in selecting my topics, especially their nuances. Any researcher knows how crucially important that is – to study what you are genuinely curious about. I was given a piece of very good advice (I do not quite remember who it came from) about selecting a topic that I now pass on to my protégées – bachelor's, master's and doctoral students: choose a topic that you are really passionate about, because, after a couple of months studying it, you are bound to hate it and this is when you will search for what got you interested in the first place. It is similar to relationships – after many years, it helps if you can remember why you fell in love with the person in the first place.

Two of my "bosses" at COBIK have done a great job of leading and empowering my career. Miha was a very good mentor and supervisor, especially at the beginning, when I was pretty much his only PhD protégée and he had sufficient time and energy to help me. He led by example, so my work was also driven by his success. He also showed me the importance of proactivity – to jump on every (research and consulting) opportunity (which I think later turned out to be a challenge for him, because there are only 24 hours in every day), to also watch for your time and to aim high. He told me at one of our first meetings that "Obtaining a doctoral title is not difficult, if this is your only ultimate goal" – honestly, at that time, I was pretty sure that that was the ultimate goal. I soon realized that it was not really like that. Our approach resulted in a lot of work, but this work was manifested in many research results and publications.[7]

On the other hand, I also had an excellent role-model in our Head, Marko Jaklič. The proactivity and being practically-oriented is one of the key things he transferred to me. I have learned always to try to be practical and to think in what way the things we do (research, teaching) help the business sector, students in practice, companies, etc. Thinking this way helps me not to get stuck in research just for the sake of research.

DOCTORAL STUDIES AT FELU

My doctoral studies consisted of a three-year program at FELU; I enrolled in 2010.[8] My general impressions are positive – the program at FELU is not bad at all, actually: with regard to the content, structure and professors, it is definitely one of the best in the region and quite comparable to those from some of the best business schools in Europe. It gives you broad knowledge and skills, and a sense of a research community (especially among PhD students, as well as the FELU faculty). The best thing for me is that it is quite international: there are many foreign professors, some top-notch in their respective fields, and by doing research, I got the opportunity to collaborate with people from all around the world.

In general, one of the best things about being in academia is being internationally connected. Visiting scientific conferences, interacting with foreign professors and students at the FELU doctoral program, as well as trying to publish in international journals really helped me in my professional development. Interacting with people I met at conferences, and with people my supervisor or other professors connected me to, presented a significant boost in my career. An example of such excellent collaboration is with BI Norwegian Business School in Oslo. It started with their professor Anders Dysvik when he first came to Ljubljana in May 2011. Our collaboration progressed as Miha got the adjunct associate position there, and the connection with BI became more intense.[9] It consisted of collaborative research that I had never experienced before, joint/collective participation at conferences, publishing papers together and conducting research seminars in Oslo.

The best thing about visiting BI was to witness first-hand the collaborative research, such as that emphasized by Shani and Coghlan (2008). How individuals help and encourage each other within departments was something new to me. Just the fact that they are co-located (all together in one part of the BI building) helps a lot. In addition, they have offices with glass "walls" in order to "break" boundaries and increase interactions among them. The physical presence and closeness is very important in stimulating collaborations, something that we all should strive for in the future. On a related point, Anders' first visit to Slovenia consisted of him delivering an interesting seminar on HRM, and then Miha introduced us and we decided to take him on a little excursion to the Škocjan caves and Piran. In addition to the social side of doing collaborative research and interacting with your business partners in a very friendly manner,[10] I also informally learned a great deal about research and the mindset they have about it at BI. For example, thinking about the psychometric background of everything (validity, reliability), making causal claims, etc. Those are some points that I now try to pass on to my younger colleagues.

During my PhD studies, I gradually grew in self-confidence and realized that I was no worse than my colleagues. I always thought: doctoral studies as a highest level of formal education must be extremely difficult. Some of the smartest, hardest-working people must apply. I quickly saw that, while, of course, very smart, hard-working and ambitious individuals in fact joined this program with the aim of obtaining the highest academic degree, I was just as hard-working, and even perhaps had a better support system around me (i.e. my supervisor, the COBIK–LOIS team, a good employment agreement and the micro research community, which are extremely important in academia; Surry et al., 2013). However, it was not all about the work and studying.

In addition to our business relationship, a lot of my PhD colleagues became my friends and we shared quite a few great days and nights hanging out. I was really lucky that I did not have to face a lot of the obstacles that my colleagues had to during their studies. In addition, I perceive myself as a proactive and quite persistent person, always ready to learn and to search online for what I do not know. In particular I find this latter to be a very good quality that perhaps some people lack. This is so because when you learn something on your own rather than asking someone for every little piece of advice, you not only really learn it for the long run, but also build up your self-efficacy beliefs. Supporting this point, Loyens and colleagues (2008) have found that students with self-directed learning in problem-based study developed superior skill of coping with challenges and had higher self-efficacy beliefs.

A DEFINING MOMENT IN THE HOLY LAND … AND THE SUBSEQUENT AMJ PUBLICATION

Doing research is an inescapable part of the academic life. It represents an intertwined process of not only thinking, reading, analyzing and writing, but also traveling and networking. Trying to make an international appearance, I had a couple of fortunate breakthroughs. Before describing my touchdown moment (i.e. a positive career shock) in Israel that really made a difference, I need to recall my very first academic conference abroad – the Organizational Learning, Knowledge and Capabilities Conference (OLKC) in Hull, UK (2011). I remember that I was not really sure how to approach anyone, but luckily others were not as shy and I quickly made new colleagues and friends. Meeting the same people at various conferences revolving around some of the things you are mutually interested in provides you with a great sense of a global community. At a couple of conferences, I took one of Anders' pieces of advice and looked up people that were going to be there in advance – although at one particular venue in Rotterdam, at the EURAM mini conference on management innovation, I almost felt like a stalker with all the names/pictures/ biography profiles printed out. So I became a bit more "normal" after that.

A particularly defining moment and a fortunate event in my academic life was the first Israel Organizational Behavior Conference in Tel Aviv. This particular conference was advertised as involving a bunch of famous Organizational Behavior [OB] people – one of them also being Adam M. Grant, a professor at the Wharton School of the University of Pennsylvania, a "wonder boy" of management and OB research, whose papers we modeled our own against. I went there with Miha in December 2011 – we sent a paper on the curvilinear relationship[11] between authentic leadership and employee creativity, suggesting that leaders can be "too authentic" and that too high levels of authentic leadership lead to less employee creativity than with only moderately authentic leaders.

The first day of the conference was not that special – I presented our paper, we got some nice feedback, witnessed a couple of useful presentations, hung out with Israeli professor Yoav Vardi, who has also been a visiting professor at FELU for several years now, and had an enjoyable tour of Jaffa, the old part of Tel Aviv. Then came the second, horizon-opening day of the conference.

Miha and I were discussing introducing ourselves and talking to Adam. But we were not completely sure whether or not to do so, or what we could actually get from doing so (although knowing Miha, I was pretty sure that we would). Our perspective shifted in the morning. Adam delivered a brilliant keynote speech. In the second part of the speech, he referred to one of his recent papers on the "too-much-of-a-good-thing effect in management" (Grant & Schwartz, 2011) and how it has only recently become interesting for researchers to examine the negative aspects of positive constructs and vice versa. And then he went on to say that there were only two papers in this conference that follow this supposedly ultra-modern trend – one from a prominent scholar whose name and paper I, of course, have forgotten – and ours!

We were shocked and just could not believe that Adam M. Grant mentioned our paper in his keynote speech in front of a crowd of famous researchers from all around the globe! Miha and I were sitting on opposite sides of the hall, and we immediately exchanged looks – we both knew this meant something big. And we also both knew that we needed to talk to Adam that day. So, right after the keynote, we went and introduced ourselves, and he was super-friendly. We briefly presented our research, and he immediately looked very interested. I remember a very nice thing he said, after we thanked him for his time – he said, "Thank you for doing such fascinating research". Truly a great guy, a giver, completely. Because he did not have a lot of time, we made plans to meet in the lunch break.

In the meantime, Miha and I prepared a bit, talked about everything we needed to tell him, and gathered our grips because we were talking to such a famous person (he is to us researchers what Michael Jordan is to basketball fans). During lunch, he was again very friendly and full of advice and willingness to help. In particular, we presented our latest research on knowledge hiding and creativity that showed that if you hide knowledge, you hurt your own creativity (authored together with Anders and Christina Nerstad, also from BI) because your colleagues retaliate. He liked it a lot, particularly because of the focus on the "negative" construct, knowledge hiding, as opposed to knowledge sharing. We had talked before about submitting it to the *Journal of Organizational Behavior*, a very good journal, but not the best in our field at the time. We were pretty confident. We had also conducted both a field and an experimental study, but simply had no experience in publishing in top-tier journals. But Adam suggested submitting to the *Academy of Management Journal* (AMJ), one of the best in the management field, where he was also one of the associate editors. We did not need a lot of convincing to do so.

We submitted the paper to AMJ and were immediately pleased that we got Adam as an action editor. We knew we could not expect any favors and that he would do this to an extremely high academic standard, but still, at least he knew the paper and thought the idea was good enough for AMJ. It took a year and three rounds of reviews for the paper to finally get accepted. Such a rigorous process is not unusual for top-tier journals, as their rejection rate climbs to 90%. For example, Glick and colleagues (2007) report that in 2000 the AMJ rejected 92.5% of original submissions and *Administrative Science Quarterly* rejected 90% of original submissions.

The reviews were extremely challenging – I think in the end, not a single sentence remained unchanged. And, in every round, in addition to 15+ comments from each of the three reviewers, we got another 15+ comments/suggestions (that were extremely developmental) from Adam. *It involved a lot of work.* We had to re-do all the analyses, rewrite the entire paper, re-do the experimental study, etc. But it was more than worthwhile in the end. It was such a tremendous accomplishment for the whole group, but for me in particular. Not many PhD students have their work accepted for publishing in AMJ, especially not those studying outside the United States. I had also become the first Slovene leading author on an AMJ paper (Špela Trefalt [2013] followed quickly after, although her paper was actually in press before ours). Looking back, with all the hard work that went into rewriting the paper, it was definitely the main idea, the story of the paper that got it accepted, not the fancy analyses or the style of writing. Judge et al. (2007) write about that in their own AMJ paper. The hook, the main story is everything in the paper.

During my two and a half years of doctoral studies, I not only learned and absorbed knowledge like a sponge, but, also as a consequence of my supervisor's goal-driven attitude, I wrote a lot. Writing, writing, writing ... that's how you get better at academic writing. I had papers in proceedings of ten international scientific conferences (also got two Academy of Management Annual Meeting best paper proceedings, in 2012 and 2013), and defended my thesis in February 2013.

During my doctoral adventure, not everything was rosy and without pressure. On the contrary, I felt pressure quite a lot. And it was not necessarily inflicted by someone else, but rather by myself. I knew that I had been given a great opportunity at COBIK, and I knew that the positions at FELU were rather limited because of the general economic situation in Slovenia at that time. On the other hand, I also knew that my supervisor could have chosen anyone for this position, and I knew that he was very successful research-wise and had high expectations. I wanted to meet those expectations that I thought senior colleagues had set for me. Perhaps I got this from my mother – she was the Head of the Research and Development department in the Slovene manufacturing and processing company Kolpa, and the creator of a composite material called Kerrock. I think I am similar to her in that way. Obviously something is pre-determined by our genes.

What was a significant driver during my studies and what I wanted to contribute to is bringing Slovenia to the world map, and FELU and COBIK to the research map (I got this comment at many conferences actually, mostly from people who had never heard of Slovenia or did not know where it was). Naturally, I could not have done it without the support of my micro research community: FELU and the COBIK faculty and students played an important role as well. I have to mention Darija Aleksić and Sabina Bogilović, a couple of Miha's PhD students (therefore, my "academic sisters"), who were also my colleagues already at bachelor's and master's studies. They are very talented young scholars with an undoubtedly bright future ahead of them who I have shared many (academic and friendly) talks with. The way I am wired (and it also shows in various personality tests) is that good "positive" relationships mean a great deal to me. I especially do not like confrontations, and also have difficulties in saying "no" (although I am improving in that segment). An inclusive, mastery and friendly climate is a key factor for my work and happy personal life. Therefore, personal and work-related "communities" of people that I can trust and feel a part of are very important to me – and I have so far been fortunate to have that in my life, both personally and professionally. This has undoubtedly been one of the key success factors for me.

TRANSITION TO JUNIOR (AND LESS JUNIOR) FACULTY

After finishing my PhD, I had quite a good idea of what I wanted to do in my near and far future, but my career was nonetheless not set in stone. I held the assistant professor position at FELU, but my contract was (for various reasons related to practicality) not indefinite. Even though it would be by all objective standards foolish from FELU's perspective to let me go, being a rather risk-averse person, I cannot say that it did not bother me that I did not have a permanent contract. That being said, my key priority was definitely a desire to stay at FELU and continue contributing to placing the institution on the research map.[12] I also love teaching at FELU a lot.

Nonetheless, there was (and still is, always) the opportunity of going abroad. Spending at least three months abroad is also a part of the requirements for obtaining higher-level titles (of an associate and a full professor), and in the summer of 2016, I went to Canada to visit our knowledge-hiding research colleague Catherine E. Connelly. I have been offered positions (a research fellow, a visiting professor or a tenure-track position) pretty much everywhere I have been – but I have not quite found a place that would be as suitable for me as Ljubljana and FELU. Although I have to emphasize that the working conditions at FELU are very nice and improving every year, a lot of it has to do with my family and social environment, as well as just the general appeal of Ljubljana and Slovenia as places to live.[13]

After being promoted to the position of associate professor at FELU in 2018, and keeping in mind my reluctance to move from Slovenia, my research path seems quite set. I have been involved in many fascinating projects since my doctoral studies. Fair Labor in the Digitized Economy,[14] along with colleagues from BI Norwegian Business School (Sut I Wong and Christian Fieseler, and others), was definitely one of those that had a big impact on my research evolution, as I am increasingly diving into positive and negative aspects of digitalization. My next goal is definitely related to potentially acquiring a European Research Council grant related to the negative aspects of digitalization, and how to overcome them. Another one is examining innovativeness among public sector employees (funded by the Croatian Science Foundation), which also helped me intensify (and extensify) my collaborations with Tomislav Hernaus and colleagues at the University of Zagreb. A not-so-gratifying (research-wise) experience is coordinating AACSB (American Accreditation of Business Schools)-related initiatives at FELU, which involves a lot of administrative work – but at the same time also allows me to get to know the school and its people much better.

It happens sometimes that you get caught up in something, especially if you are good at it, and end up forgetting to ask yourself what you still want to do. Therefore, I will also write about some other motivations that I continue to have. A lot of them are related to research and curiously exploring the world around me. Mentoring next generations of researchers also comes to mind – I love doing that, although it is not always easy with different backgrounds, motivations and personalities being involved in these processes. Translating my knowledge and experience and passing it on to younger generations who are eager to walk in my footsteps is close to me – I enjoy helping others in order for them to get better. Some of my aspirations are naturally also related to teaching – besides trying to be the best I can at FELU, I also want to contribute to overcoming creativity-blocking barriers, not only in higher education, but also in primary and high schools. It is almost sad to see students come to university with such a set mindset of structured problem-solving, wanting to follow very specific instructions, and wanting to listen to lectures and remember facts without thinking too much or developing their open-ended problem-solving skills.

I also have quite a few business motivations that are (almost) completely unrelated to my current path – but not completely, as I think it is very important that we, academics, are not narrowly focused only on our topics.[15] I have always wanted to be a writer (which in a way I am now, of course, with all the academic and professional papers and book chapters), but not only academic – I still want to write some fiction as well. Children's books, perhaps something related to my French bulldog, Sushi, or some short stories, I am not sure yet. In this regard, Yoav Vardi is an inspiration with the poetry he has written in addition to his academic work.

I have also not given up on entrepreneurship just yet. I now spend some (mostly research) energy on contributing to the development of a national and regional ecosystem favorable to the stimulation of entrepreneurship, mostly high-tech or high-growth; however, not nearly as much as some of my colleagues. In any case, perhaps I will re-install my little book of ideas that I used to carry around and write them all down. After all, academic life is not a very profitable business. But it is rewarding in all other aspects. If you do something you love, then you never really work – I am living proof of that. For me, the academic work is certainly a calling. On the other hand, I do (not) work all the time – but also try to have sufficient work–life balance and flexibility in work that I can do whatever and go wherever I want, almost whenever I want. And this is something I value the most.

A LEARNING EXPERIENCE: KEY SUCCESS FACTORS

People frequently ask me: What are some of the key success factors that enable some doctoral students to graduate so fast, to publish something in high-ranked journals, and to generally be successful? I offer a couple of explanations, and I feel this might serve nicely for the new generations of potential researchers deciding whether or not to embark on this route.

A very, very important lesson I have learned is the importance of trying – trial-and-error. All in all, I received 20+ rejections of my papers during my doctoral studies (some at conferences, but mostly at journals – desk rejections, rejections in the first round of review, or even after the first round). I think the first rejection came from the *Leadership Quarterly* (LQ), where I submitted a paper based on my master's thesis. I still remember – I was at Amsterdam airport returning from the aforementioned OLKC conference when I got it, waiting for my returning flight. The rejection was actually quite nice, very friendly, based on the quality of that paper, which was, from the present perspective, nowhere near close to being good enough for LQ (or any other Social Sciences Citation Index (SSCI)-ranked journal, for that matter). When I finally got it accepted by the *Australian Journal of Management* (Černe et al., 2014a), it was a completely different paper, with a different study, and the same as with the AMJ paper (Černe et al., 2014b), almost no sentence remained unchanged. I dealt with this rejection in a positive manner. As more rejections came along the way,[16] I learned that it is a numbers game – you have to move very quickly, rewrite based on what you think was relevant feedback and send it back into the system – re-submit or submit to another journal. Some researchers naturally have a different, a more in-depth approach, with a bit more deliberation attached to it – which might be a more academic approach.

Another, perhaps more crucial key point related to this experience is the value of optimism – trying to overcome all obstacles hands-on and with a positive attitude. I have always been like that, at least since I read some books on positive psychology in high school. I liked this notion so much that I chose authentic leadership and positive psychology as "my" topics for bachelor's and master's theses. And, in my experience, findings of those research streams are true – positive attitude helps so much! It does not help "attract" positive things happening to you *per se*, but helps with dealing with whatever comes at you in a more efficient manner, not worrying about stupid unimportant things (e.g. cheap talk and rumors, lack of confidence and similar). It also helps you interact with others – no one likes somebody that is constantly complaining or talking in a negative manner.

Another key success factor is persistence and hard work. Some people probably do not realize it, but I have spent numerous hours learning the research methodology and various analytical techniques, researching online how it is done, scrutinizing them and trying different analyses out. In order to learn how to conduct a specific analytical technique, I definitely found that merely reading is not enough. Moreover, it can be counterproductive, especially when you read about a particular methodology in detail, study the nuances and get lost in an overload of information. A much better way is to learn the techniques first-hand,[17] trying them out on your own data, for your own specific problems, using tutorials, searching online, and then going in-depth only on particular matters that are relevant for your own research problem.

Therefore, I see research as a circular process that has to combine research problem framing, data gathering and analysis simultaneously at all times. And this process does not happen overnight – it can take months for someone to be able to master a particular analytical technique, gather data, master the literature and write a decent paper. I have also spent countless hours reading papers, from my fields, about writing and publishing, such as the AMJ series on writing for that journal published in 2013, Sutton and Staw (1995), and Whetten (1989), or papers which have applied similar research designs or analytical techniques that I aspired to.

I also have to emphasize one thing – besides resulting from a student's own personal initiative, success also depends on the supervisor. I was lucky (or, perhaps said better, well-informed) and came into a very good situation that fitted my needs and desires. I always got support when I needed it, from my supervisor and the micro community of researchers around me, and was directed towards the right things. And I am very grateful for that – even though I worked extremely hard and a lot, and this is certainly the key point.

In the end, I will refer back to the title of the chapter – a series of fortunate events. As you have been able to read throughout the chapter, I have been lucky. There have been a lot of what-ifs[18] in my academic career so far. I am not sure what would have happened with my academic career if I had not met Sandra in the first year of bachelor's studies, if I had not met Miha just when he was looking for a research assistant at COBIK, if we had not gone to Israel and met Adam there to guide us towards AMJ. Therefore, minor things do in fact determine people's fates. But for the ultimate conclusion, I will relate to something that I have been highlighting and is completely opposite – that we can determine the outcomes with our efforts, or at least influence the probability of succeeding to a significant extent. Therefore, I will sum up with Virgil's proverb (an ancient Roman poet) that is quite commonly used in our area: "Fortune favors the bold." My colleague and friend Aleš Pustovrh told me, after we had successfully submitted the PACINNO[19] application (that we later on actually got approved and which brought around six million euros into the Adriatic region), an even better version of that proverb originated by Louis Pasteur: "Fortune favors the prepared mind."[20] I believe this to the utmost extent and tell it to any of my potential protégées or students: if you work really hard and invest a lot of time and effort into something, good things are bound to happen, sooner or later.

NOTES

1. The title of this chapter is a parodistic reference to a *A Series of Unfortunate Events* – a series of children's novels by Lemony Snicket (the pen name of American author Daniel Handler). While many academic lives might not be (in parody, of course) that much different from those described in the tales written by Lemony Snicket, I was fortunate and flexible enough to (at least up to now) navigate the academic waters successfully and avoid potential misfortunes that many young academics face, such as uninterested, self-gratifying or manipulative PhD supervisors and senior professors, malfortune in the publish-or-perish game related to terribly long review processes, a lack of opportunity to get sufficient knowledge, insufficient support from their institutions, etc. An interesting research stream that deals with the role of luck and coincidences in careers can be found within fields examining protean and boundaryless careers.
2. The Centre of Excellence for Biosensors, Instrumentation and Process Control was established in 2009. During 2009–2013, the centre of excellence operation was financed by the EU (European Regional Development Fund – 85 %) and the Republic of Slovenia (Ministry of Education, Science and Sport – 15 %).
3. Novo mesto (literally "New town"), my hometown, is a town of a little more than 20 000 people located on a bend of the Krka River. It is situated in southeastern Slovenia (Dolenjska region), close to the border with Croatia.
4. Matura exam at the end of high school.
5. I actually became the first student in Slovenia to finish their bachelor's studies after the "Bologna Process" was implemented (the Faculty of Economics was the first school to overhaul its programs), co-creating the European Higher Education Area under the Lisbon Recognition Convention. I later on repeated this feat at the master's level in 2009.
6. Later on, I learnt that this invitation was also based on the very positive referral of my bachelor thesis mentor, Sandra Penger. Apparently, it seems that everything you do counts sooner or later.
7. Feel free to check out my website: www.matej-cerne.com. The main motive for having the website was that I wanted to increase my visibility as an academic – we meet many people that we might end up collaborating with in our research, and we need to be able to be found in this globalized world.
8. I did not really play with the idea of doing my PhD abroad. When I got the COBIK opportunity, one of the preconditions was that I would enroll into the doctoral program at FELU and have Miha as my supervisor. Nonetheless, even though I had been thinking about doing the PhD before that, going abroad did not really become a viable option. This might have been the case because I simply did not have enough insight into academic research at the time and did not really know all my options and their potential consequences. With the way everything turned out, of course, I can say that I am happy that I did my doctoral studies at FELU.
9. I also have to mention one of the most fun experiences related to these trips to Oslo: watching *PhD: The Movie* (https://phdmovie.com/ [accessed November 2, 2012]) in the BI apartment in Oslo with Miha. This movie, along with other satiri-

cal (but all too often very realistic!) portrayals of PhD life (e.g. PhD comics https://phdcomics.com/, Lego Grad Student https://brickademics.com/ etc. [accessed November 2, 2012]), I believe helps take research and everyday occurences within academic life a bit less seriously.

10. In Anders' words: "Since we work so hard all the time, we have to unwind from time to time and drink a glass of wine over good food and great company."

11. An acknowledgement has to be made here: the idea to examine curvilinear relationships in general actually came from Miao Quing, who was a visiting professor at FELU, and I wrote this particular paper on the curvilinear relationship between authentic leadership and creativity as a part of one PhD course at FELU.

12. We're doing quite well – in 2018, FELU made it into the *Financial Times'* list of top 95 European Business Schools for the first time.

13. For example, Save the Children's *End of Childhood Report 2017* (Geoghegan, 2017) ranked Slovenia as second in terms of the best countries to have children in.

14. A four-year research project funded by the Research Council of Norway, https://www.bi.edu/research/find-departments-and-research-centres/research-centres/fair-digital2/ (accessed September 18, 2018), it focuses on how society can ensure fair labor conditions while transitioning into a fully digitized economy, and involves partners such as BI Norwegian Business School, Berkman Center for Internet and Society at Harvard, and Erasmus University Rotterdam.

15. That is, "Fachidiot", which" literally translated into English means "subject idiot", and is defined by the Goethe Institute as: "Someone who knows a lot (and solely) about a particular field, in a similar way to a single-track specialist."

16. In November 2018, following a visit to my friends at the University of Tilburg, I counted them all and "celebrated" my 100th rejection from SSCI-ranked papers, tallying my success rate to about a one-in-three.

17. It also helps that, at FELU, research seminars or parts of various courses are conducted by (mostly visiting) top-notch professors that are able to present different methodologies and answer questions that doctoral students might have.

18. There's an interesting history book on that matter, edited by Robert Cowley (2001): *The Collected What If: Eminent Historians Imagine What Might Have Been.*

19. PACINNO (Platform for trans-Academic Cooperation in INNOvation) is a strategic project funded by the IPA (Instrument for Pre-Accession Assistance) Cross-Border Cooperation Programme.

20. Louis Pasteur, French chemist and microbiologist renowned for his discoveries of the principles of vaccination, microbial fermentation and pasteurization, seems to be the original author of this proverb.

REFERENCES

Černe, M., Dimovski, V., Marič, M., Penger, S., & Škerlavaj, M. (2014a). Congruence of leader self-perceptions and follower perceptions of authentic leadership: Understanding what authentic leadership is and how it enhances employees' job satisfaction. *Australian Journal of Management, 39*(3), 453–471.

Černe, M., Nerstad, C. G. L., Dysvik, A., & Škerlavaj, M. (2014b). What goes around comes around: Knowledge hiding, perceived motivational climate, and creativity. *Academy of Management Journal, 57*(1), 172–192.

Cowley, R., ed. (2001). *The Collected What If: Eminent Historians Imagine What Might Have Been.* New York, NY: Putnam's Sons.

Dimovski, V., Penger, S., & Peterlin, J. (2009). *Avtentično vodenje v učeči se organizaciji* [*Authentic Leadership in a Learning Organization*]. Ljubljana: Planet GV.

Geoghegan, T. (2017). *Stolen Childhoods: End of Childhood Report* 2017. London: Save the Children.

Glick, W. H., Miller, C. C., & Cardinal, L. B. (2007). Making a life in the field of organization science. *Journal of Organizational Behavior, 28*(7), 817–835.

Grant, A. M., & Schwartz, B. (2011). Too much of a good thing: The challenge and opportunity of the inverted U. *Perspectives on Psychological Science, 6*(1), 61–76.

Hay, L. (1991). *The Power Is Within You.* Santa Monica, CA: Hay House.

Judge, T. A., Cable, D. M., Colbert, A. E., & Rynes, S. L. (2007). What causes a management article to be cited – Article, author, or journal? *Academy of Management Journal, 50*(3), 491–506.

Loyens, S. M., Magda, J., & Rikers, R. M. (2008). Self-directed learning in problem-based learning and its relationships with self-regulated learning. *Educational Psychology Review, 20*(4), 411–427.

Shani, A. B., & Coghlan, D. (2008). *Handbook of Collaborative Management Research.* Thousand Oaks, CA: Sage Publications.

Surry, D., Baker, F., & Rausch, T. (2013). The role of micro communities in educational research. *Society for Information Technology & Teacher Education International Conference,* pp. 2453–2456.

Sutton, R. I., & Staw, B. M. (1995). What theory is not. *Administrative Science Quarterly, 40*(3), 371–384.

Trefalt, Š. (2013). Between you and me: Setting work–nonwork boundaries in the context of workplace relationships. *Academy of Management Journal, 56*(6), 1802–1829.

Whetten, D. A. (1989). What constitutes a theoretical contribution? *Academy of Management Review, 14*(4), 490–495.

8.   Future work selves in academia

Karoline Strauss

Estimated reading time: **27 minutes and 7 seconds**.

CHAPTER HIGHLIGHTS

* Worrying about the future will cost our well-being in the long run. However, you should be prepared and proactive.
* Having a clear future work self offers a sense of direction as individuals "navigate through the fog of multiple career trajectories".
* Engage with administrative work on your own terms (administrative roles should not be resource-draining activities).
* Having a clear sense of your future work self means that you can evaluate opportunities in terms of whether they bring you closer to being who you want to be in the future or take you further away.
* Be a positive influencer.

> *No star is ever lost we once have seen,*
> *we always may be what we might have been.*
> Adelaide Anne Procter

INTRODUCTION

I worry about the future. I worry about the polar bears dying as the climate is changing, about society collapsing and having to defend my life and property against marauders, about the future of business education, of women's reproductive rights, of democracy in the Western world, and of the European Union. While I am trying to worry less in general and I am making some progress, I still worry about a great many things I cannot control, and some that I can. There is, as you may be aware, a cost to worrying about the future, in terms of our well-being (Borkovec et al., 1998). Ample research shows the benefits of paying attention to the present rather than the future (or the past, for that matter) (Brown & Ryan, 2003; Hülsheger et al., 2014). But my obsession with the future also comes with benefits. In research on proactivity, one of my main research interests, authors often refer to a quote which states that there are three kinds of people in the world: those who make things happen, those who watch what happens, and those who wonder what happened (proactive people being the first kind, of course) (Parker & Bindl, 2017). "Making things happen", i.e. trying to bring about change in ourselves or in our environment of our own accord, necessarily involves some anticipation of the future (Parker et al., 2010). Imagining the future enables self-regulation[1] (Taylor et al., 1998) and allows us to prepare for problems before they occur (Aspinwall & Taylor, 1997). Being focused on the future and the role our behavior plays in shaping it should also make it more likely for us to exercise and eat healthily (Joireman et al., 2012), so at least there are some advantages to thinking about the future. I can certainly see a further upside: wanting to understand how thinking about the future can help us make things happen continues to inspire my research program, as it has done since my PhD. In my doctoral research I developed the concept of "future work selves", our representations of ourselves in the future which reflect our hopes and aspirations in relation to work (Strauss et al., 2012).

Future work selves are not just career aspirations. They form part of who we believe we are, and often go beyond extrinsic career goals such as advancing to a particular position. They incorporate our ideas of the kind of person we want to be, the kind of relationships we want to have, and the experiences we want our future selves to have (Strauss et al., 2019). The clearer and the easier for us to imagine our future work self is, the more likely it is to promote proactive career behaviors, such as career planning, networking, and the development of skills that may be needed in the future (Strauss et al., 2012; Taber & Blankemeyer, 2015). Spending time imagining one's future work self can also promote other types of proactive behavior, such as efforts to shape the future of one's organization, at least in some people (Strauss & Parker, 2018).

I have been studying future work selves and their impact on people's proactive behavior for a little over ten years at this point and I continue to be intrigued by our future selves and their interplay with motivation, behavior, and well-being. In my own career I mostly felt that I had a clear future work self, a clear idea of who I wanted to be in the future I was actively working towards, even though this future work self underwent (and still undergoes) frequent revisions (Strauss & Kelly, 2017). Careers do not necessarily follow linear plans but are influenced and shaped by chance events (Bright et al., 2005; Černe, Chapter 7, this volume). However, as Louis Pasteur said: "Chance favors the prepared mind."

Having a clear future work self can at the very least provide meaning (Zhang et al., 2017); it offers a sense of direction as individuals "navigate through the fog of multiple career trajectories and enables them to align their job and their career with their values" (Strauss et al., 2012, p. 582). In this chapter, I will use future work selves as a framework to reflect on my career so far. I will explore how my own future work self was shaped through experiences, role models, and the many setbacks inherent in academic life, and how it nonetheless continues to provide a sense of purpose and direction. Finally, I will consider how as scholars and teachers we in turn influence others' future work selves as they navigate the changing landscape of academic life.

MY FUTURE WORK SELF ... HAS A PhD

I first started thinking about doing a PhD in 2004. I was in the third year of a five-year master's in psychology at the University of Vienna and had come across a flyer advertising the Personality and Social Psychology doctoral program at the University of Michigan. It showed Ann Arbor in autumn, and students in wool jumpers were clutching books under maple trees whose leaves had turned bright red. This could be my future self, I thought. Maybe my future work self would not be in Michigan (which seemed somewhat out of reach), but maybe there were other options. I was a teaching assistant[2] in the department of economic psychology at the University of Vienna and this meant I was part of department meetings where research strategy was discussed, I was sharing an office with some of the department's doctoral students, and I was teaching research methods workshops.

Academia began to seem like a path that was possible for me. I was quite ready to give up on the future work self I had previously held, which involved working as a management consultant and corporate trainer. After a series of internships in this field I was increasingly sure that this wasn't what I wanted. Academic research seemed to be about studying what was genuinely interesting, about solving puzzles, and about being independent of a paying client's agenda. It also incorporated elements of a long lost future work self of mine. Before I had decided that psychology was a degree which would at some point offer at least some employability I had wanted to become a writer of some sort, maybe a journalist, maybe a novelist, but definitely someone who was paid to write. Being an academic started to evolve as a desirable future work self, so the next step was finding a PhD position.

I did not know a lot about PhD programs and university rankings so I looked for a PhD position on a topic that I was interested in, rather than for a PhD program that placed well, i.e. whose students ended up with faculty positions at research universities. I applied for, and was offered, a PhD position at a university in Switzerland but I waited to hear back from the Institute of Work Psychology at the University of Sheffield where Mark Griffin was advertising a PhD position in the area of leadership. With both offers eventually on the table, I decided to go to Sheffield. This was probably the single best decision

I made for my early career, choosing the right PhD advisor. I knew that journal papers were the currency of academic careers, and Mark had published widely in the journals I dreamed of publishing in. I had also tracked down the CV of a recent PhD student of his and had worked out that she had published papers with Mark during and after her PhD, so hopefully I would be able to do the same. I have seen people succeed who did not have this advantage but, as I would later find, working with someone who is publishing in journals you are hoping to target yourself means you can learn from them, instead of working the rules of the game out yourself.

While I was aware of the Institute of Work Psychology as a well-known research center in occupational and organizational psychology which counts many talented and productive scholars among its alumni, I had never been to the UK, I did not know anyone there, and I did not really know where Sheffield even was. I watched *The Full Monty* in preparation, a late 1990s British comedy about a group of former steel workers in Sheffield who founded a male striptease act in order to make a living, and brushed up on my English by reading a lot of Oscar Wilde (it turned out that neither is all that accurate a representation of life in the North of England in the mid-2000s). I bought a one-way ticket to the UK, booked myself into bed and breakfast accommodation near campus for a week, which I figured would be long enough to find a place to live, and left Vienna.

Studying for my PhD in England was nothing like I had imagined. Few of the university buildings looked like something out of Harry Potter, and particularly the first year involved a lot more reading than writing. For me, the first period of my PhD was the most challenging, trying to find a topic, getting excited about a new idea only to find out that there is already a well-developed body of research on the topic, seemingly moving around in circles without really achieving anything. Mark Griffin was, however, a fantastic PhD advisor. He was kind, generous, and patient with me as I arrived at our meeting each week with a new model. He shared a data set with me during my first year which resulted in my first paper, published in the *British Journal of Management*. He found funding for me to go to the Academy of Management Annual Meeting and supported me as I wanted to develop the concept of future work selves even though he was, as he recently admitted to me, not really sure about the idea in the beginning.

Mark's wife Sharon K. Parker took over the direction of the Institute of Work Psychology just as I began my PhD and together they used their resources and network to bring prolific and emerging scholars to the Institute, primarily from the US, but also from all over the world. There was a vibrant community of researchers and doctoral students who would come together for barbecues on the lawn and for "cake day", a weekly event where we would celebrate even small successes over, well, cake. This is where I met collaborators and friends and I continue to benefit from the connections to this community to this day.

Sheffield itself was a wonderful place to live. Far from the smog-choked industrial city I had imagined, it is the gateway to the beautiful Peak District national park where I learned to rock climb, went on long hikes, often by myself, and where I sat overlooking dry-stone walled fields full of sheep and heather turning purple in autumn to clear my head. For a while, anything seemed possible. I was going to publish papers and get a faculty position and altogether have an exciting career.

Then my first paper was rejected and I lost all confidence in my future work self. Maybe I wasn't cut out for this. Clearly I wasn't meant to be an academic if my first steps in this direction resulted in failure. I walked around the department, distraught, for weeks. One of the older professors in the department unhelpfully told me that by trying to publish at this point in my academic career I was aiming too high and that this would only ever result in disappointment. I am not sure how I eventually bounced back from this setback and reconnected with my future work self as an academic. It certainly took a while, and it will certainly have been helped by my advisors, Mark Griffin and Sharon K. Parker, sharing their own experiences with rejections, which made them seem more normal and less disastrous. The rejected paper eventually formed the basis of my paper in the *Journal of Applied Psychology* but this was several years after this first rejection. Particularly in the early years of our careers, so much hinges on the success of each paper, and any rejection not only feels threating to our future work self but also has real consequences for the kinds of jobs we can apply for. I was lucky to work with Mark and later also with Sharon on additional projects during my PhD, which meant I at least did not have all my eggs in one basket as I applied for positions after my PhD.

MY FUTURE WORK SELF ... HAS A FACULTY POSITION

PhD programs in the UK traditionally do not have a very substantial taught element. Instead, students begin to work immediately on their PhD project and PhD scholarships are typically limited to three years. This means that postdocs are a common option in order to be able to compete on the job market. I finished my thesis within three years and for a while I thought I would be able to move to the US immediately after my PhD, ideally to a business school strategically located near areas offering rock climbing and other outdoor sports. I would get one of these houses with a deck wrapping all around, and drive an SUV. I did not have much success on the US job market, and for a while my future work self seemed somewhat up in the air. Where would I go? What would I do if I was not able to find a position?

At the same time the relationship I had been in during my PhD ended and the chaos in my personal life meant I had little time left to worry about my professional future. For a few weeks, I did little else but go rock climbing. Rather than worrying about my future I was focused on the more immediate worry of falling off some rock face. Then, just at the right time, Sharon K. Parker won a research grant that would fund my postdoc position and a year of breathing space opened up in front of me. I soon had better luck on the UK job market, particularly as my paper on future work selves in the *Journal of Applied Psychology* (eventually published as Strauss et al., 2012) was progressing towards an acceptance.

Before my postdoc year was up I was in a position to choose among two offers for a faculty position in the UK. For a while I saw my future work self in a cottage in the Welsh countryside, driving to teach an MBA class in a Land Rover with a sheepdog sticking its head out the window. I would have raised chickens and learned to sea kayak. Instead, now having had ample career advice, I chose the more highly ranked school and stayed in Sheffield. Getting a faculty position in the place where you did your PhD is not uncommon in many European countries, but essentially unheard off in the US. However, Sheffield provided excellent conditions to new assistant professors (or lecturers, as they are still called in many UK universities). My teaching load was light and I could continue to work on the grant that had funded my postdoc position, now as a PI (a principal investigator, essentially the lead researcher on a grant or a lab).

While the Institute of Work Psychology was an independent research center during my PhD, it was now part of the management school and I found myself in a business school environment rather than a psychology department for the first time. I started teaching a leadership course on the MBA program but most of the courses I taught were part of the Master's in Occupational Psychology. It was not until my next job change that I felt I had truly left psychology departments behind.

MY FUTURE WORK SELF ... IS ON THE MOVE

I had been an assistant professor at the University of Sheffield for less than three years when I was invited to apply for a position as associate professor at Warwick Business School (WBS). WBS was undergoing some substantial changes and I joined a department where a number of faculty had either recently left or were in the process of leaving. At the same time there was some rapid growth. At WBS expectations in terms of research and teaching were high, and I decided to keep my head down and get on with my research program. I was happy to be at a prestigious and well-resourced school but I was still commuting the 150 or so kilometers from Sheffield. Faculty at WBS were mostly in the office only when necessary so I, too, only came to campus for one or two days a week. While at Sheffield and particularly the Institute of Work Psychology I had felt like part of a community, for a number of reasons this was less the case at WBS.

After two and a half years at WBS I was ready for a change and I started to reimagine my future work self. Our future selves are the most flexible and adaptable part of our self-concept (Cross & Markus, 1991), allowing us to take a playful approach to thinking about who we may want to become (Ibarra, 1999). There was nothing holding me in the UK (not counting my friends, mortgage, and what you would generally refer to as a life), and I was contemplating a move to a new country and to a new school. I mentioned this in a conversation with a friend and co-author, and in another one of these instances where chance comes into play with, as Pasteur put it, a prepared mind, he suggested I should apply to ESSEC, one of the leading business schools in France where he had just spent some time in a visiting position. He had good things to say about ESSEC and its potential fit for me. Faculty seemed to have the breathing space to pursue ambitious and risky research projects and have plenty of autonomy.

Unlike the UK-based business schools I had worked at, the top business schools in France are traditionally standalone institutions, not attached to a university and so not subject to being governed by a larger and multidisciplinary institution. A university-based business school is supporting less profitable departments, while a standalone business school typically has more autonomy and more agility. UK universities and their business schools are also subject to benchmarking and assessment exercises (the Research Excellence Framework, the Teaching Excellence Framework, and soon the Knowledge Exchange Framework) (Pidd & Broadbent, 2015) which shape their behavior and that of their researchers (Smith et al., 2011). Much has been written about how the way UK universities are managed influences academic work (see Deem et al., 2007, for a critical perspective).

In contrast, ESSEC, while of course subject to rankings, felt like a more dynamic environment. This was becoming more important as I began to look for ways to contribute to my institution through an administrative role. I wanted to change something, implement something new, create something out of nothing, and ESSEC's entrepreneurial culture made it seem like a good place to do so. Somewhat out of the blue, without really being on the job market, I applied to ESSEC just ahead of the closing date, gave a job talk on my way to Austria for Christmas, and received an offer on Christmas Eve. I moved to ESSEC in August 2015, and on the day I am submitting this chapter (September 1, 2018) I have become a full professor there. ESSEC has a transparent policy on the academic evaluation (and potentially the promotion) of professors, but also encourages a diversity of profiles, essentially enabling plenty of "job crafting" on part of professors (Bakker et al., 2017; Wrzesniewski & Dutton, 2001).

As part of my job-crafting efforts at ESSEC, I also found an administrative role that allowed me to write the rules rather than merely implement them, and I became the academic director of the Global BBA (Bachelor of Business Administration) dissertations. I feel lucky to have been able to engage with administrative work on my own terms, at a point in my career where my research program was well established and I was an experienced teacher. I have seen friends and colleagues under pressure from their institutions to take on large administrative roles early on in their career, and I have seen assistant professors spend their valuable time on activities that will make a difference to the institution or to their students but that will ultimately not be of much use when they are looking for a promotion or for a new job. Of course I would not suggest to anyone to selfishly look out for themselves only. I struggle to say "no" myself when asked for help at work, and research shows that this tendency can result in women finding themselves with a larger number of smaller and more diverse roles (Ely et al., 2011). But having a clear sense of my future work self means that I can evaluate opportunities in terms of whether they bring me closer to being who I want to be in the future or take me further away, and that I feel more confident turning down tempting and lucrative offers of additional roles because they are not compatible with my future work self.

MY FUTURE WORK SELF … IS A PRIORITY

My future work self mostly involved what was the less comfortable option. As you may have guessed from the opening paragraph, being constantly worried about the future does not make you the most adventurous person. I did not travel around Southeast Asia with a backpack the way many of my friends seemed to do at some point in their 20s. I would worry about food poisoning and being kidnapped by militia and about exotic diseases I don't even know about. Granted, I used to scuba dive and I rock climb, but only with excellent insurance and with mountain rescue on speed dial. It is not so much that for me the glass is half empty, it is more that I worry that there may be a shark at the bottom of it (I am paraphrasing from Sarah Kendall's Australian Trilogy[3]). But in pursuit of my future work self I moved country, twice, and exposed myself to all kinds of metaphorical sharks. I could have remained in Vienna, and then in Sheffield, and then in Warwick, and sometimes I wonder what my life would be like now if I had stayed put. But longing for the self we would have been if we had not left, say, our home country largely does not help us adjust to new environments (George & Strauss, 2018), and I am glad I moved as I did.

During my master's at the University of Vienna my somewhat eccentric developmental psychology professor told a story in one of her lectures about her female doctoral students and research assistants seeming reluctant to take opportunities to relocate that would further their career because of their relationships while their male counterparts had no such hesitations, as their female partners usually came with them. Anecdotal as this was, it ties in with a persistent pattern of career decisions in heterosexual couples where it is still common that the man's career takes precedent (Ely et al., 2014). I took note of that anecdote. "This is not going to be me", I thought. I was ready to move when it would benefit my career, and ready to expect my partner to support me in this. Failing that, I would have been quite happy to follow Avivah Wittenberg-Cox's (2017) advice and remain single rather than be with a partner who would not support my career, not just in words but in actions.

My own personal decision is, of course, in no way a judgment of women who make different choices (although see Stone & Lovejoy, 2004, on the myth of women's "choice" to opt out of their fast-paced careers), and my various moves were certainly made easier by the fact that I am not a caregiver. Making my future work self a priority means, however, that shortly after I met my partner and fell in love I moved to another country. It means that we only see each other on the weekends, taking the train back and forth between London and Paris and spending most weekends in our house in a quiet French village near ESSEC's main campus. (There are worse living situations, I have to say.) It means I missed a family event this year because I was giving a keynote speech in China, and I am writing this chapter in the early mornings of what is technically supposed to be a summer holiday in the Alps. It has taken some searching for someone who supports my future work self even if it is not convenient for them, and who would be ready to come with me should I move again.

MY FUTURE WORK SELF IS ... LIKELY INFLUENCING OTHER FUTURE WORK SELVES

I have paid little attention in my research so far to where future work selves come from but earlier research on possible selves highlights that they are shaped by role models (Ibarra, 1999), not necessarily by distant heroes, but by being able to see people like ourselves succeed in a particular profession or industry (Lips, 2007; Oyserman & Fryberg, 2006). I knew I wanted to be a professor from the point where I considered doing a PhD. There were female professors at the Faculty of Psychology at the University of Vienna, not a great many, but enough to make this path seem like an option for myself. It sometimes seems that gender equality has come such a long way that representation is no longer much of a consideration but I recently read a letter of application for a faculty position at ESSEC that opened with "Dear Sirs", so it seems that at least for some it is still completely normal to imagine all-male recruitment committees and professorial bodies. A young researcher I work with recently told me that she had only started to imagine a career in academia for herself once she came to ESSEC because there she saw people like herself who were professors. Business schools remain comparatively male-dominated environments. The 34% female faculty in the 2018 *Financial Times* rankings make ESSEC one of the more gender balanced schools.

I think about the influence I may have on my doctoral students' future work selves. I want to inspire them to imagine their best possible future work self, to help them believe in the quality of their work and in their potential, in my actions and in my words. Incidentally, we likely process feedback about our future work selves somewhat differently from feedback about our current selves because the greater psychological distance[4] future work selves induce makes it easier for us to focus on how we can develop ourselves rather than on how we can feel better about ourselves (Anseel et al., 2018), making it more likely that the feedback will actually help us improve (Anseel et al., 2015). This means in giving feedback I try to emphasize doctoral students' future selves, rather than critiquing their current selves (Anseel et al., 2018).

While I try to inspire my doctoral students to think about their best possible future, I am also mindful of just how likely it is for papers and grant applications to get rejected and I worry about their future work selves and about their well-being in general. Academic life is probably more stressful than it has ever been and the PhD is a particularly risky time for mental health (Evans et al., 2018; Levecque et al., 2017). It is my job, of course, not to show them that I worry, and to give them a sense of optimism and confidence, the way Mark Griffin has done with me, all the while thinking through backup plans in case samples are not recruited, hypotheses are not supported, and papers are rejected. A good friend of mine, working in another discipline, was working with a PI who was not only forever worrying but also constantly shared these worries with her team, unsettling everyone she worked with. This also meant that she continued to change the direction of research projects, trying to hedge her bets, and resulted in studies that weren't nearly as well designed and focused as they could be. Worry has no place in shaping your research program; experiencing negative rather than positive emotions does not exactly broaden your thinking about new ideas (Fredrickson, 1998).

I try to encourage my students to look after themselves and take time away from their PhD because only when we mentally switch off completely from work can we recover from it (Sonnentag et al., 2008). This runs somewhat contrary to the idea of an "ideal worker" myth as completely devoted to their work that forms part of many professionals' identity (see Williams et al., 2016, for a wonderful discussion on this topic and research in this area). But maybe the best we can do as supervisors is to put our own concerns about our image and ego aside and normalize setbacks, to tell the stories of our own rejections and mistakes, and of how they did not derail our future work selves, at least not those parts of them that are most important.

MY FUTURE WORK SELF IS … FOREVER IN TRANSITION

When I present my research on future work selves I am often asked if they are ever achieved. Do we ever become our future work self? Sometimes I find myself thinking that I have indeed become who I wanted to become. This is often a fleeting moment when I am working intensely with one of my talented doctoral students or with collaborators whose company I enjoy, when a class is going well and I can see things click for my students, or when I get to travel the world to talk about my research. In these moments I feel incredibly grateful and privileged, but they involve a reflection on my past future work self. As humans we are notoriously bad at estimating just how happy an anticipated future will make us (Wilson & Gilbert, 2003), so it may be for the best not to dwell on how well our past future work self matches reality. My sense is that future work selves are forever in transition. We find new future selves for ourselves across our lifespan (Cross & Markus, 1991). Bandura (1989) highlights this ability to set new goals for ourselves, to purposely create a disequilibrium, a state of discomfort, in order to mobilize our efforts, as a key component of human agency.

In my latest research I am trying to gain a better understanding of the dynamics of our future work selves (Strauss et al., 2019). In earlier studies I found that future work selves that are not only clear and easy to imagine but also complex, i.e. that contain multiple different elements, are more strongly associated with proactive career behaviors such as networking and career planning (Strauss et al., 2012). This is presumably because when we think about ourselves in terms of a greater number of different aspects we are less vulnerable to setbacks affecting any one of these aspects (Linville, 1987). So how do future work selves change and adapt over time, and how do we maintain a sense of consistency over time? Do we hold on to core elements that will always be critical to who we want to be and change only those aspects that feel too difficult to attain, or no longer valuable? I love being a professor but maybe there is a future work self out there that does something else entirely. Wherever she is, I imagine my future work self will always involve those parts of me that are most important to who I want to be. She will continue to solve puzzles, to write, and to work with young people on bringing about their respective future selves.

NOTES

1. Self-regulation refers to the "processes involved in attaining and maintaining (i.e., keeping regular) goals, where goals are internally represented (i.e., within the self) desired states" (Vancouver & Day, 2005, p. 158).
2. Teaching assistant positions were short-term, part-time positions typically held by master's students.
3. A trilogy of shows by multi-award-winning storyteller Sarah Kendall, each of which takes us on a trip, giving us a unique snapshot of small-town life in Australia in the late 1980s and early 1990s. At a time when most people were seeing Australians through the filter of the TV series *Home and Away* and *Neighbours*, Sarah presents a darker underbelly to the stereotype of the sun-loving, happy-go-lucky Aussie teenager.
4. Psychological distance is the "subjective experience that something is close or far away from the self, here, and now" (Trope & Liberman, 2010, p. 440).

REFERENCES

Anseel, F., Beatty, A. S., Shen, W., Lievens, F., & Sackett, P. R. (2015). How are we doing after 30 years? A meta-analytic review of the antecedents and outcomes of feedback-seeking behavior. *Journal of Management, 41*(1), 318–348.

Anseel, F., Strauss, K., & Lievens, F. (2018). How future work selves guide feedback seeking and feedback responding at work. In D. L. Ferris, R. E. Johnson, & C. Sedikides (eds.), *The Self at Work: Fundamental Theory and Research* (SIOP Organizational Frontiers Series) (pp. 295–318). New York, NY: Routledge.

Aspinwall, L. G., & Taylor, S. E. (1997). A stitch in time: Self-regulation and proactive coping. *Psychological Bulletin, 121*(3), 417–436.

Bakker, A. B., Demerouti, E., & Wang, H. (2017). A review of job-crafting research: The role of leader behaviors in cultivating successful job crafters. In S. K. Parker, & U. K. Bindl (eds.), *Proactivity at Work* (pp. 95–122). London, UK: Routledge.

Bandura, A. (1989). Human agency in social cognitive theory. *American Psychologist, 44*(9), 1175–1184.

Borkovec, T. D., Ray, W. J., & Stöber, J. (1998). Worry: A cognitive phenomenon intimately linked to affective, physiological, and interpersonal behavioral processes. *Cognitive Therapy & Research, 22*(6), 561–576.

Bright, J. E. H., Pryor, R. G. L., & Harpham, L. (2005). The role of chance events in career decision making. *Journal of Vocational Behavior, 66*(3), 561–576.

Brown, K. W., & Ryan, R. M. (2003). The benefits of being present: Mindfulness and its role in psychological well-being. *Journal of Personality and Social Psychology, 84*(4), 822–848.

Černe, M. (this volume). My academic life: A series of fortunate events.

Cross, S. E., & Markus, H. R. (1991). Possible selves across the life span. *Human Development, 34*(4), 230–255.

Deem, R., Hillyard, S., Reed, M., & Reed, M. (2007). *Knowledge, higher education, and the new managerialism: The changing management of UK universities*. New York, NY: Oxford University Press.

Ely, R. J., Ibarra, H., & Kolb, D. M. (2011). Taking gender into account: Theory and design for women's leadership development programs. *Academy of Management Learning & Education, 10*(3), 474–493.

Ely, R. J., Stone, P., & Ammerman, C. (2014). Rethink what you "know" about high-achieving women. *Harvard Business Review*, *92*(12), 100–109.

Evans, T. M., Bira, L., Gastelum, J. B., Weiss, L. T., & Vanderford, N. L. (2018). Evidence for a mental health crisis in graduate education. *Nature Biotechnology*, *36*(3), 282–284.

Fredrickson, B. L. (1998). What good are positive emotions? *Review of General Psychology*, *2*(3), 300–319.

George, M., & Strauss, K. (2018). *The self left at home: How hypothetical home selves influence expatriates*. Paper presented at the Academy of Management Annual Meeting, Chicago, IL.

Hülsheger, U. R., Lang, J. W. B., Depenbrock, F., Fehrmann, C., Zijlstra, F. R. H., & Alberts, H. J. E. M. (2014). The power of presence: The role of mindfulness at work for daily levels and change trajectories of psychological detachment and sleep quality. *Journal of Applied Psychology*, *99*(6), 1113–1128.

Ibarra, H. (1999). Provisional selves: Experimenting with image and identity in professional adaptation. *Administrative Science Quarterly*, *44*(4), 764–791.

Joireman, J., Shaffer, M. J., Balliet, D., & Strathman, A. (2012). Promotion orientation explains why future-oriented people exercise and eat healthy: Evidence from the two-factor consideration of future consequences-14 scale. *Personality and Social Psychology Bulletin*, *38*(10), 1272–1287.

Levecque, K., Anseel, F., De Beuckelaer, A., Van der Heyden, J., & Gisle, L. (2017). Work organization and mental health problems in PhD students. *Research Policy*, *46*(4), 868–879.

Linville, P. (1987). Self-complexity as a cognitive buffer against stress-related illness and depression. *Journal of Personality and Social Psychology*, *52*(4), 663–676.

Lips, H. M. (2007). Gender and possible selves. *New Directions for Adult and Continuing Education*, *114*, 51–59.

Oyserman, D., & Fryberg, S. A. (2006). The possible selves of diverse adolescents: Content and function across gender, race, and national origin. In C. Dunkel, & J. Kerpelman (eds.), *Possible Selves: Theory, Research and Application* (pp. 17–39). Huntington, NY: Nova.

Parker, S. K., & Bindl, U. K. (2017). Proactivity at work: A big picture perspective on a construct that matters. In S. K. Parker, & U. K. Bindl (eds.), *Proactivity at Work: Making Things Happen in Organisations* (pp. 1–20). New York, NY: Routledge.

Parker, S. K., Bindl, U. K., & Strauss, K. (2010). Making things happen: A model of proactive motivation. *Journal of Management*, *36*(4), 827–856.

Pidd, M., & Broadbent, J. (2015). Business and Management Studies in the 2014 Research Excellence Framework. *British Journal of Management*, *26*(4), 569–581.

Smith, S., Ward, V., & House, A. (2011). "Impact" in the proposals for the UK's Research Excellence Framework: Shifting the boundaries of academic autonomy. *Research Policy*, *40*(10), 1369–1379.

Sonnentag, S., Binnewies, C., & Mojza, E. J. (2008). "Did you have a nice evening?" A day-level study on recovery experiences, sleep, and affect. *Journal of Applied Psychology*, *93*(3), 674–684.

Stone, P., & Lovejoy, M. (2004). Fast-track women and the "choice" to stay home. *The ANNALS of the American Academy of Political and Social Science*, *596*(1), 62–83.

Strauss, K., & Kelly, C. (2017). An identity-based perspective on proactivity: Future work selves and beyond. In S. K. Parker, & U. K. Bindl (eds.), *Proactivity at work: Making things happen in organizations* (pp. 330–354). New York, NY: Routledge.

Strauss, K., & Parker, S. K. (2018). Intervening to enhance proactivity in organizations: Improving the present or changing the future. *Journal of Management, 44*(3), 1250–1278.

Strauss, K., Griffin, M. A., & Parker, S. K. (2012). Future work selves: How salient hoped-for identities motivate proactive career behaviors. *Journal of Applied Psychology, 97*(3), 580–598.

Strauss, K., Loermans, A., Mell, J., & Anseel, F. (2019). Future work selves as dynamic networks of future-oriented self-representations. *Academy of Management Annual Meeting Proceedings*.

Taber, B. J., & Blankemeyer, M. (2015). Future work self and career adaptability in the prediction of proactive career behaviors. *Journal of Vocational Behavior, 86*, 20–27.

Taylor, S. E., Pham, L. B., Rivkin, I. D., & Armor, D. A. (1998). Harnessing the imagination: Mental simulation, self-regulation, and coping. *American Psychologist, 53*(4), 429–439.

Trope, Y., & Liberman, N. (2010). Construal-level theory of psychological distance. *Psychological Review, 117*(2), 440–463.

Vancouver, J. B., & Day, D. V. (2005). Industrial and organisation research on self-regulation: From constructs to applications. *Applied Psychology: An International Review, 54*(2), 155–185.

Williams, J. C., Berdahl, J. L., & Vandello, J. A. (2016). Beyond work–life "integration". *Annual Review of Psychology, 67*(1), 515–539.

Wilson, T. D., & Gilbert, D. T. (2003). Affective forecasting. In M. P. Zanna (ed.), *Advances in experimental social psychology* (Vol. 35, pp. 345–411). San Diego, CA: Elsevier Academic Press.

Wittenberg-Cox, A. (2017, October 24). If you can't find a spouse who supports your career, stay single. *Harvard Business Review Digital Articles*. Retrieved July 10, 2018 from https://hbr.org/2017/10/if-you-cant-find-a-spouse-who-supports-your-career-stay-single.

Wrzesniewski, A., & Dutton, J. E. (2001). Crafting a job: Revisioning employees as active crafters of their work. *Academy of Management Review, 26*(2), 179–201.

Zhang, C., Hirschi, A., Herrmann, A., Wei, J., & Zhang, J. (2017). The future work self and calling: The mediational role of life meaning. *Journal of Happiness Studies, 18*(4), 977–991.

PART IV

Academic balancing and role switching

9. Multiple paths for scholarly impact

Ante Glavaš

Estimated reading time: **38 minutes and 49 seconds**.

CHAPTER HIGHLIGHTS

- Test out both published and unpublished research with students, get feedback, and then revise.
- You should continuously question yourself about the impact that you want to make.
- One's path might come from unexpected places, one just has to be open to it.
- It is important to have meaningfulness both in work and at work.
- A lot is about luck and being at the right place at the right time. But you have to know how to recognize the opportunity.

Every oak tree started as a couple of nuts that stood their ground.
Henry David Thoreau

INTRODUCTION

This chapter is intended for scholars at all stages of their careers. I wrote it not only to help scholars starting out on their journey but also for scholars at later stages to reflect on their own learnings. My hope is that the sharing of my own path and learnings will help those reading this. In the end, this chapter actually had the biggest impact on me, as it was a great way for me to reflect on my career to date – and for that I thank the editors of this volume.

Having said that, I encourage each reader to read what is written here, then disregard it, and only use what I wrote as a starting point to think more deeply about their own unique path and learning. Therefore, an underlying theme throughout the entire chapter is that there is a fine balance between what we think should be done (e.g. what is considered to be a smart decision in the process of publishing) vs. what we really want to do (e.g. our own purpose, values, passion).

The chapter is outlined as follows. I first explicitly state my assumptions regarding what constitutes traditional and non-traditional research paths. I then describe my own research path. That is followed by some potential obstacles on the research path (e.g. dark sides of research). Finally, I conclude with lessons learned.

As a forewarning, I have written very little about the more traditional aspects of my journey. I do not see a lot of learning that can come from my own relative successes above and beyond what much more knowledgeable scholars have written about how to successfully publish (e.g. Andre & Frost, 1997; Billsberry et al., 2019; Frost & Taylor, 1996).

THE PATH – "TRADITIONAL" VS. "NON-TRADITIONAL"

Before I outline my own path, I would like to overtly state my assumption of what an ideal traditional path should be. By no means is this what I am suggesting, but it is rather what I think the recommended advice would be for scholars who would like to have a well-established research track.

In brief, the first assumption is that tenure track would be the ideal path because it usually allows more time – and sometimes other resources – for research. I also find that teaching is important because it is a key source of impact. Also, I often test out both published and unpublished research that I have on students, get feedback, and then revise. However, in this chapter, the focus is more on research so I will not write much about teaching. The second assumption is that there should be a balance of quality and quantity of peer-reviewed publications. Ideally, this would be mixed with some applied articles in which research is translated for those in practice.

However, by no means is the traditional path the ideal path. I have many colleagues, who are of a similar age, and have their PhDs, who are in corporate, consulting, or independent (e.g. authors). A good case can be made that they are having at least as strong an impact as I am.

MY OWN PATH

Building on the prior section on paths, the fundamental question I ask myself is the impact that I want to make. This is something I continuously question in a healthy way. I see my colleagues having great impact in practice, while sometimes I question my impact when I am working on an article for nine years and it is yet to be submitted.

In order to provide a context to what impact means for me, it is important to give the background context. Also, by providing my background I hope to show that each journey is unique and why it is important to tailor impact depending on what drives a person. As a warning, what I will write is very different from the traditional path I described above. I am explaining my path on purpose – to show that there are many paths one can take.

So, what drives me started off when I was young. Without going into all the details of my youth, in brief, I grew up in a family of very, very dedicated activists for social justice. I will purposefully leave out the details of what the social justice issues were because that would (a) deserve another entire chapter and (b) it would detract too much attention from this chapter. My entire life revolved around that growing up – and that is an understatement. Due to the causes that my family fought for, many of my family's friends were killed and my own family barely stayed alive – some of which I was witness to and I am fortunate and blessed that we survived. So, I grew up with this strong desire to change the world in order to avoid the crazy stuff I had witnessed growing up. If I wasn't helping the world, I felt like I was wasting time. For me, this is something that drove every decision I made.

Pre-academic Years

I was born and raised in the US for the first 18 years. My family is Croatian and they dedicated their lives to fighting for social justice. As a result, my family was often in danger and this greatly influenced my childhood as well as my drive to do good in the world. Then in 1991, when Croatia gained its independence, we moved to Croatia. To make a long story short, I spent the next 13 years, mostly in Croatia, but also living for stints in Brussels and London, as well as a shorter time in Italy, working in various sectors but all related to helping improve the world, and especially Croatia. Being educated in business and finance, I worked mostly on how to change corporations so they can benefit society and the planet.

As a brief overview of some of the jobs, I was a senior executive in a Fortune 500 company – rated the world's most socially responsible company at the time.[1] Then I founded and led three different social enterprises that worked towards improving Croatia and the region. It was a dynamic time which I would need another chapter to describe. In brief, I could paint a picture of the cup half full or half empty, depending on how you look at it. On the positive side, we were doing incredible change. Tens of thousands of youth from war-torn towns were involved in our leadership programs. These youth not only impacted their surroundings but changed their own lives. Corporations then really liked what we were doing and then wanted us to run these same leadership programs for their own employees. So, we would run these programs and then funnel the profits back into the work for youth. This resulted in working with over 100 organizations, many of which were among the largest in the world – and we worked with all levels from top management to employees on the ground. This is one of the social enterprises that I founded. That then led into founding two more social enterprises, which had similar themes, both of which had huge impact. I also received numerous international awards and recognition for my work as well as a Presidential Medal of Honor. The point here is not to explain the work itself, but to get a flavor of the lifestyle I was leading.

However, to "paint the cup half empty" and show the other side, the more impactful our work became, the more trouble I found myself in. Too much power came into play as we became stronger, so I was not able to continue my work. At the same time, another fortunate coincidence happened. I had just completed a certificate course on change management at Case Western Reserve University. During that course, I became close to a PhD student there, Bauback Yeganeh. He kept telling me that I should get my PhD. However, being an academic was completely opposite to the life of I had been leading for the prior 13 years. So just as I was going through bankruptcy – and being extremely frustrated with my situation, because I was trying to help others and did not find it fair that this is what I got in return – Bauback called again saying it was three weeks to application time. Also, my good friend and closest partner in my work, Zeljko Mavrovic,[2] encouraged me to go to the PhD program. He said that I could only do so much by myself but that I could do more if I multiply that knowledge by educating other youth. So, combined with my desire to just get away, I decided to apply to Case Western Reserve University, not thinking that I had much of a chance given my non-academic background. Then to fast-forward five months later, I was chosen as one of seven finalists from 80 applicants, then went through interviews and ended up being given a scholarship along with two other colleagues, who are now very good friends – which is another lesson I learned: academia can be lonely so make sure you surround yourself with good friends.

PhD Years

During my PhD, I had a fortunate experience, one I would not have wanted to miss, but it was very non-traditional. Among many great things that happened in the program, one was that I ended up being the Executive Director of the Center for Business as an Agent of World Benefit. It was a result of many coincidences (some that seemed very negative at the time) and being in the right place at the right time – another theme that often happened in my life. The Center was a huge effort led by the founding faculty director, David Cooperrider, a great team, and had huge support from the school. We organized largely impactful conferences with hundreds of CEOs and hundreds of academics, together with the UN Global Compact and the Academy of Management. Numerous initiatives emerged, including the founding of the Principles of Responsible Management Education. In addition, we had a project called World Inquiry, through which 4 000 interviews were conducted resulting in hundreds of mini-cases on win–win examples of how companies can create business value while helping society and the planet.

While all this was exciting, I was not publishing as much as I would have liked. Thus, I was doing the opposite of all well-intentioned advice, which was to create a pipeline before you finish your studies. Nor was I honing my research skills. Also, I thought I was not suited to be an academic anyway. I liked the work at the Center because it was similar in nature to my work back in Europe.

However, something changed when I was in the phase of intensively writing my dissertation. Although the *output* is not great scholarly work, I loved the actual *process*. I loved the intellectual aspect of figuring out patterns in my data – I was conducting a grounded theory study into why employees engage in corporate social and environmental responsibility as well as the effects – and seeing the potential for impact on both scholarship and practice.

This was another lesson I learned, which is that one's path might come from unexpected places, and that one just has to be open to this. I never saw myself as an academic. Yet, I realized that I could have a huge impact on others through this work. The reason I did not think academia was for me was because of the rhetoric surrounding publishing – and this still strongly exists today – in that publishing was the major end goal. For me, that did not matter because if an article is read by only a few people, most of whom just skim it, then what is the point of spending so much time and energy when there is more that I can do in the world. However, if I reframed the publication as just a starting point, then that changes the equation. If my work can have impact on practice such as on multiple people doing their own projects, then I am having a stronger impact than I can by doing one project at a time, such as I was before. On top of this, I was seriously struggling and battling to even keep those projects afloat in terms of time, money, and especially corruption.

A model from one of my professors in my PhD program, David Kolb, helped illuminate how this impact happens. He is known for his experiential learning model (Kolb, 2014), among others. The model puts forward that experiential learning starts with the concrete experience. Then one reflects on the learnings from that experience. After that, an abstraction process occurs through which one is able to distill applicable themes and practices that can apply to future experiences. Then the learner tests those out in practice. This all then closes the loop back to the beginning and one then goes through the process in iterative cycles (see Figure 9.1).

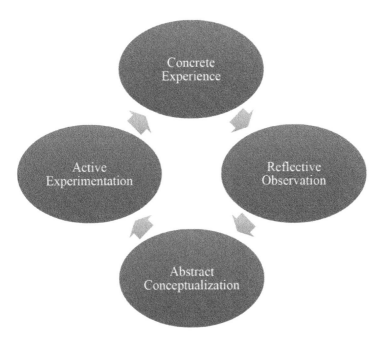

Figure 9.1   Kolb experiential learning cycle

This model was relevant for me in defining impact because I thought of all the great change agents I had met through all the work I had done as well as the networks in which I was involved. These individuals were doing amazing work in the world. They all were going through amazing *Concrete Experiences*. However, they were all so busy that they barely had time for *Reflective Observation*. At best, they might have time while traveling or having some down time. Occasionally some of them might write a blog. But rarely is there any time for or even knowledge about how to engage in *Abstract Conceptualization* – that is where I see my impact. These change agents have so much valuable knowledge. As a scholar, I can help distill that knowledge so that others might learn from their successes and failures. As such, their knowledge is multiplied. At the same time, I personally am able to make an impact. I used to be one of those change agents that never had time to distill my learnings. In this way, instead of the impact I am able to have as one person, I am able to amplify my impact to many change agents. Then this not only influences my research, but also my teaching. Currently, I am using this in my courses in the MBA and undergraduate programs.

Tenure Track

Again, this was a "coincidence" of being at the right place at the right time. I originally had plans to do a post-doctorate at MIT (Massachusetts Institute of Technology), mostly working with Peter Senge, who is considered the father of the Learning Organization (Senge, 1990; Senge et al., 1999) and was named a "Strategist of the Century" by the *Journal of Business Strategy*. Much of my work would have been amazing projects in the field. However, at the same time, I was increasingly drawn to spending more time doing research (i.e. the research I mentioned previously in terms of distilling impact from change agents). Somewhat unexpectedly, Carolyn Woo, the Dean of the Mendoza School of Business at the University of Notre Dame wrote to me. She had seen that I had inquired about a position at the school, which was not tenure track but nevertheless an interesting position working on business and society. She invited me to consider a visiting professor position, which was essentially a post-doctorate during which I would teach one class and have the rest of the year to further my research. I went there and interviewed and fell in love with the place. In parallel, my wife was also offered a position in their Executive Education, which is what really made the difference.

As another related learning, none of this would have been possible without the support of my wife. I cannot state that enough. Not just helping me physically, but mostly emotionally and mentally. We had first met during my doctorate and married before I defended.

During that year of visiting at Notre Dame, I was then offered a tenure track position. At that time, the business school was ranked #1 in Bloomberg and also the research in the management department was world class (it still is at the time of writing this). If I am being fair, I did not deserve to be hired based on my publishing record. Typically, one would need at least one, if not multiple top-tier publications. And, the business school had a very tight list of only a few top-tier journals. They told me that I fit the values of the school and that they would take a risk because my research path was non-traditional, but also high risk, high reward. I was fortunate that they were so honest with me. They bluntly told me that it is difficult to publish on corporate social responsibility (CSR) in top-tier management journals and that tenure would be extremely difficult. In fact, many others outside Notre Dame encouraged me not to go tenure track because they said it would just force me to publish traditional research and thus not pursue my true passions. However, I was driven to do the research that I love and thought I could do that at Notre Dame due to the values fit and the great platform that Notre Dame has through which I could spread my research.

Phase I

The first phase lasted about three years and it was during the first phase of my tenure track, revolving mostly around publishing a review article in the *Journal of Management* (JOM; Aguinis & Glavaš, 2012). The primary reason for this was because there was little published in top-tier management journals on CSR, especially at the individual level of research. A secondary reason, and just as important to me, was that I was confused with the field of CSR and thought a review was needed. This came from my doctoral studies during which I read – well, often I actually skimmed – 2 000 publications, hoping to gain clarity; but in the end, I actually became even more confused. This is not surprising given that CSR is vast, diverse, and cross-disciplinary. Irrespective of a particular discipline, this pattern follows Einstein's idea on simplicity of complexity, i.e. "Out of complexity, find simplicity!"

The seemingly confusing nature of CSR meant that many scholars outside CSR just viewed it as a context and not a legitimate field of study. This made it difficult to publish anything related to my PhD which was in Organizational Behavior. So, I submitted a proposal for a review article to JOM, which was accepted. However, I had just defended my PhD and did not have the experience or skills to write such a review article. Usually, senior scholars would write one. Thus, I coordinated with Herman Aguinis to be equal co-authors. With his guidance and that of the Action Editor, Deborah Rupp – who was later also the Editor-in-Chief at JOM – I was fortunate to have exceptional support in getting this article published.

That article has gained great traction and has about 1 244 citations in Web of Science (by October 2020). It arguably helped open up a whole field of micro-CSR – which is research on CSR that includes the individual level – by legitimizing it and providing a research path. So, in hindsight, it was a good move that helped build my reputation and impact as a scholar. However, at the time, I was strongly advised not to write such an article. The reason that most scholars write reviews only after tenure is because (a) one is more experienced and (b) it takes up all of one's time. I remember when I reached out to another scholar who had written a review article at JOM and he told me how it had taken two years of his life, during which he lost count of how many hours he spent after 1 500 hours! I naively thought I could do it much quicker. Instead, it took much longer.

Also, I was barely able to work on any other research during that time. Taking into consideration that I spent a lot of time having a great experience in my doctorate (i.e. running the Center for Business as an Agent of World Benefit), but not directly related to research, it meant that I did not have a research pipeline coming out of my doctorate. Then working on the review article, I was not able to form a pipeline until after I finished the review. That meant that half-way through my tenure track, I was only beginning my pipeline. Assuming that it takes a few years to publish once one starts a pipeline, I had set myself up for "failure" by traditional tenure track standards. And I was already embarking on a path of publishing in CSR, which was arguably much more difficult than other research paths. There was simply no way I could get tenure at the University of Notre Dame – which had the most rigorous standards (e.g. JOM was not even considered an "A" level journal). To their credit, they were creative in trying to find ways for me to stay and I am extremely grateful for my time there; but I really did want to stay on tenure track.

Phase II

This phase lasted about three to six years and (depending on how you want to define it) was when I really built my pipeline. To save space, I will not write much about this phase because it was typical by most standards. There has been so much written by others about publishing (e.g. Bond, 2018; Clark et al., 2016) that there is nothing new I could say. There are perhaps two things that I would point out. First, my pipeline usually had about ten research projects at any given stage (e.g. some were being revised for resubmission, others were just beginning with data collection). Second, I was strongly advised not to engage in qualitative research because it takes so long to publish. I wish I had not listened to this advice because many of the questions I have regarding CSR need inductive research.

Also, during this phase, I moved from Notre Dame to Kedge Business School in France. This was partially due to personal reasons, but also because they offered an Associate Professor position, I had freedom to research what I wanted, and the CSR group at the school was world class.

Phase III

This is the current phase – and it began about two years ago – at the time of writing this chapter. I moved back to the US, to the University of Vermont, partially due to personal reasons, but also due to the research support US universities provide. The reality is that many business schools around the world cannot afford professors who do research. If one just does the math, if a professor teaches half the number of classes of other professors (e.g. three to four classes a year as opposed to six to eight classes) and does research the rest of the time, then that means the school needs to hire twice the number of professors. It is actually more complicated than I explained, but, more or less, the economics are difficult for research in the current economic environment. But, for me, I really want space to do research. The main reason is that I feel like I am just scratching the surface. I am engaging in more qualitative research at the moment (e.g. Aguinis & Glavaš, 2019; Glavaš & Willness, 2020), trying to understand more deeply what drives individuals to engage in CSR. We do know a lot already, but it's only the tip of the iceberg. For example, how do social intrapreneurs influence the organizational culture and vice versa? How do we create organizations that work towards a higher purpose? What is the role of employees at all levels, not just top management? Then how can we change our own teaching and curriculum to help develop such employees who can transform organizations? Those are only but a few of the questions that I have.

On a related note, I received tenure at the University of Vermont. This allows me the freedom to do research that I think will be impactful. It's not to say that I wasn't doing impactful research before, but there is something about tenure that creates an inflection point – part of it is due to the process of writing up my own research dossier – and has made me think deeply about the type of impact I want to have.

THE DARK SIDE OF RESEARCH

Although I am using the popular term "dark side", in reality what follows are neither dark nor light sides. Points made below are inherent challenges and mostly very subjective. For me, it has varied. On bad days, they have been huge obstacles. On good days, I took them as opportunities for growth. Anyway, every job has its challenges and I am fortunate that the challenges we have in doing research are quite minuscule compared to a lot of challenges that people face around the world.

Publish or Perish

There has been a lot written about this. In a nutshell, it really comes back to Kerr's (1975) classic Organizational Behavior (OB) article: "On the folly of rewarding A, while hoping for B". What we measure and reward in organizations is often what we get. As a parallel, I have seen many corporations want to engage in CSR, but because they are still basing performance on quarterly financial results, often employees will primarily pursue profit at all cost, including costs to society and the environment. Similarly, if the primary measurement in some business schools is research productivity, then teaching and service tend to suffer. At one point, I found myself caught up in this cycle.

That is why it was important to explain my background before academia. I am always driven by impact on the world. However, I was spending most of my time in an office. It even got to the point that I was strongly advised not to even do media interviews because they were detracting from my research. As I was told, every hour spent on anything else is an hour less on research. I also received informal advice that my teaching ratings were too high and that I was spending too much time on teaching. Rather, I should optimize that time, do enough to get good ratings, and spend the rest on research. In the end, I do not think that advice helped my research and actually think that my research suffered because I had been out of touch with reality for so long. That is also another reason I want to do more qualitative research because I want to be out in the field, interviewing people, observing, and ideally doing action research.

Contribution to Theory

The most difficult was the question of contribution to theory. This is because I always first started my research by approaching it phenomenologically with what practice needed. To me, this is due to my background and passion. Then I tried to tack on theories to justify. For me, to this day, I still have challenges with this. It is counter to what I teach.

For example, I teach design thinking and one of the key messages I have is that the key problem that many organizations have is that they do not start with the customer or other stakeholders first. They create an idea in a closed environment and then try to test it out to see if it works. Rather, the approach should be to truly get to know the customer and then see how an organization can leverage its strengths to meet those needs. In that way, the organization is not working outside its scope and also it is actually delivering something that the customer really needs, which in the end ensures greater success of the service/product.

I feel as if the same approach should be taken with our research. If we are creating theory no stakeholder cares about, then I think what is the point? It is then just an exercise of mental stimulation which academics do for our own sake. It took me a while to not judge that and see that as being OK. As I will explain later, many people find meaningfulness in doing things that they enjoy. So do many academics. There is nothing wrong with that. In fact, positive psychology encourages us to focus on our passions and what we love doing.[3] However, given my background and drive, this was not enough – impact on those outside academia was missing.

Feedback Loops

Another difficult challenge I find is that feedback takes a long time and is usually negative. In my prior work, I was used to almost instant feedback from stakeholders. Instead, I would work on a research project usually for at least a year, sometimes longer (e.g. I have one that has taken ten years and I am about to finally submit a paper). Then, if I do not get a desk rejection, I wait for months to get feedback. If I am lucky, I am happy to not be rejected and instead am sometimes provided with a few lines of what I did well, but always provided with many pages of what I did wrong – that is a best-case scenario. As a result, this can easily lead to self-doubt. It was counter to what I was used to where I was directly changing people's lives and seeing the fulfillment in their eyes. Being an academic leaves too much time for us to be inside our own heads. That is the double-edged sword of our jobs – you need your head to do positive things, but at the same time, being in your head the whole time can lead to mental tiredness.

As I will explain later, that is why practices of positive reinforcing cycles of self-reflection are healthy and necessary. In addition, the most important lesson for me is to enjoy the process and worry less about the outcome. If I do what I am passionate about and if it is of good quality, the results will eventually come.

Ego

Like many fields, academia is driven by ego, which is not necessarily negative. A self-concept based on being a good person, for example, can be good for the world. But it can also be a slippery slope if we let ego drive and define us. Academia has a lot of traps that can lead to that. Thus, I had to be careful to play that line where I am attracted to these aspects but at the same time am not defined or driven by them. As a few examples of illusions of ego, along with a little self-deprecating humor related to the reality:

- **Publishing**: If I publish an article, then I feel really proud. But, in reality, usually there is an Action Editor and three reviewers per article at the types of journals to which I submit. So, if I publish, that means that four people were able to support my work, often after multiple rounds of pointing out what was wrong with it. It is not the vote of the general public on whether they think my article is useful, just that group of about four, and so many rounds of review – which take years – are lost on only appeasing that group of reviewers.
- **Recognition**: If I am recognized, a network of a few hundred scholars in my domain follow my work and thousands more might have heard of it. At the time of writing this chapter, I have about 5 000 citations in Google Scholar. In my circle, that number seems to be a decent number for a mid-career scholar. However, in the broad scheme of things, that is a very small number of people. In my prior work, I was directly influencing that many people daily in most of my jobs, and, in some, the numbers were larger.
- **Networking**: I go to conferences, present, take part in networks, review papers, am on editorial boards, etc. However, despite the time spent preparing for conferences, often I will present to rooms with 10–20 people. Currently I am reviewing seven papers and I spend a lot of time making sure I am fair and thorough. Out of those reviews, most will be rejected,

and I will be lucky if the authors even take anything of what I wrote into consideration.

There are many other parts of an academic role that I have not listed that take up a lot of time. But the point is that academia is a closed loop of scholars who often self-reinforce their own views. I have been rejected multiple times with the message being that CSR has no place in business. Sometimes this has been implied and sometimes this has been actually explicitly stated. To be fair, there are many academics that I know who are open-minded and like to be challenged. However, in the end, it is a field that is self-governed. We decide what gets published in our own journals, who gets to present at conferences, and who leads our networks.

This is an important realization, because it also means that, if one's work is not accepted, it does not mean that the work is necessarily bad. It just means that it does not fit into what your peer group thinks is acceptable. At the same time, it also shows how it can be an illusion and dangerous for one to place one's own identity, self-concept and ego based on what others think. If you are driven by what others think, then you are missing internal drive. That makes this academic journey, which is extremely self-driven, much more difficult. Rather the drive should be internal and if the external recognition comes, that is a bonus. Like most people, I personally do like external recognition and much prefer someone complimenting my work than telling me how awful it is. Anyway, that is the approach I try to take. Some days it is more difficult, some days it is easier. But I work hard to try to keep myself centered and grounded.

LESSONS LEARNED

Lesson 1: Internal Drive

The flip side of the previously mentioned obstacles is that it takes huge internal drive. The path can be lonely with a lot of negative feedback loops – both from others as well as our own internal dialogue. That is why, at least for me, I found it crucial to engage in research that I love. It is a tough enough job to stay mentally engaged the whole time. So why make it tougher? I have seen a lot of colleagues just focus on publishing – and often rationalize why they are taking that path – while doing something they do not love. However, I cannot judge them because some of them have a pragmatic approach of getting promotion first (e.g. tenure) so that they could do what they love after promotion. But for me, if I am not doing what I love, then why would I be in academia in the first place? I was doing impactful work before so the last thing I want to do is to be stuck in an office writing articles that only a few people will read.

Perhaps the most useful models for me personally came from my research on work meaningfulness. What especially resonated with me are two models. The first is Wrzesniewski's (2003) work on meaningfulness. She built on the work of Bellah and colleagues (1985) to propose that employees have three different orientations or paths for finding work meaningfulness. Each person might be influenced by some combination of these orientations:

- **Job orientation**, where just having a job is meaningful. For example, someone can feel as if they are a provider for their family. For me, having a job at a university aligns with my own ego needs – ego is not always a bad thing just as long as I do not let my ego influence all my decisions. Also, being paid enough is important – I have a lot of debts still left over from bankruptcy and other matters. Finally, and I realize this is very old-school thinking, but I do like being a provider. That was an interesting realization because I have studied feminism and I think I am really open-minded and respectful of everyone. But I did grow up in a family that comes from a patriarchal culture and part of me likes the fact that my wife does not have to work unless she wants to – even though she is amazing at what she does and does not depend on my financial support.
- **Career orientation**, where promotion and recognition provide meaningfulness. For me, it was important to be an Associate Professor in France and then again to go through the process and get tenure and Associate Professorship now in the US. It showed recognition that I was on the right track and that I'm having an impact in my profession.
- **Calling orientation**, where working for a higher purpose is a source of meaningfulness. This one is the most obvious for me and, as I have written, it has been the biggest driver.

What surprised me when I began to study the work meaningfulness literature is that I realized that I have a combination of all three orientations. Obviously, the calling orientation has been the strongest driver. But I had to be honest with myself and say that I also had the influence of job and career orientations. For a lot of people that do similar work to me, it is almost something negative to say that one could be influenced by money, prestige, and recognition. But being honest with myself and knowing what drives me helps me stay motivated. So, while I used to always put my job and career needs secondary to my calling, I now make sure I also get what I think is fair in terms of job and career.

On a related note, the model of Pratt and Ashforth (2003) of meaningfulness in/at work also helped illuminate my personal sources of meaningfulness. The authors put forward that people can find meaningfulness *in* work (i.e. in their jobs) and/or *at* work (i.e. from being part of an organization). For example, some people can find meaningfulness *at* work because they work for a socially responsible organization. What I realized is that, for me, it was important to have both meaningfulness *in* work and *at* work. Because I do not want to publicly state something negative about past organizations, I will leave names out to remain politically correct. But there was one organization where I felt that I did do impactful work *in* work (i.e. in my job), but I felt the values of leadership were completely opposed to my own and quite unethical. I could not stand working there because I felt that every day that I did not try to counter them, I was just letting them continue with their unethical and often illegal behavior. I tried to work constructively with them but, when that did not work, I left the organization because the value mismatch was unbearable. On the flip side, I also have experienced the situation of reaching meaningfulness *at* work, where the organization was doing good in the world, but had none of it *in* work. This might be due to my past experience, but, if I am not having an impact on the world through my job, I feel as if I am not fulfilling my calling.

Finally, another model also helped me understand my drive. It is an old model in psychology, but was really put forward to me by a professor in my PhD program, Richard Boyatzis. Among other models he has, what resonated was the distinction of ideal vs. ought self. The ought self is how we are conditioned to think we should be vs. what we truly want to do (Boyatzis & McKee, 2005). Despite my whole upbringing and career usually being focused on following my ideal self, I did find myself at times almost wandering to the "ought self" of an academic and being too concerned with doing what is expected of academics instead of truly thinking about impact.

Lesson 2: Kairos

> Kairos: the perfect crucial moment; the fleeting rightness of time and place to create the opportune atmosphere for actions, words or movement.[4]

This has been a theme of my life, literally. One of the most defining programs of my youth was actually called Kairos. It was a peer-service program that the Jesuit high school I went to created. During my junior and senior years, I personally went through the program and then helped others also on their own journey. Then fast-forward to Croatia, on a separate continent. I ended up being constantly drawn to this island-town in Croatia, called Trogir, which is a 3,000-year old town that used to be a Greek colony in ancient times. I vacationed there in the summers. I stopped when I moved to the US for my PhD. But then I met my wife early in my PhD program, who is from Croatia and has a family-owned vacation home just 50 meters down from where I would vacation. So, we spend our summers there now. I was always drawn to this place, but only afterwards found out the fascinating coincidence that Kairos is actually the cultural symbol of the town – and, as mentioned above, Kairos means to be able to recognize those fleeting moments of coincidence and make the best of those opportunities.

So, this is one lens that I use to describe my life. A lot is about luck and being in the right place at the right time. But you have to know how to recognize the opportunity. Often times, the opportunity might seem negative at first, so it takes a lot to try to see the positive in those times. And that is not enough. You then have to have the courage to act on it. First, everyone thought I was crazy for moving to Croatia during the war and giving up a great education in the US and a potential good career, but I felt like it was the right time to go. Then when I found a great job in London, I left the corporate sector to move back to Croatia and found social enterprises. Then I went into my PhD, which was also a fortunate series of events, which also people said was crazy. Even crazier, I fell in love with it and stayed, despite all recommendations for me not to, that it was not part of my true personality. So, one might say that I am crazy, others might just think that I am stubborn, but what I believe is that I did what I was truly drawn to and loved. Also, another thing I learned is that recognizing an opportunity means having a positive opportunistic lens. Many things that I thought were negative events actually opened the door for new opportunities.

Lesson 3: Staying Grounded and Centered

For me personally, it has been crucial to stay grounded and centered. There is no one approach and it varies by person. For example, it can be family, spiritual practices, sports and exercise, reading, watching stupid movies, etc. A powerful practice is walking in nature. For instance, I practice a lot of meditation. I also have a lot of really goofy friends – fortunately, most of them are in Croatia and far away from the US classrooms where I teach because they have threatened to invade them and tell the students stories about what we used to do. I also have a very loud and collectivist family, similar to the ones you see in movies like *My Big Fat Greek Wedding*. But all this keeps me grounded.

Being such a person is important to me for three reasons. The first is it keeps me internally driven and not sucked up in the external drive. It can be very easy to be drawn into the positive and negative of academia. There is a positive allure to being recognized in networks and among colleagues. Also, the negative external criticism from reviewers and others can weigh on a person. Staying grounded allows me to not take myself too seriously nor let others define me. It allows me to listen to the content of what others have to say but block out the other noise that comes with the messages.

The second reason is that, as academics, we are too much in our heads. And not just that, we are too much in our left brains. This can be a cycle, one that is hard to get out of. Moreover, the whole language and our work is very left-brain focused. This means that we are often not in touch with all aspects of our selves. So, I find my best work is when I can be grounded and centered, tap into not only both sides of my brain, but my whole self.

The third and final reason goes back to my prior point on design thinking. If we are too much in our heads, then we tend to listen much less and to project our own thoughts on others. Instead, a design thinking approach means listening to what is truly going around in the world and then seeing how we can address that with our own strengths. On the other hand, I find myself doing this sometimes and see this also in academia, where we come up with certain ideas and then try to force them on others. We use ourselves as the starting point and not others. So, our work becomes very self-serving in this way rather than being other-serving. There are no recipes, only idiosyncrasies, idiosyncrasies and idiosyncrasies …

CONCLUSION

If I could summarize most of what I wrote, it is that I have usually been guided by impact and then let everything else fall in place. Up to now, it has turned out OK for me in terms of my scholarship. However, that might not be the case for others. So, if there is one message I hope that the reader gets from this chapter is that everyone's path is unique. Thus, I think we should all take the great advice we can get, but ultimately decide what drives each of us.

NOTES

1. Based on my experience in this company and also subsequent entrepreneurial experience, the workload in academia was equal to other sectors. I had longer hours in the office before, but now I find I actually work more hours, but am able to do most of them from home. The stress was the same, but in different ways. In other sectors, there was more daily stress to achieve short-term goals. But in academia, there is more long-term stress – which can arguably be just as difficult – because feedback times on articles are very long, and upon receiving them you usually only focus on the critiques. Thus, academia is a good life with a lot of independence, but you have to deal with the mental fortitude of rarely getting positive feedback, and usually having to wait for long periods for critiques.
2. He is a Croatian former professional boxer. In 1998, as an undefeated challenger and three-time European champion, he faced and lost to Lennox Lewis for the heavyweight title. After the fight, he retired and became a social entrepreneur, with a focus on healthy lifestyles and food.
3. For more on positive psychology, see, for example: https://ppc.sas.upenn.edu (accessed January 18, 2019).
4. Numerous definitions exist for Kairos but most center around it being a fleeting moment, one that is crucial, and that it can be opportune if recognized and seized. Also see https://creatingkairos.wordpress.com (accessed January 18, 2019).

REFERENCES

Aguinis, H., & Glavaš, A. (2012). What we know and don't know about corporate social responsibility: A review and research agenda. *Journal of Management, 38*(4), 932–968.

Aguinis, H., & Glavaš, A. (2019). On corporate social responsibility, sensemaking, and the search for meaningfulness through work. *Journal of Management, 45*(3), 1057–1086.

Andre, R., & Frost, P. J. (eds.). (1997). *Researchers Hooked on Teaching: Noted Scholars Discuss the Synergies of Teaching and Research.* Thousand Oaks, CA: Sage Publications.

Bellah, R. N., Madsen, R., Sullivan, W. M., Swidler, A., & Tipton, S. M. (1985). *Habits of the Heart: Individualism and Commitment in American Life.* New York, NY: Harper and Row.

Billsberry, J., Kohler, T., Stratton, M., Cohen, M., & Taylor, M. S. (2019). From the Editors: Introduction to the Special Issue on Rhythms of Academic Life. *Academy of Management Learning & Education, 18*(2), 119–127.

Bond, J. (2018). *Scholarly Publishing: A Primer.* Woodbury, NJ: Riverwinds Publishing.

Boyatzis, R., & McKee, A. (2005). *Resonant Leadership: Renewing Yourself and Connecting with Others through Mindfulness, Hope and Compassion.* Boston, MA: Harvard Business School Press.

Clark, T., Wright, M., & Ketchen Jr., D. J. (eds.). (2016). *How to Get Published in the Best Management Journals.* Cheltenham, UK and Northampton, MA, USA: Edward Elgar Publishing.

Frost, P. J., & Taylor, M. S. (eds.). (1996). *Rhythms of Academic Life: Personal Accounts of Careers in Academia.* Thousand Oaks, CA: Sage Publications.

Glavaš, A., & Willness, C. R. (2020). Employee (dis)engagement in Corporate Social Responsibility. In D. Haski-Leventhal, L. Roza, & S. Brammer (eds.), *Employee Engagement in Corporate Social Responsibility* (pp. 10–27). London: Sage Publications.

Kerr, S. (1975). On the folly of rewarding A, while hoping for B. *Academy of Management Journal, 18*(4), 769–783.

Kolb, D. A. (2014). *Experiential Learning: Experience as the Source of Learning and Development.* Upper Saddle River, NJ: FT Press.

Pratt, M. G., & Ashforth, B. E. (2003). Fostering meaningfulness in working and meaningfulness at work: An identity perspective. In K. S. Cameron, J. E. Dutton, & R. E. Quinn (eds.), *Positive Organizational Scholarship: Foundations of a New Discipline* (pp. 309–327). San Francisco, CA: Berrett-Koehler.

Senge, P. M. (1990). *The Fifth Discipline.* London, UK: Century Business.

Senge, P. M., Kleiner, A., Roberts, C., Ross, R., Roth, G., & Smith, B. (1999). *The Dance of Change: The Challenges of Sustaining Momentum in Learning Organizations.* New York, NY: Doubleday/Currency.

Wrzesniewski, A. (2003). Finding positive meaning in work. In K. S. Carmeron, J. E. Dutton, & R. E. Quinn (eds.), *Positive Organizational Scholarship: Foundations of a New Discipline* (pp. 296–308). San Francisco, CA: Berret-Koehler.

10. Walking the line: in search of academic balance

Tomislav Hernaus

Estimated reading time: **31 minutes and 48 seconds**.

CHAPTER HIGHLIGHTS

- Anyone can teach, but the quality of the teaching process is what really makes a difference.
- Changing focus will enable you to keep your motivation at a high level.
- The key question we need to find an answer to is not where we are in relation to others but where we are in relation to ourselves; do not compare with others – instead, determine and follow your idiosyncratic growth path.
- Being creative and innovative – developing and proposing something new, which no one before has concluded or done – is not easy at all. However, it is almost equally demanding to transfer the new knowledge to others in an articulate manner.
- It is necessary to separate everything that a professor knows from what students should know.

Any order is a balancing act of extreme precariousness.
Walter Benjamin

ROAD TO THE UNKNOWN: THE BEGINNING OF AN ACADEMIC CAREER

Every beginning is uncertain, precarious and difficult. This is particularly true for academic career development. Similar to a *greenhorn* in the Wild West,[1] young scholars find themselves faced with numerous academic challenges while they are still insufficiently skillful and quite inexperienced, without a clear vision and purpose. I was the same – young, indecisive and unaware of the road I had taken.

During my student days, i.e. undergraduate and graduate study, I did not even once give a thought to pursuing an academic career. Although I was attracted to the position of a teaching assistant (which I had never applied for), and I enjoyed reading management literature and writing student papers, I did not know myself well enough to be able to say I wanted to become a member of academia. However, due to certain circumstances and fate (i.e. fortunate events), as well as the judgment of a few professors who noticed my class efforts, an opportunity arose and, utterly unintentionally, I entered the academic world.

Similar to an infant, in the first months of my academic life, my main goal was to learn how to walk or, in other words, to avoid a failure at my first professional test. After only a few days of being employed at the Faculty of Economics and Business, University of Zagreb, I was "thrown into the fire" and very soon realized that I was to undertake highly demanding work. Following my instinct, I grabbed relevant books, and started cramming and preparing teaching materials. Having autonomy in designing seminar lessons, I tried to be creative and I approached the set task primarily from the students' perspective (taking into consideration what they would find interesting, but at the same time useful). I used the summer break for preparation and, quite satisfied with myself, in mid-September, to the great surprise and pleasure of the course lecturer, I finished the hundred-page-long working material of the *Seminar Syllabus*, which was my preparation for the upcoming task, i.e. the first academic year that I was to spend on the other side of the lecturing rostrum. Thorough preparation made the beginning of my teaching experience much easier, which proved to be crucial for the development of my academic career.

First teaching experiences presented a significant challenge as well as a huge burden. Namely, a 15-minute presentation of a seminar paper to colleagues and friends proved to be quite different from facing 120 unfamiliar students, only two to three years younger than me, and trying to get their attention and teach them. Just before entering the classroom for the first time as a teacher, I was excited and nervous but at the same time motivated and prepared. I remember that I told myself: "You're neither the first nor the last to hold lectures. Thousands of lecturers each day teach their students, and if all those people can do it, there is no doubt you can do it also." Naturally, anyone can teach, but the quality of the teaching process is what really makes a difference. Quite self-critical and a bit more experienced, having won a few "battles" and suffered a few "defeats", and with some positive student reactions on my side, I managed to keep my head above water, although it seems that I more often "floated" than really "swam" in the direction I intended.

At the beginning of my career, I was primarily focused on teaching- and student-related activities, while research was secondary in importance. I was very much attracted to research, but before being able to start writing, I realized that I first needed to devote my time to reading. An exception was the comprehensive empirical research on workplace relations conducted for the purpose of writing my bachelor's thesis, which served as the basis for my first scientific paper (Pološki Vokić & Hernaus, 2005). It was obvious that at that time I was still not capable of writing scholarly papers on my own, but I managed to accomplish that with selfless help and a significant contribution from a more experienced colleague. While preparing the paper for submission, horizons of a new world started opening to me – the world of scientific research and academic publishing.

Shortly after my employment at the Faculty of Economics and Business, I enrolled into the scientific postgraduate study program in Organization and Management and not long after that I also became the program secretary. That was certainly the first important, if not the crucial, moment of my personal and professional development. The new administrative role took me a substantial amount of time, yet provided me with an opportunity to collaborate intensively with my future PhD supervisor. Consequently, I began developing an interest in and passion about organization design topics, thus following the steps of my future "academic father". This new role also helped me to obtain the feeling of obligation and responsibility for institutional development.

Very quickly (maybe even too quickly) I gained the opportunity to actively participate in providing consulting services. It was an additional responsibility, but also a new and valuable experience. Working on numerous tasks and in various project teams, I could gain first-hand experience of business practice, become familiar with the project management methodology, and had the opportunity to integrate theoretical knowledge and practical solutions.

Planned or casually, quite conveniently, early in my career I was faced with diverse teaching, research, consulting and administrative assignments. Naturally, initially not all pieces of the puzzle fell into place, but as the time passed I realized that an academic job position can be very complex and manifold, without firm, clear boundaries between various types of activities. Nevertheless, it is the variety and complexity that really attracted me. Not only did I feel an inclination towards academic work (both teaching and research), but I also noticed that I had progressed, which was a sign that I was on the right track.

ACADEMIC BALANCE DYNAMICS

The following years of my academic career are best described with the words "harmony" and "dynamics". I tried to simultaneously drive towards four determined tracks (i.e. teaching, research, consulting and administration), which were not always headed in the same direction, let alone straight and driven along at the same speed. However, different tasks were often intertwined; they mutually supplemented and influenced each other, thus facilitating or limiting my further professional development. In any case, I can say that the "wild horse" I was trying to saddle was not easy to steer and the ride was at moments quite exhausting, although really exciting.

If I had been able to choose (and I might have chosen it unconsciously), things could have been much simpler. Besides all fixed and formally determined teaching responsibilities, all other assignments were quite flexible and indefinite. I could have reduced research activities, consulting services or administrative assignments to a minimum, which would have made my life easier. However, I chose something different – my way. I was determined to persist and "push" into all the four directions of my academic career development and to give the maximum, which was not always easy.

Actually, it is very difficult, almost impossible, to simultaneously be focused on a large number of various activities. Multitasking is a myth; it causes our performance to deteriorate (Kirchberg et al., 2015). Luckily, I feel like being a polychronic person, so I do enjoy switching between various aspects of my academic work. The situations in which I could focus on only one aspect, for instance teaching or research, were rare. In any case, the nature of academic work dictates that numerous tasks be performed simultaneously and as soon as possible, so I had to be similar to contemporary managers, either "the quick or the dead". Since the named challenges were accompanied by job complexity and task variety, I could not complain about my job being (un)challenging. However, eventually I managed to organize my obligations in accordance with the seasonal nature of certain tasks and congruently to my own working habits and affinities. It did not happen overnight, but only after a few years, during which using the method of trial and error I utilized time, energy and intellectual resources more or less successfully.

Learning by doing was not always pleasant nor fun. Numerous sleepless nights, missing social gatherings, working at weekends and holidays, and feeling as if I was neglecting family and friends left a sour taste in my mouth. The price for the ambition to build an academic career was certainly high. I was constantly wondering: What am I doing wrong? What should I do differently? How to organize myself better? It was absurd, even tragicomic, that I am professionally involved in organization theory and practice, but I could not find the adequate work–life balance. Although I had been teaching generations of students that *successful managers do not carry (or should not bring) their work home*, in my case, bringing work home has become a rule, not an exception.

I realized that it was crucial to manage priorities, but that it was also not possible to predict and plan all business obligations in advance. I often had problems with the very simple managerial concept *urgent and important* (referred to as the Eisenhower Matrix; see Covey, 2013), where urgent tasks regularly used to "suffocate" the important ones. For important, most often intellectually demanding and time-consuming tasks, I had to use afternoons and evenings, i.e. Saturdays and Sundays and/or holidays. Additionally, since there was no strict hierarchy between teaching, research, consulting and administrative aspects of my academic life, running deadlines were the only criteria for organizing the workload.

Nowadays, things are somewhat different. There are almost no sleepless nights and I attempt to solve priorities differently. I try to put greater emphasis on distinct aspects of my work in different periods. For instance, winter semesters are primarily reserved for teaching. Teaching workload (up to 20 hours per week) and intensive work with students do not leave much free time for other activities, which does not mean I neglect them completely. During those winter months I also try to work on at least one scientific "project" in the background – a book chapter or a journal article, studying professional and scientific literature and planning future projects.

Summer semesters are predominantly focused on research, primarily reserved for writing, professional training and consulting services. In addition to administrative tasks related to the postgraduate program and the related lectures, I am focused on further development and realization of my ideas, learning statistical methods, conducting empirical research and attending scientific conferences. Certain activities, such as mentoring students, are present throughout the year, as well as a series of other, mainly less demanding although enduring administrative tasks, which are a constituent and unavoidable part of our profession.

Greater focus on particular aspects of academic work in certain periods has significantly increased my scientific productivity and the feeling of contentment. In my work, there is a certain dynamics meaning that, similar to the seasons of the year, teaching and research semesters alternate. In the process, the feeling of being suffocated with one and the yearning for the other inevitably occurs. Therefore, at the beginning of February, after an intensive period spent with students in a lecture hall, I eagerly wait to jump into the world of books, papers and statistics and to start writing, i.e. preparing new texts and teaching materials. At the end of July and especially in mid-September, I can no longer wait to meet new generations of students and welcome the opportunity to transfer my knowledge and acquired experience. In that way, by changing focus, I always manage to keep my motivation and flow at a high level.

Of course, periodical reviews (that is, making checkpoints) of accomplished results are extremely important. Psychological studies have shown that performance feedback (especially when received quickly) is a relevant source of motivation (Hackman & Oldham, 1976; Marthouret & Sigvardsson, 2016).

For instance, student evaluation results, decisions on accepting a scientific paper or reviewer's comments, recognition and rewards and the supervisor's and colleagues' support have significantly influenced my work enthusiasm. Either positive or negative, those were signals which indicated what I had done well, and what needed changing and improving. However, in addition to external evaluation and extrinsically-driven motivators, I have always tried to be self-critical enough. As a rule, twice a year, before summer holidays and at the end of December (around New Year holidays), I zoom out to look at my CV and try to evaluate accomplishments in the previous half-year period as well as over my entire career. I do it in order to determine certain areas or activities I should put greater emphasis on in the upcoming months. That way, with the aim of maintaining academic balance, I try to focus on activities I might have neglected or dealt with less in the preceding months.

In addition to the described "strategic" break down and the focus on specific aspects of the academic work in individual periods (months), I also apply a series of "tactical" and "operational" techniques making my daily functioning easier. These are small tricks which, if applied correctly and simultaneously, can result in significant time savings. For instance, I try to adhere to "the five minute rule" and perform minor and less demanding activities (such as answering emails, telephone calls, writing memoranda, photocopying and similar) immediately. A few years ago, I also started writing down all obligations and ideas in order not to mentally exhaust myself by thinking about what else is to be done and whether I have forgotten something. Anyway, there is the saying "smart people memorize it, while wise people write things down".

What also proved to be very practical and useful is dividing a working day into phases, in which I try to separate the time only for myself, and the time for the things that are my biggest business priority at a certain time. Since I get up relatively early in the morning, and my mind is fresh and clearest during the morning hours, I use that time for intellectually demanding and creative tasks, the so-called "*organic*" tasks, such as reading scholarly articles, writing papers or preparing new teaching materials. As the day goes by, the nature of tasks that I do changes in order to achieve a high level of workday productivity. That means that tasks such as filling in the electronic bibliographic database, maintaining student registers, browsing scientific databases in search of articles, searching the Internet, graphic editing of teaching materials and similar activities, the so-called "*mechanical*" tasks, I usually leave for afternoon hours.

I am convinced that the key to accomplishing desired results is systematic and well-organized work, which results from and is based on knowing your *daily biorhythm*. In that respect, I have developed my own system, owing to which I rarely work under pressure or use force, and in that way I also avoid situations which additionally deprive me of energy and reduce my academic productivity.

BUILDING ETHICS OF RESPONSIBILITY

The dynamics of accomplishing the balance described above can be seen only as the technical part of academic work. As such, it is certainly not enough or self-sufficient; instead, it should be extended by a sociological and a psychological dimension. Like in sports, if one wants to be a successful young academic, one has to be mentally strong and psychologically stable. Specifically, this means that a striving individual has to build his/her own viewpoint and find inner peace which will accompany him/her, and calm and encourage him/her in difficult, frustrating and discouraging moments. The role of a personal value system, as well as of "driving" thoughts and ideas, which show us the path we should take is particularly important.

Young academics often have their role models, regardless of whether these are their mentors or someone else, such as a leading scholar in their field of interest they admire and they want to become alike. However, I believe that if you have a single role model you can eventually be only a good replica. Unfortunately, replicating the "best" practice does not lead to success. The "best" practice is a myth because while you are trying to copy that practice, it is changing and becoming even better. Each individual should have his/her own path and build his/her personal style and academic profile. That profile in certain aspects can be based on or be similar to profiles of other successful people, but eventually the mosaic is only yours.

My approach and work philosophy is that I always try to give the maximum in given circumstances in order not to have the need to reprimand myself. Since *I want to learn something new each day*,[2] I try to maintain the process of self-improvement, because, if I stop, it will be very difficult to start again. On the other hand, when I do something, I try to make my work beneficial to society, i.e. the financial rewards are not self-sufficient. Taking into consideration the profession we are in, I feel a desire, a need and the responsibility to "make a difference" – to educate young people, improve business systems, and inform the academic and professional audience. These are social values and *prosocial behavior* which have been comprehensively studied in recent years by Adam M. Grant and his collaborators (e.g., Grant, 2008; Grant & Ashford, 2008).

The named scholar, the youngest professor in history with the highest title at the Wharton School of Business, in his book *Give and Take: A Revolutionary Approach to Success* (Grant, 2013), distinguished among three categories of people: *givers*, *matchers* and *takers*. I try, although without the ultimate success, to be a giver, and selflessly share my knowledge, experience and time. That is not always simple, and I have noticed that occurrence of such behavior to a certain extent depends on the context – a specific problem in hand or people involved.

I still do not manage to limit the number of obligations I accept and take responsibility for. I believe that this is a common problem for many, especially young(er) scholars. It often happens that we procrastinate, that is, promise much but simply physically are not able to realize everything, at least not by the due date. In that way, we compromise our own integrity and academic credibility, as we do not manage to grade exams on time, write reviews or send a paper for publishing within the set timescale. In order to avoid that, one should always remind oneself of the slogan "less is more" (see Bertolucci, 2014). For instance, it is better to accept a fewer number of mentorships and be a high-quality, devoted mentor than have tens of students and be able to dedicate less than ten minutes to each when the time comes. The same applies to the number of scholarly papers, which is often inversely proportional to their quality, and it is similar to teaching overload, due to which the quality of the teaching process is often not at the optimal level. If we promise and do not meet the promise, we create a negative image although we work with 150 per cent capacity, investing enormous efforts yet delivering suboptimal results.

Finally, as a part of personal ethics of responsibility and own value system, I would point out two personal traits that I consider essential for academic success – *perseverance* and *courage*. With regard to the first, I am fairly sure that my results are to the greatest extent the outcome of multiyear persistence and continuously invested efforts. To draw a parallel with sports, we may say that if talent contributes 10 per cent the remaining 90 per cent of success depends solely on hard work and invested time resources. So far, I have never noticed an article being written by itself or students holding a lecture without me.

The second key individual characteristic, courage, means a readiness to take a road less taken, such as to risk when choosing a research topic, a method or an idea we want to deal with. That means that sometimes we need to swim against the mainstream. As an example of such a situation I can provide my decision on choosing the methodology for my doctoral research. For some time I could not decide whether I should use hierarchical linear modeling as a data analysis method. It was novel at that time and a very demanding statistical method (especially from the aspect of data sampling and interpretation), which I did not know much about. However, I took the plunge and the risk that eventually paid off multiple times, because not only did I expand my methodological knowledge but also conducted comprehensive research that ensured me a series of quality publications. Although it was easier to apply some more familiar method, in that way I would miss the learning part, and probably would not discover a new, multi-layered dimension of scientific research nor acquire a better insight into contemporary business practice.

The two abovementioned personality traits are certainly not the only ones that make a difference. There is a series of other personal characteristics desirable for the academic profession (e.g. self-efficacy, openness to experience and others). However, there is no unique profile of a successful scholar. In other words, the key to success is equifinal, and it results from knowing yourself and harmonizing the personal value system with personality traits and developed competencies.

SOURCE OF INSPIRATION AND SUPPORT

Ups and downs are a part of academic life. Just as it is not possible to get everything we want, it is also not realistic to publish all that we write. Rejected papers, dismissed project proposals and received critiques on the one hand, as well as successful publications, recognition and rewards on the other, remind a scholar of humility because there is always someone better. The key question we need to find an answer to is not where we are in relation to others but where we are in relation to ourselves. Whether we really give our best, do we do all it takes at a certain moment and do we develop and grow throughout the process?

In ancient times, Aristotle concluded that a man is in his nature a "social animal" that cannot function without other members of the same species (Lord, 2013). A similar thing applies to the academic community. I owe my professional development as a scholar primarily to the variety, i.e. the fact that I was exposed to various opinions, theories, practices and ideas of leading world and Croatian scholars. Systematically following and attending doctoral workshops, professional seminars, educational programs and conferences, I had an opportunity to directly listen and communicate to cutting-edge thinkers in the field of organization science such as, for instance Jay R. Galbraith, Arnold B. Bakker, Susan A. Mohrman, Edward E. Lawler III, Thomas G. Cummings, Christopher G. Worley, Paul S. Adler, Richard M. Burton, Borge Obel, Lex Donaldson, Charles C. Snow, J. Barkev Kassarjian, Amy Kates, Ann Majchrzak, Omar El Sawy and others. Not only was I at the source of knowledge and in touch with leading minds in my academic discipline, but I could very clearly see that all of them share the same values – simplicity, openness and modesty.

It would be unfair not to mention numerous other scholars I talked to and who, to a lesser or a greater extent, directly or indirectly influenced my personal and academic *habitus*. However, I was impressed the most by the cooperation with Susan A. Mohrman during my six-month study visit to Los Angeles at the Marshall School of Business, University of Southern California. Discussions with Sue at the time of writing my doctoral thesis proposal were an invaluable experience for me. Looking back at it now, I can say that those were probably the beginnings of my scientific maturation (which actually never stops), filled with a series of self-revealing moments.

Besides getting familiar with different theoretical perspectives and method-ological approaches, I realized the deeper sense of academic contribution and started thinking more intensively about my style of writing scholarly papers. I learned that each written word is important. Actually, in a certain way, I started perceiving writing as a magic and highly creative game of composing words, arguments and ideas. I believe texts should not be written superficially, but they need to have a "soul", i.e. a greater depth. It is achievable if we critically review each paragraph, sentence or word, and even each letter, if it shows itself to be wrong or unclear. The majority of people, as well as a sig-nificant number of scholars, unfortunately take the existing texts and quotes for granted, without critically thinking them over and estimating their value, objectivity or justifiability.

My study visit to the United States offered me a very cathartic experience, and has given me some time to reflect on my first years in academia. Not only did I learn a lot about science and my profession but I got to know myself better and formulated a clearer picture of how I wanted to position myself in the following years. It additionally fueled my desire and inspiration to provide quality within my work, i.e. to, if needed, take the longer but the right way. I gained a good insight into a different (North American) practice, which addi-tionally helped me understand the world of academia.

However, certainly the deepest impact on my career so far has been left by my long-time mentor. I was very lucky and honored to work with Professor Pere Sikavica. Our relationship, primarily based on mutual respect and immense trust, was crucial, as much for my personal, as for my professional development. From him, I have learned a lot not only about our profession but also about human values and life in general. In numerous situations he was by my side providing me with selfless support. He trusted me and provided me with the freedom to be creative, to be myself. Whenever it was necessary he advised me and directed me not to stray away. To make a long story short, I would recommend such a mentor to everyone.

The choice and the relationship with a mentor are crucial for a young scholar's success. This has been true for a long time. For instance, it is indicative that the greatest Ancient Greek philosophers – Socrates, Plato and Aristotle, who founded a series of scientific disciplines – were mutually firmly related. More precisely, Socrates was Plato's teacher, while Aristotle[3] was Plato's student. The similar practice is present today because if we look at, for instance, the field of organization science, a number of contemporary leading world scholars also had leading academics of their time as mentors (for instance J. D. Thompson mentored J. R. Galbraith, L. W. Porter mentored T. G. Cummings and E. E. Lawler III, S. R. Clegg obtained his doctoral degree under the mentorship of D. J. Hickson, while J. W. Boudreau was mentored by E. E. Lawler III). H. Zuckerman (1977) through her research additionally confirmed the importance of excellent mentors, i.e. high-quality scientists, in forming a future scientific super elite (Prpić, 2000). She has clearly shown that a significant number of the Nobel Prize winners were students of previous laureates (Ben-David & Sullivan, 1975). Obviously, for the development of a successful scientific career it is useful and advisable to have a quality mentor, although it is not and cannot be a guarantee of success.

Despite the fact that a mentor probably influences the development of a young apprentice the most, I would like to return to variety. Owing to the great trust of my mentor, alongside him, I had an opportunity to work with other professors in relation to different aspects of academic work (teaching, projects, books, articles). I have learned different things from those collaborations. The fact that many of them wanted to work with me was a great recognition but also presented a great responsibility. My workload increased significantly and I could not or did not know how to say "no". By refusing one offer you potentially close one door, but, again, it leaves you time and energy for some other, maybe even more important, activities. It is a matter of decisions that each individual has to make based on his/her own judgment, set goals and plans at a certain moment.

Dilemmas are particularly common in relation to providing consulting services and conducting professional project studies. While, on one hand, in addition to the financial benefit, it is a great opportunity for expanding professional knowledge and acquiring a more detailed insight into the existing business practice, on the other hand, there is less time to do research, the latter being particularly important and required at the beginning of an academic career. However, through careful coordination of assignments it is possible and necessary to establish a balance. Even more, there should be a synergy between teaching and consulting, as well as between consulting and research.

Although the issue of balance between different academic roles has already been elaborated (see Hernaus and Černe, Chapter 2, this volume), I would here like to emphasize my positive experience from IMTA – International Management Teaching Academy at Bled in 2011. By participating in the two-week seminar not only did I realize that around the world there are people with the same or similar problems and dilemmas but I also became additionally aware of how inspiration and enthusiasm are essential for performing multiple aspects of academic work.

The feeling of belonging to an academic community and cooperation with colleagues with whom we share the same values certainly can be a source of great inspiration and excitement. Through the exchange of opinions and by giving/receiving feedback, it is easier to evaluate our own work efforts. International and domestic recognition and awards are also good indicators of accomplishment that can significantly increase the self-esteem of a young scholar and motivate him/her to strive towards academic excellence. Each award I have received, in addition to thrilling me and making me proud, has also been a great encouragement and "obligation" not to lose impetus. In general, reputation holds an important role within academic circles (confirmed by the Matthew effect; see Merton, 1968). It ensures new opportunities and challenges, encouraging one not only to keep the existing quality level, but to also take a new step forward and justify the expectations.

Finally, we should not forget the role that family has in building an academic career. Family members provide us with peace and safety, and give us great support. They sympathize with us, and often sacrifice a lot for our academic dreams to come true. It is not easy to be a successful scholar if you do not have family and/or a broader social support. Having understanding and the support of the environment (in the emotional, cognitive, time-consumption and even financial sense) is desirable for pursuing an undisturbed and successful academic career. In other words, social (family) support is definitely a necessary, although not the only precondition.

NOTES ON THE ACADEMIC CRAFT

Scholars use various theories, approaches, tools and techniques in order to elaborate a certain theme, solve a research problem, realize set goals and make a societal contribution. Each individual needs to learn the academic craft on his/her own and decide how to organize his/her own "laboratory". But, it can also be useful to listen, read and be acquainted with the academic (both research and teaching) experiences of others.

Application of research platforms is something that I have recognized as useful for determining my own academic path. Some authors (for example, Glick et al., 2007) argued that scholars can simultaneously focus on two or a maximum of three different areas, within which they elaborate on themes they find interesting. In my case, those are the domains of organization theory and design, business process management, and work design. Within each named area, I have recognized a few problems I try to study in more detail. Additionally, I try to connect the three platforms and through a multilevel approach encompassing various scientific disciplines (economics, psychology, sociology, information sciences). Thereby, I attempt to reach new scientific knowledge through an integrative, interdisciplinary approach. Such an approach is contrary to the prevailing opinion according to which young scientists need to have a narrow focus that they eventually expand during their career (Darley et al., 2007). I believe it is not necessarily wrong, just different, and to a certain extent it is a more interesting, although more demanding approach.

Being creative and innovative – to develop and propose something new, that no one before has concluded or done, is not easy at all. However, it is almost equally demanding to transfer the new knowledge to others in an articulate manner. Here, I would like to primarily emphasize written communication. The purpose of writing should be to create such a manuscript that others would like to read and will be able to understand. When writing academic papers, it is advisable to use a simple text structure and avoid long sentences and unfamiliar words. It is necessary to avoid "typing",[4] and instead try to write "intelligently" – clearly, simply and appropriately (Lee, 2011). An author needs to constantly have his/her target audience (e.g. students, scholars, practitioners, the general public) on his/her mind and adjust accordingly both the writing style and the level of complexity. Regardless of the target audience, each text should be fluent, and have a clear leitmotiv directing the reader towards desired cognitions. In that sense, during the process of writing my own papers, I use hidden titles for each paragraph (which I subsequently erase) which contribute to a clearer chain of thoughts, reduce redundancy in the text and facilitate its logical consistency. In other words, I try to tell my readers a compelling and useful story.

Oral communication is by no means less important than written communication. It provides us with greater freedom of expression and the easier/quicker introduction of new content into the discussion. For instance, very often when I read something new and interesting, I have an urge to share it with my students and colleagues. Why should not somebody else benefit from that information or knowledge? But, there is also a trap in such behavior because it is necessary to separate all that a professor knows from what students should know. However, that does not mean that knowledge and information should not be shared in other ways. For that reason, I have decided to start an Internet site aimed at spreading knowledge in the field of organization design[5] so that everyone interested could keep track of the latest events, information and developments.

When it comes to teaching, I adhere to an unwritten rule that each year at least 10–20 per cent of teaching materials need to be updated (Nahavandi, 1997). By doing this, my lectures are relevant to students and more fun to me. In the process, I have realized it is useful to manage *a teaching dossier or a portfolio* containing syllabi, tasks, exercises, business cases, slides, exams and other materials I have collected and made during the years. Having all materials systematically documented in one place, I find it easier to organize my teaching plan. Additionally, at the beginning of a semester, I ask students to send me their CVs, based on which I make a list with their photos and names. Afterwards, I try to memorize the list because I believe it facilitates a more open and participative learning atmosphere. All the above mentioned I do with the purpose of avoiding the method of turning on the "automatic pilot" in the classroom (the concept devised by Cameron, 1997), which is quite widespread in practice.

Finally, it is almost impossible to find a person seriously involved in science that will tell you that he/she has too much spare time. Although we differ and are not all equally capable, the mode in which you organize your time is a key prerequisite for being satisfied with yourself. I personally like working on more than one task/project at once. By constantly rotating tasks from various domains of academic work, I attempt to remain mentally fresh during the day/week and in that way achieve more (the exception is situations that require strong focus and a high level of concentration or when there are strict deadlines). In order to avoid reading the same article accidentally two to three times (which happened to me during the writing of my doctoral thesis), or not knowing where notes and material related to a certain topic are, in addition to using the EndNote software for electronic resources systematization, I have developed a personal system of processing notes, which significantly makes the manuscript and teaching preparation easier.

Owing to the systematic approach to reading books and scientific papers I take out useful parts of texts (quotations, ideas, facts and similar) from what I have read and, together with the related comments, I organize them depending on the theme. In that way, if I decide to write on a certain topic, I can quite easily access the most important ideas and findings within a field, which have been recorded and stored over several years. I have recently also started managing a "Project" schedule (recommended by Rocco, 2011) in MS Excel, where each sheet of a file represents an individual project (for instance an article, a book or a research project) or academic work category (for instance reviews, mentorships, councils and similar). Having everything in one place, I can more easily control the scope of my job and upcoming deadlines related to individual activities, as well as analyze later what and in which period I did this.

All previously mentioned tools and techniques make my daily academic activities significantly easier. However, they are not and cannot be a substitute for the desire, motivation and readiness to be involved in academic work. Motivation drives people, the same as the lack of motivation determines their (dis)satisfaction. Therefore, at the end of this chapter and as a recapitulation of my previous 15-year working life in academia I can only conclude that intrinsic motivation is my major driver. Because, no matter what, the fact is that I really love my work, i.e. my work is part of me.

NOTES

1. The German novelist Karl May begins his famous, three-volume (1963–1965) novel *Winnetou* (May, 2006), one of my favourite childhood books, by explaining the expression *greenhorn*: "According to the explanation, a *greenhorn* is a person still green, i.e. young and inexperienced, who has to spread his horns

carefully if he does not want to experience a nuisance ... a *greenhorn* believes that turkey-tracks are bear-prints ... he is the man who noted down eight hundred Indian expressions, but when he meets a real Indian he realises that he by mistake sent the list of Indian expressions home in his last letter while he kept the letter ... he memorises contents of books he reads well and believes he is a bright young man, instead of actually tasting life, and fifty years later finds out what the real wisdom is ...."

2.   Already a hundred years ago the psychologist E. Coué said that "Day by day, in every way, I am getting better and better" (Yeates, 2016).

3.   For a number of years Aristotle mentored Alexander the Great, the greatest conqueror in world history who had never lost a battle.

4.   The attitude that "authors often instead of writing, just type" was introduced by Murphy (1996, p. 131).

5.   For the time being the website is only in the Croatian language: www.orgdesignhub .com (accessed August 10, 2017).

REFERENCES

Ben-David, J., & Sullivan, T. A. (1975). Sociology of science. *Annual Review of Sociology*, *1*, 203–222.

Bertolucci, D. (2014). *Less is More*. London, UK: Hardie Grant Books.

Cameron, B. J. (1997). Learning to teach: An ongoing process. In R. Andre, & P. J. Frost (eds.), *Researchers Hooked on Teaching* (pp. 160–177). Thousand Oaks, CA: Sage Publications.

Covey, S. R. (2013). *The 7 Habits of Highly Effective People: Powerful Lessons in Personal Change*. New York, NY: Simon & Schuster.

Darley, J. M., Zanna, M. P., & Roediger III, H. L. (2007). *The Compleat Academic: A Career Guide*. Washington, DC: American Psychological Association.

Glick, W. H., Miller, C. C., & Cardinal, L. B. (2007). Making a life in the field of organization science. *Journal of Organizational Behavior*, *28*(7), 817–835.

Grant, A. M. (2008). Does intrinsic motivation fuel the prosocial fire? Motivational synergy in predicting persistence, performance, and productivity. *Journal of Applied Psychology*, *93*(1), 48–58.

Grant, A. M. (2013). *Give and Take: A Revolutionary Approach to Success*. New York, NY: Viking.

Grant, A. M., & Ashford, S. J. (2008). The dynamics of proactivity at work. *Research in Organizational Behavior*, *28*, 3–34.

Hackman, J. R., & Oldham, G. R. (1976). Motivation through the design of work: Test of a theory. *Organizational Behavior & Human Performance*, *16*(2), 250–279.

Kirchberg, D. M., Roe, R. A., & Van Eerde, W. (2015). Polychronicity and multitasking: A diary study at work. *Human Performance*, *28*(2), 112–136.

Lee, M. (2011). Finding voice. In T. S. Rocco, & T. Hatcher (eds.), *The Handbook of Scholarly Writing and Publishing* (pp. 102–114). San Francisco, CA: Jossey-Bass.

Lord, C. (2013). *Aristotle's Politics*. Chicago, IL: The University of Chicago Press.

Marthouret, E., & Sigvardsson, S. (2016). *The Effect of Quick Feedback on Employee Motivation and Performance: A Qualitative Study on How To Formulate Effective Feedback*. Unpublished doctoral dissertation. Linköping: Linköping University.

May, K. (2006). *Winnetou*. New York, NY: Bloomsbury Continuum.

Merton, R. K. (1968). The Matthew effect in science. *Science*, *159*(3810), 56–63.

Murphy, K. R. (1996). Getting published. In P. J. Frost, & S. M. Taylor (eds.), *Rhythms of Academic Life: Personal Accounts of Careers in Academia* (pp. 129–134). Thousand Oaks, CA: Sage Publications.

Nahavandi, A. (1997). Teaching from the heart. In R. Andre, & P. J. Frost (eds.), *Researchers Hooked on Teaching: Noted Scholars Discuss the Synergies of Teaching and Research* (pp. 197–212). Thousand Oaks, CA: Sage Publications.

Pološki Vokić, N., & Hernaus, T. (2005). Interpersonal relations at work perceived by Croatian and worldwide employees and by different age, gender, education, hierarchical and company size groups: Empirical evidence. *Management: Journal of Contemporary Management Issues*, *10*(1), 23–49.

Prpić, K. (2000). The publication productivity of young scientists: An empirical study. *Scientometrics*, *49*(3), 453–490.

Rocco, T. S. (2011). Reasons to write, writing opportunities, and other considerations. In T. S. Rocco, & T. Hatcher (eds.), *The Handbook of Scholarly Writing and Publishing* (pp. 3–12). San Francisco, CA: Jossey-Bass.

Yeates, L. B. (2016). Emile Coue and his method (III): Every day in every way. *Australian Journal of Clinical Hypnotherapy & Hypnosis*, *38*(1), 55–79.

Zuckerman, H. (1977). *Scientific Elite: Nobel Laureates in the United States*. New York, NY: The Free Press.

11. Dissociative identities in academia: notes on paradox and multimodal role-play

Alf Rehn

Estimated reading time: **29 minutes and 9 seconds**.

CHAPTER HIGHLIGHTS

- Playing multiple roles can serve as a productive challenge, and even a method of inquiry.
- Many identities are rewarded in contemporary academia. Having the capacity to adjust your identity to various demands, and being comfortable with the identity dissociation this entails, is a competency – for some even a core one – and can become a commodity.
- Many academics need to accept that they will not excel in all things a contemporary academic is asked to excel in.
- By being visible one is more likely to be remembered, invited and included in things.
- Be a player of many roles if you can, and, if you cannot, be clear about why you've opted for a more narrow professional identity.

> *Man is least himself when he talks in his own person.*
> *Give him a mask and he'll tell you the truth.*
> Oscar Wilde

INTRODUCTION

I have always been fascinated by the notion of multiple personality disorder, the often sensationalized and also criticized idea that an individual can develop several internally stable but externally exclusive identities or personality states. In the psychiatric literature it is today called dissociative identity disorder (see Howell, 2011) to better illustrate the manner in which it works. Rather than a person actually having several identities (with which we tend to refer to a relatively complete and enduring notion of self), the disorder refers to how a person might have personality states that are dissociated from each other, to the point where the person in a more or less conscious way starts treating these as actual identities, complete with their own names, preferences and histories. Now, the existence and functioning of such a disorder is challenged by many in the psychiatric profession, and there are problems with both the definition and the research done into the disorder. Whilst it has often been deployed in popular culture, for instance in movies such as *The Three Faces of Eve* (1957) or *Split* (2016), the actual prevalence and existence of such a disorder is less certain – which of course has had little to no effect on people, like myself, being fascinated with it.

Beyond its capacity for titillation, a key reason this notion persists in our cultural consciousness is in all likelihood the fact that we all feel somewhat dissociated from time to time. We take on various roles, both professional and personal, which can feel more or less fake. We shift between identity states and personality states, and although very few of us start believing that our professional selves are clinically separate from our personal selves, this doesn't mean that the idea is wholly alien to us. Further, as we are subjected to increasing and often mutually exclusive demands on our professional time, we may come to question what the core of our professional identity is, and if such a thing even exists.

I will in this chapter contend that contemporary academia, and the plethora of roles the modern academic is desired to occupy, makes this field of ours well suited for inquiring into the dissociation of professional identities. I will not, however, argue that this is a pathological state, but in a rather more provocative manner suggest that there might even be ways in which playing a multiplicity of roles can serve as a productive challenge, and even a method of inquiry. It should be noted that I am making this argument as someone who plays a great many roles, and as someone who has benefited from this – your mileage may vary. It should also be noted that some academic disciplines seem better suited for such tricksterish liminal play, with my own field of management being one such. I will return to these issues, including the moral and ethical consequences thereof, and will now go on to discuss many roles and identities of the modern academic.

ROLE-PLAY IN THE GROVES OF ACADEME

Today, in an age when the world of academia is going through profound upheaval, it is important to note the sheer number of roles that the modern academic is supposed (expected) to occupy in order to be seen as fully realized.

The professors of yore were supposed to be scholars and teachers, where the latter part could be ignored if too burdensome. Some might engage in supervision, if they felt they had found a suitable pupil. Others might decide to forego research, and instead focus on holding the occasional seminar and otherwise live the life of a gentleman of leisure. Others again might devote themselves to research, yet only publish once they felt they truly had something to say. These halcyon days in what Horace called *silvas Academi* today sound more like times of myth and legend, but reading through e.g. memoirs of British academics from the first half of the twentieth century establishes that there really were such carefree days.

Today, the notion that a professor, or any academic wishing for a successful career, could manage this simply by playing a singular role seems a quaint impossibility. Rather, the contemporary academic is presented with a laundry list of roles to play, and although no-one is expected to play all of them, there is in both the public debate and the upper management of the modern university a clear preference for adopting as many of these as one with at least some success can. I have in the following presented a partial list, and the reader is welcome to insert additional ones in the space provided:

- Scholar
- Researcher (as separate from scholar)
- Teacher
- Supervisor
- Doctoral supervisor
- Administrator
- Leader of a research project
- Leader of a research team
- Leader of a research group
- International networker in the establishment of the three aforementioned
- Principal investigator, aka writer of funding applications
- As above, but on an international level
- Academic entrepreneur
- Academic intrapreneur
- Supporter of entrepreneurship/intrapreneurship, academic or not
- Participator in the public debate
- Guru
- Public intellectual
- Writer of white papers
- Creator of reports
- Expert on policy
- Advisor to politicians or civil servants
- Keynote speaker

- Blogger
- Radio personality
- Talking head on TV
- Actual star of TV
- Writer and columnist (popular)
- Consultant
- Social media maven
- Influencer
- Participator in professional organizations
- Thought leader
- Builder of companies (aka a regular entrepreneur)
- Innovator
- Commercialization connoisseur
- Expert mingler
- Good company at dinners
- And so on, continue here:
- –
- –
- –

Whilst no one academic is asked to be all of these things, at least not at the same time, there is an increasing number of academics who are voicing dissatisfaction with implicit or explicit demands to be as many of these as possible. This development has at least three drivers. One, there is a small number of superstar-academics who seem to navigate all these different roles, and even do so with ease. Often a kind of exceptionally skilled academic entrepreneur, they have created a system where they seem to be able to both deliver award-winning teaching, produce exceptional research, popularize this, attract heaps of funding, and run a company or make a TV series on the side, all without breaking sweat. Whilst such talents should be lauded – if for nothing else then out of respect for the hard work that has gone into it – it can also establish an unrealistic target for other academics.

Two, university administrators and politicians within the field of higher education are, for various reasons, keen to see academics broaden their portfolios. In part this is for simple economic reasons, as universities become more and more dependent on external funding and valorization. In part this may stem from a desire to "optimize the machine". If the choice is between an excellent scholar and an excellent scholar with media presence and entrepreneurial skills, choosing the former would seem quite odd – at least if we assume that media and entrepreneurship will not by necessity degrade scholarship.

Three, as the two aforementioned drivers have become more prominent, the capacity to adopt an increasing number of these roles has become a valuable asset on the job and promotions market. Academics have thus themselves started to adapt to the playing of several roles, in effect creating an arms race of academic role-play. Taken together, these three drivers emphasize the need for academics to at least consider getting into several different roles during the span of their career.

My interest here is not to judge whether this, on the whole, is a good or a bad thing. There are arguments for both. This fragmentation and dissociation of professional identities can, if handled in a clumsy manner, drive academics to less impactful research, less engaged teaching, and mental health issues such as burnout and depression. On the other hand, and as previously mentioned, it is difficult to argue that academics engaging e.g. in the public debate or in popularizing research would by necessity be a bad idea. It seems, at least to me, that the issue of dissociated identities is one of how these are handled, rather than that they are symptoms of a pathology. Then again, I would be the kind of person to say exactly that.

STUCK IN THE MIDDLE WITH ME

I have, as I write this (2018), just moved on to be a professor of innovation, design and management as well as head of a unit of innovation and design engineering, but before this I was a chair of management and organization, and had been so for nigh on 15 years. I am 47 years of age. Readers of a mathematical disposition can from this ascertain that I was rather young when I was made a chair. This, in and of itself, is not particularly interesting, nor the reason I was asked to write this chapter. What tends to intrigue people more is that, in addition to being a chair, with the attendant roles of being a teacher, a researcher, a supervisor, and a (terrible) administrator, I play numerous other roles more in the public eye.

I have been referred to as a management guru, a thought leader, a public intellectual, and an "influencer". I do not claim to be any of these things, as it is very difficult to ascertain by what metrics one can lay claim to such lofty titles. I am merely pointing out that I have been called these things, and many other things as well – not all of them laudatory ("charlatan" and "media clown" come to mind). The reasons why such accolades (and such denigration) have been heaped upon me stems from the fact that I for over a decade have taken part both in the broader discussion on management and in the public debate, with some degree of success.

I have keynoted huge conferences with thousands in the audience, and spoken in front of royalty and heads of state. I have been a warm-up act for people such as Michael Porter and Arnold Schwarzenegger, two individuals seldom mentioned in the same sentence. Media outlets such as Fox News, Financial Times, Boston Herald and Handelsblatt, to mention but a few, have quoted or mentioned me. I have a healthy social media following, and have been listed as one of the 100 most influential people in my home country of Finland (being quite active on Twitter and Facebook has been a key factor here). I have written a bestselling book that was translated into eight languages, as well as commentaries that have been debated at parliamentary levels. I have been on TV, more than a fair few times. In fact, I have been asked to become the presenter of my own TV show, although other matters scuppered the idea. I am not writing this to impress you, as I do not myself see it so much as impressive as surprising and somewhat amusing, but rather to establish my *bona fides* as an academic who has played around in many fields, adopting many roles. No matter what you think of my research, I have spoken to and influenced a wide range of people, far beyond what a "normal" academic will do in their lives. Again, I am not saying this is a good (or bad) thing, I merely state it as a fact. In a busy year, I give some 80 keynotes for professionals and corporations, in addition to the students I teach and the people I address through my plethora of columns, blogs for professional media outlets, other media work and general punditry.

What this means, from the perspective of professional identity, is that I sometimes feel like I have a controlled form of dissociative identity disorder. There is Alf the Professor, happily bumbling along in the corridors of the university, lecturing like any other academic, dealing with the minutiae and the hundreds of tiny things that a modern academic has to deal with. That identity teaches and supervises, repeats the same lectures at times and patiently talks to students about their master's theses. Then there is Professor Rehn, who is a different identity altogether. This is the identity media approaches, the professional if sharp-tongued public intellectual, always ready either with a witty one-liner, or prepared to give a more philosophical interview. This identity is both more measured and more acerbic, designed for media-friendliness, and also comes to the fore when writing one of his many, many columns and commentaries. Then there is Alf Rehn, Management Guru (ARMG for short). This is quite an extroverted identity, one who struts about on stage and talks with great pathos about things such as the challenge of creativity or building innovative organizations. This is the "thought leader" that companies invite for speeches and events, and who never fails to amuse and provoke from the stage.

These three identities also have their own sub-identities. Alf the Professor is subtly different when teaching and when doing admin, and Alf Rehn, Management Guru is quite different when keynoting big external events and when doing internal training sessions. There are shifts and spillovers, memories from one identity leaking over to another. Sometimes ARMG is pushed in front of a camera, which prompts a quick if at times incomplete shift to Professor Rehn. Sometimes Alf the Professor is asked to comment on being ARMG. The different identities remain separated, but not without affecting each other. Interesting, at least to the identities themselves, is that they do not always even like each other. ARMG appreciates the benefits of Alf the Professor, but also dislikes the slow pace and Byzantine logics of that world. Professor Rehn does not like being confused with ARMG. Oh, and there's of course a fourth identity, lurking in the background. Alf at times wishes all these roles would disappear, as he just wants to be at home with his kids and/or girlfriend, not caring a whit about the role-play of academia. Still, this is where we are. These are who we are.

Note that I do not claim any one of these to be better, or more true, or more genuine than the others. Nor can I state that one of these was a choice and the others reactions to trauma. Sure, I can try to narrate them, to elevate myself or to excuse myself, but that would not be very honest. I no longer think I can explain why they emerged, and as any such explanation might well be a defense mechanism rather than a true telling of facts, I have chosen not to provide such explanations.

THE PARADOX OF PROFESSIONALISM

The reason for these many identities is simple – they are rewarded in contemporary academia. Having the capacity to adjust your identity to various demands, and being comfortable with the identity dissociation this entails, is a competency – for some even a core one – and can become a commodity. I have myself in effect been headhunted to a position specifically because I can span several professional identities, with the attendant improvements in, for instance, compensation. It should, however, be noted that there is a paradox inherent in all this.

Whereas professionalism has usually been taken to mean that one strives for excellence within one, clearly delineated profession, this blurs in cases such as the one I am referring to here. With academics increasingly being pushed towards fulfilling several, potentially conflicting professional identities, there exists the possibility that, in order to be more professional, one needs to be less professional. What I mean by this most confusing statement is the following: It is self-evident that an academic, in order to be successful and enjoy the respect of their peers, should publish in well-regarded outlets (starting from *Academy of Management Journal*, *Journal of Management* and other four-star journals). Whilst this is of course not the only way to be a true scholar, it is a simple and often used proxy, a sort of easy basic function of contemporary research excellence.

Now, for a researcher to excel at other aspects of modern academia, for instance outreach, the time to become excellent at the same is by necessity deducted from time dedicated to writing and publishing. This might seem self-evident, but little attention has been paid to the time it takes to become well-versed in e.g. industry outreach. Similarly, the inherent challenge in attempting to be professional in several, at least in part mutually exclusive domains, may be commonly discussed among academics, but rarely inquired into more formally. Whilst it can be argued that engaging with e.g. industry outreach can have some positive effects on one's research endeavors, it is still the case that using less time in the area of publishing will constitute a lessening of one's professional performance. Hence the paradox.

An academic plotting out their career will thus often be in a difficult situation making choices regarding e.g. research vis-à-vis teaching or outreach. An immediate supervisor might be quite insistent you focus on teaching, a research leader might demand you dedicate yourself to publishing in high-ranking journals, and administrators may at the same time suggest you have not dedicated yourself sufficiently to building contacts in industry. Some might now say that this has always been the case, but I contend that the groves of academe have become far more prone to making conflicting demands on the professionals therein.

One way to solve this paradox is of course simply to excel at all the varied professional demands that face the modern academic. This, however, demands either astonishing skills at both time management and a level of competence in highly separate areas only very few people hold, or a dedicated team of underlings, and to run the latter you would also need both skilled delegation and significant resources to execute the work in a professional manner. Whilst there obviously are people who can adeptly manage this (some of the more successful US business school professors come to mind – Clayton Christensen's team[1] is so big that he has a separate "Chief of Staff"), the stark reality is that many academics need to accept that they will not excel in all things a contemporary academic is asked to excel in.

The way in which one does this will of course differ greatly from academic to academic. For some, possibly most, the favored strategy is to simply ignore the "new" suggested professional identities. To this group, notions of even trying to be a "guru" or a "thought leader" is anathema, and something similar goes for notions such as being professionally active on social media, writing for a general audience except as an occasional amusement, and working with e.g. industry outreach. Note that I am not stating this as an indictment, as I see this as a perfectly normal strategy in the face of paradoxical demands. Others, again, seem to adhere to a more cynical strategy, one where you "play the game" and occasionally engage in things such as outreach or more public affairs, but where this is done in a manner that communicates that one's true, core professional identity is still very much that of an academic, keeping other identity states at a cynical distance.

Some of us, however, have embraced the paradox, and adopted a mode of working with multiple professional identities. A key aspect of this is an acceptance of the fact that, in order to become more professional, we have to be less professional. In my case, for instance, I have recently finished a book on leadership for a general audience. Whilst the manuscript was rather short for a book – 36 000 words, i.e. not too long for the harried businessman – crafting it still took considerable time away from things such as the serious research project I am currently running. Now, some of my colleagues would say that the choice to write a popular book in such a situation is simply wrong. To them, communicating with the outside world should never hold priority over more academic matters. I, however, profess a notion of professionalism wherein it is important to at least attempt a decent performance in the varied, dissociated identities I play with. To not try to be a decently active thinker also in the more general field would, to me, be a rejection of a new kind of professionalism, one which we may have to become more accustomed to. Note that I am not claiming that I've achieved perfect success in such endeavors (or, really, any endeavor), only that I am trying to sketch out a new notion of academic professionalism, one more attuned to an age of transparency and ever-present media.

THE HEART OF DARKNESS

Friedrich Nietzsche ([1886], 2002) famously warned us about looking too deeply into certain things, stating: "He who fights with monsters should be careful lest he thereby become a monster. And if thou gaze long into an abyss, the abyss will also gaze into thee." It is a chilling but astute observation about the plasticity of ethics, and the manner in which we can start rationalizing atrocities whilst believing we're only reacting reasonably to other atrocities. I also find it a good reminder of how adopting an identity or role can start changing you, possibly in ways you do not quite notice yourself.

Looking back at my own work, I can sense that there are monsters lurking in the deep waters of contemporary professional identity. Take social media, for instance. As part of being a professor who communicated ideas outside academia, I have taken to using Twitter a fair bit. I've also used Facebook to some effect, often commenting on politics in Finland and occasionally achieved some fame (or notoriety) whilst doing so. As an example, I was both flabbergasted and highly amused when a rather acerbic Facebook-posting I had done was quoted in the Finnish parliament the day after I had written it. The fact that it was by a representative of a somewhat xenophobic populist party made it even better.

But here, specifically, be monsters. It is of course always nice to notice that one is being noticed. I have also taken some joy out of having quite the social media following, at least if I compare myself to my professorial peers. When someone has challenged me on this, I've stated that I believe it to be a good thing that professors (and other academics) take part in the public debate, for several reasons. One, as a person who enjoys a great deal of freedom and is in a safe professional position, I can speak for people for whom this might not be the case. Two, as a professor (who also has some modicum of fame) I enjoy more visibility and should use this to e.g. highlight problems in society or business. Three, I can, in my own little way, show the surrounding world that not all professors are the caricatures that still dominate people's ideas about academics. I've even gone so far as to say that I feel particularly professors have a *responsibility* to use their position in such a way. With all we are given – time, a platform, legitimacy – it would be a sin to waste this. Further, what fun is it to have such freedoms if one only uses it to repeat oneself and for feeding the machine?

Such high-minded sentiments aside, I do also need to acknowledge that there is an element of vanity, not to mention marketing, to it all. Being visible on social media, and gaining attention through it, has its pleasures. As academics often suffer from being if not ignored then at least left mostly to their own devices, the kind of instant attention that social media affords can be quite enticing. This aside, visibility can have more direct benefits as well. For someone who, as a sideline, speaks professionally, social media is a way to stay "top of mind" with potential clients, as well as a way to build one's network. By being visible one is more likely to be remembered, invited, included in things. The downside of this is that as a multimodal professional, I can feel both an urge and a pressure to keep up my activities, and, at times, ramp them up. If one provocative statement leads to being mentioned in parliament, why not craft one more? Maybe several times a week? Maybe all the time? Whilst social media can be a great tool in building one mode of your professional identities, it can lead you towards trying to be visible for visibility's sake, provocative for the sake of provocation.

Something similar might be said about working as a professional speaker. On one hand it is wonderful work, particularly for one who enjoys being on stage and in the spotlight. It can pay very well indeed, and you get to see much of the world. Once you've honed your skills you can get by with less and less preparation, and if you become really good it can become so easy and natural to you that the only real work you put in is the travel (which can be very tiring, though) and the hour or so you are on stage. This can tempt you, possibly away from academia altogether, and make you believe that all work should be as simple as presenting a well-honed speech over and over again.

Put somewhat more bluntly, the fact that you've learned to deal with dissociative identities does not mean you fully control them. I have myself battled with the challenge of being both Alf the Professor and Alf Rehn, Management Guru (not to mention "Professor Rehn"). At times, I have felt nigh on disgusted with ARMG, and vowed I would focus more on academic things. At times, I have been fully disgusted with my academic identity and said I will leave academia and devote myself to business, stating that I would do so because business is more ethical, moral, and honorable than academia can ever hope to be (a sentiment that shocked some people, but which I still hold to from time to time). What is important to realize is that each of the many partial professional identities that an academic can adopt has its own set of attractors, and that the difficulty of living with dissociative identities is not how to adopt them, but how to successfully and in a controlled manner be able to switch between them without one becoming too dominant (unless one opts for that, of course). We all make our own choices, pick our own masks, or choose not to test out new ones.

DISSOCIATIVE IDENTITIES: YOUR MILEAGE MAY VARY

Is it, then, a good thing or a bad thing that the demands put on academics can push one towards a sort of dissociative (professional) identity disorder? On one level it is clear, at least to me, that the manifold roles that a contemporary academic is meant to occupy and even master is a serious cause of stress and confusion. Many if not most academics I know communicate that they feel a great deal of stress in their work, and much of this stems from having to "juggle hats" (you should note that I've not really addressed the role of "Administrator" in this text, but it is for many a key part of the multimodal role-play). Overall, I wish for academia to move more towards a model in which great teachers can be great teachers and where people who are bad at administration do not end up doing lots of it. A model where there would be several tracks for people to develop and excel, and where switching between them would be celebrated rather than frowned upon (compare, for instance, how moving into more of a leadership role is often seen as "leaving" research behind).

That said, I believe that paradoxical demands put on a contemporary academic are not likely to lessen, and may in fact increase in intensity. If this indeed is the case, academics will have to learn to live with something akin to dissociative identities – being a scholar one day, an entrepreneur the next. This will not be an easy transition, as academia as a culture is not particularly good at transmitting this kind of knowledge, and as most senior academics still lack some of the core skills of this assumed academic-to-be. There is a risk that this will create new splits within the field, between those comfortable with multimodal role-play, and those who stick to the more traditional professional identity of the academic. We're already seeing this playing out in business schools, where particularly some of the more critical scholars find themselves sidestepped and marginalized.

But it is also exactly here that the promise of the dissociated identity might lie. I am, myself, what one would consider a critical scholar. My research has touched upon things both critical and esoteric, and had dealt with matters such as power and ideology, alternative economic forms, popular culture, childhood, and zombies (yeah, really). I've taught critical management studies, introduced feminist and queer theory into staid business school courses, and supervised highly critical and theoretical PhDs, the kind that are often criticized for lacking "business relevance". I have, however, also written a bestselling book on creativity, and both worked with and taught management consulting. To some this is paradoxical, and possibly the hallmark of a confused mind. To me it has been a revelation.

By applying myself to fields not normally associated with someone with my title and research background I have not only been able to get insight into a world that most academics only talk about in hushed, vague terms, I have also become a better teacher. Rather than pontificate about the vagaries of strategy work and the power games in an executive team, I have been able to draw on my own experiences and through this enliven my more theoretical engagements. Rather than talking about what management consultants do, I've been able to illustrate it with both what I have done as one, what my friends who are management consultants do, and what boards and/or executives look at when they hire them. I could go on, but will instead move onto a second, possibly more surprising benefit.

Although it sounds counterintuitive, I have found that my dissociated identities have actually given me more freedom as an academic, not less. Early on I learned that the biases people in industry held towards people in academia could actually be used in a productive manner. Coming from academia, even though I was quite young for a professor, meant that the expectations were that I would be quirky, forgetful, boring, incomprehensible, somewhat asocial, and otherwise a caricature of the fumbling professor. This has dual benefits. Any time I wished to be critical or provocative, I could simply wrap this up in my professorial persona, and know that things that would be taboo for others to do or say would be forgiven since I was a "professor" and therefore couldn't be expected to behave properly. Thus I could ask the questions no-one else dared, challenge notions that were otherwise taboo to talk about, and say whatever I wanted to whomever I wanted. On the other hand, the very low bar set for professorial performance also meant that I could happily confuse and delight people. Professors and academics are meant to be boring and self-important, so I started opening my lectures with self-deprecating jokes, and pepper them with various, often dirty, jokes. Professors are meant to stand behind pulpits, so I started pacing around stages. Professors are meant to wear a suit and a tie, so I would turn up in sneakers and a t-shirt (plus a jacket, most of the time). I found that the assumed professional identity of an academic was both a handy thing to hide behind, when I so wished, and a delightful counterpoint to challenge and distance myself from. This created space and freedom for me in the world outside of academia.

Inside academia, curiously enough, something similar happened. As I, at least in Finland and at my university, now was the "famous one" and "the one that works with all those companies", I found that my work was rarely if ever questioned. On the contrary, since I fulfilled one of the roles that a contemporary university wishes to see fulfilled, I was given pretty much *carte blanche* when it came to other endeavors. No-one minded that I had my students read Marx and queer theory, because I also gave a practical course in management consulting and could help the university when they needed contacts to a CEO or to get a government minister to come speak at an event. I even felt that other professors were supportive of all this, as the fact that I had so much outreach activity meant that they didn't have to worry as much about it. I remember sometimes thinking that I was a sort of a "sin-eater"[2] for academia. In my case, I felt that what I might be doing when adopting the identity of ARMG was something akin to this. I played the trickster on stage, so that other professors didn't have to. I made racy comments on the radio, so that other professors would be left in peace ... I am not writing this to claim I am holier than they, not at all; I am merely pointing out that the benefits of a dissociative professional identity might at times extend beyond the person adopting the same.

All this is to say that one doesn't need to go into the multimodal role-play I have discussed here, but one should not ignore or look down upon it either. The world needs some of us tricksters, but not everyone should be one. Just like in every culture, the slightly mad jester can play an important role in academia, one that challenges boundaries and norms, and the jester deserves a modicum of respect. It is a skill, of sorts, to be able to switch between identities and switch between contexts, but it can also be a rather difficult professional identity to maintain. So be a player of many roles if you can and, if you cannot, be clear about why you choose your own professional identity. Respect the skills inherent in all of the roles a contemporary academic is supposed to perform, but be aware of their pitfalls and seductive properties. And, if you go so deep into your different roles and dissociated identities that you start having little conversations with yourself, remember the wise words of my father, who whenever he was asked if he was talking to himself would answer: "Well, it is the only way to have an intelligent conversation around here, isn't it?"

NOTES

1. A professor at Harvard Business School who became famous through his work on "disruptive innovation" and who is today counted as one of the top innovation and management gurus in the world.

2. A "sin-eater" is a person who, often by eating a meal at the house or burial site of a recently deceased person, consumes and carries their sins, so that they can go to heaven with a light soul. In parts of rural England, e.g., this custom survived into the late nineteenth century.

REFERENCES

Howell, E. F. (2011). *Understanding and Treating Dissociative Identity Disorder: A Relational Approach.* London, UK: Routledge.

Nietzsche, F. ([1886], 2002). *Nietzsche: Beyond Good and Evil: Prelude to a Philosophy of the Future.* Cambridge, UK: Cambridge University Press.

12. Cooperation and conflict in academia

Sonja Rispens

Estimated reading time: **23 minutes and 28 seconds**.

CHAPTER HIGHLIGHTS

* In order to become a successful academic, collaboration is key.
* In addition to collaborating with people who ask you to get on board with their projects, it is important that you initiate some projects in which you are the principal investigator.
* When planning your days, remember to allocate the most writing time to your first-authored papers.
* Engaging in activities in multiple life domains offers you more opportunities and resources, which can be used to promote growth and performance.
* Spending time on enjoyable activities in a life domain outside work (for example engaging in sports or a dance class) can be energizing, satisfying, and offers a variety of other resources that can be used for your work, thus causing a positive flow-on effect of these resources to the work domain.

Talent wins games, but teamwork and intelligence win championships.
Michael Jordan

ENGAGING IN COLLABORATION AND CONFLICT

Science is a collaborative effort and the romantic notion of the academic researcher as a lone genius is not accurate. There is a documented trend towards fewer single-authored papers in all academic fields (e.g., Akhavan et al., 2016; Nabout et al., 2015; Simonton, 2013). In fact, I have only written one solo-authored article and this is my second solo-authored chapter. Another trend is the enhanced focus on reproducibility in science (see Baker, 2016; Fanelli, 2018; Schooler, 2014), which stimulates scholars to form collaborations in order to rigorously assess the robustness of published research (see Klein et al., 2014). Another aspect fueling collaboration is the complexity of current problems that our society faces (e.g. climate change), which demands collaborative effort of scientists from multiple fields in order to understand, prevent, manage or fix those problems (e.g., Bennett & Gadlin, 2012). Further, there is a need to bundle efforts with non-academic partners, such as partners from industry or governments (e.g. Ankrah & Al-Tabbaa, 2015). And let us not forget about collaborating with our department colleagues on courses, with our fellow faculty members on (re-)designing teaching curricula, and engaging in committee work. I think it is safe to conclude that in order to become a successful academic, collaboration is key.

Collaboration is defined as the act of working together towards the same end, and, as the saying goes: Two heads can be better than one. So how can we initiate and maintain effective, productive, and energizing collaborative relationships? That question can be daunting for new academics and/or shy academics. Here are a few pointers that can help you to move forward. Although I realize there is a distinction between collaborations between academics and those with non-academic partners, I am only going to focus on academic research collaborations.

The first step is to identify with whom you want to work. You may want to consider those people who complement your knowledge or skills, who can give you access to special equipment, or those that can help to expand your data for a certain publication. Once you've identified people you want to work with, you can assess whether you already know them (which is, specifically in mono-disciplinary research, often the case). When you don't know a certain person, perhaps someone in your network could introduce you. If the person you want to meet is outside your network, you need to contact them yourself directly (e.g. via email or introduce yourself to them at a conference). This process becomes easier when you are able to explain how you think a collaboration can be fruitful for you both, what you would like to do (or what you have to offer) and how you think you can complement each other's knowledge or skills. When there is an intention to work together, it can be advisable to first set up a low-risk project, especially when you do not know each other that well. You can, for example, offer to analyze someone's data in a different way, or ask to jointly supervise a thesis project for a master's student. If the trial goes well, you can safely move into more riskier and intensive collaborations such as writing a grant proposal together.

Students and researchers might approach you for potential collaborations as well. Because that is immensely flattering, you may want to give it some thought before agreeing. Does the project look exciting? Is it connected to your own line of work? Do you have time to take on another collaboration? Try to obtain some balance regarding your role in the different collaborative relationships you are engaging in. Most institutions value independent scholarship when making tenure decisions, which means that you need to establish your own research identity. Therefore, in addition to collaborating with people who ask you to get on board with their projects, it is important that you initiate some projects in which you are the principal investigator. Establish your own line of research, on which you work with master's students, PhD students, and postdocs. Although this sounds very straightforward, for me this was somewhat of a struggle. I really enjoy collaborating with other researchers, and I always feel that I can learn a lot from them. And for a while I was not moving my own projects and ideas along but worked hard to help realize other people's ideas. In hindsight, this was certainly not the fastest course of action to establish my identity as a researcher. For my evaluators it turned out to be difficult to assess, based on my publications, what my unique contribution to the field was. At this point in time, it does not help me to dwell on this, but perhaps my derailing can be a valuable lesson for a starting academic. Focus on yourself first. Admittedly, that was the hardest part for me because it always felt so much easier to help others first. When planning your days, remember to allocate the most writing time to your first-authored papers. Think about what you want to accomplish with your research; what are the questions that intrigue you? Let those guide your actions foremost.

Collaborating with others can be fun, inspiring, and very rewarding (both personally and intellectually). However, there are potential threats to every collaborative relationship. For example, you may have overestimated what you can accomplish within a certain timeframe. This can be problematic because your collaborators' work will be dependent on yours. Not being able to deliver can diminish your reliability and thus your reputation. Did you fall prey to an optimistic planning bias or are there unforeseen circumstances intervening your schedule? If so, inform your collaborators as quickly as possible and make a new schedule. Also, when you notice that a collaborator has difficulties meeting deadlines, you may want to inquire whether there are certain barriers, and whether you can help. Practice patience and how to bring things up in a non-confrontational way. In the next section, I will talk about the inevitability of emergent conflicts and how those are likely to influence the collaborative relationship.

CONFLICTS WITH COLLABORATORS

Working with others inevitably means that you will experience conflict. A co-author may disagree with you on the appropriate theoretical framework of your study. A departmental colleague who is involved in your course may not agree with your request to publish her slides on the electronic class environment before the class actually takes place. A student might not send his materials in time so you cannot prepare for your meeting. In general, conflict is defined as perceived or actual incompatibilities between those involved (Rispens, 2014). Conflict can be a major source of stress (Römer et al., 2012) and is found to be negatively correlated with feelings of well-being (De Dreu & Beersma, 2005; De Raeve et al., 2009; Dijkstra et al., 2005).

Different types of conflict are distinguished within the literature. A well-known distinction is between task, relationship, and process conflict (Jehn, 1994, 1995). Task conflicts are disagreements about ideas, opinions, and viewpoints regarding the task at hand, for example, when a co-author disagrees with you on the theoretical framework of your paper or having debates with your collaborators on what the preferred research method should be for your joint project. Relationship conflicts are disagreements you have with collaborators and colleagues which are not related to any task you are carrying out but are about personal issues or values, for example, disagreeing with a colleague about what political party to vote for in the upcoming national elections. Process conflicts are disagreements with collaborators on *how* to pursue the task at hand, for example, debating with your co-authors about who will write or review a section of a paper.

Meta-analytic data points out that relationship and process conflict tend to negatively affect collaborative outcomes (De Wit et al., 2012). When collaborators experience relationship or process conflicts, the range of attention within the group narrows and impairs the group's integrative problem-solving ability (Rispens, 2014). When collaborators are experiencing a lot of conflict, they are usually very busy with resolving or ignoring the conflict, or fighting over it than spending effort and time on the tasks at hand, which in turn decreases task performance (Jehn & Bendersky, 2003). On the other hand, task conflict has the potential to be a positive force (De Wit et al., 2012). Task conflicts may stimulate a critical assessment of different ideas and viewpoints, thereby facilitating an increased understanding of the task, and prevent premature consensus and confirmation biases in the decision-making process (De Wit et al., 2013).

Given that avoiding conflicts is not a very useful or effective strategy (i.e. our needs and goals are likely to differ from those on whom we are (partly) dependent; Donohue & Kolt, 1992), and because individual and situational factors are important to diminish negative and create positive consequences of conflict (see De Wit et al., 2012), it is important to become proactive conflict managers. By that I mean that we need to: (a) prepare ourselves for experiencing conflict; (b) be able to determine the type of conflict; and (c) (believe we can) find ways to effectively deal with conflicts.

How does one prepare for experiencing conflict? Research suggests that people who have a tendency to be continuously on the lookout to learn new things and to use that knowledge for personal growth are better able to benefit from having conflicts, specifically task conflicts (De Clerq et al., 2017; also see De Wit et al., 2013). Even when you do not consider yourself to be such a person, you might want to consciously try to take a step back each time you experience a conflict and to determine whether you can appraise the situation in a (more) positive light ("Can I learn something from this?"). Additionally, you might want to consider preparing collectively with your collaborators for conflict. Establishing a social norm towards conflict early on in a collaboration might help (Brett, 1984; Jehn et al., 2008). Agreeing with your collaborators that it is OK to have different viewpoints regarding the project, for example, helps all involved to indeed voice their different opinions when they have them. Be advised to agree on airing those differences in a constructive manner (Tjosvold et al., 2014) and to respect the concerns and feelings of others (Peterson & Ferguson, 2014). When you and your collaborators establish roles (e.g. author order) and tasks early on in a joint project, you will likely prevent the emergence of process conflicts at a later point in time. Taking some time to figure out whether you and your collaborators share similar aspirations and work values is very helpful. Collaborators who have similar work values tend to agree on norms regarding work, and this agreement helps to minimize the emergence of relationship and process conflicts (Jehn & Mannix, 2001).

Following on from what I wrote earlier, determining what the conflict is about is important to figure out whether the disagreement has a potential benefit or not. Having a debate with your collaborators about the best data analysis technique to analyze your project data is something academics usually would welcome. Being able to determine whether it is a task conflict may make it easier to view that situation in a positive light and to react more favorably and constructively towards the person who raises the issue. Further, being able to determine when it is a relationship or process conflict is helpful in a different way. Above all, be aware that engaging in relationship conflict is likely to increase the animosity between you and your collaborators, which makes collaborative work more difficult. When these conflicts emerge, you could try to agree to disagree and leave it at that. Some discussions on how to collaborate (scheduling, and assigning roles and responsibilities to co-authors) can be useful in the beginning of a joint project, but should be settled rather early (Greer et al., 2008). As a lead author it is wise to take the initiative in assigning roles, tasks, and deadlines.

How to engage with and handle conflicts? When you have (a) prepared for conflict and (b) determined what the conflict is about, you are already halfway there. When engaging in disagreements, try to express your point of view in a clear but polite manner (i.e. stick to facts and observations, don't make it personal; Steinel et al., 2008; Tjosvold et al., 2014). And, likewise: don't take it personally. Task disagreements can be very inspiring and useful – up to a certain point (De Dreu 2006; Jehn, 1995). You cannot debate forever if you want to finish projects and papers and, hence, you and your collaborators need to find a solution at a certain point. Again, as a lead author it is important to take the initiative and responsibility in this process.

Approaching conflict proactively, and engaging in constructive negotiations and collectively finding a solution is the preferred way to manage conflicts when you want to preserve the collaborative relationship. When you want to preserve the collaborative relationship but you don't care too deeply about the conflict issue, consider giving in or making a compromise. The same rules pretty much apply to process conflict situations. Although please be aware that when process conflicts do emerge again later on in the project, there might be some underlying issue.

Research has shown that some people may experience ego-threat while debating roles, tasks, and responsibilities ("Why isn't she letting me write the discussion section? I am the most senior here, does this mean she thinks I am bad at it?"; Greer & Jehn, 2007). You can prevent this by being clear about why each person is doing which task ("I find it important that my PhD student gets practice in writing a discussion section"). Finally, relationship conflicts are hard if not impossible to solve. As I said before, you can try to respectfully agree to disagree in order to move on the joint project. When the relationship turns sour, you may want to get a third party involved such as an independent mediator, and prepare yourself to let go of the collaboration.

CONFLICTS WITH EDITORS AND REVIEWERS

Obviously, a recurrent theme in any academic's life is disagreements with editors and reviewers who have read and commented on your work. For example, reviewers may ask for things which you consider not to be correct. Or perhaps, during the second or third round of revision, reviewers bring up new issues which may seem unfair to you. My thesis advisor used to say that the reviewer is always right and I tend to agree with her. This does not mean that reviewers are factually right, but rather it offers an opportunity to see the reviewers' point of view (Eva, 2009). A reviewer may have misunderstood something in your paper and based on that misunderstanding may request something that you find not necessary or maybe not even correct. For me, that usually means that *I* have not explained it well enough and I need to rewrite parts of the paper in order to communicate more clearly. The next step is to engage in the conversation with the reviewer (in the response letter) and to explain what you did in reply to their comment.

Sometimes a manuscript gets rejected after one or more rounds of revisions. And, yes, that is an extremely frustrating experience. I have heard about people who directly contacted the editor to negotiate a different decision. I have never done that myself and just the thought makes me feel very uncomfortable. I will air my frustrations to co-authors or supportive colleagues, and then move on by submitting the paper to a different journal.

AND SOME MORE CONFLICTS

It is perhaps easier to consider the conflicts we are likely to encounter while collaborating (or trying to collaborate) with others. However, it is not uncommon for academics to experience friction between their academic role and the other roles that they fulfill in life, and to experience a conflict with their inner critic. I will explain both in more detail below and give suggestions on how to handle these types of conflict.

Work–Life Conflict

As a PhD student, as a postdoc, or as a professor, we are likely to face conflicts with ourselves. That is, in addition to being a researcher, we are also a friend, a sibling, a daughter or son, an amateur musician or philanthropist. These different roles we take on in our lives can present us with conflicts from time to time. It is not unlikely that our work will be all-consuming and overwhelming at some points. There are always deadlines, urgencies, high-risk revisions, which can get the better of us. And attending to those demands interferes with those of our family and friends and may create conflict.

From my own experience, there was a time a few years ago in which I was working pretty much all the time, which, combined with a fair dose of perfectionism, did not bring me much. After a while, I felt emotionally and cognitively drained. Constantly working, and feeling very guilty when not working, was not good for me. I did not feel content with my life or my work, I was not happy, and in general I did not feel well. I felt I was doing a bad job being an academic, a friend, a daughter, a partner, etc., and I needed to re-define who I was and what roles were important for me.

There is vast empirical evidence that demonstrates that fulfilling multiple roles in your life increases your well-being (Barnett & Hyde, 2001; Perry-Jenkins et al., 2000; Ruderman et al., 2002), decreases stress (Barnett et al., 1992) and increases recovery and performance (Demerouti et al., 2010; Dubbelt et al., 2016; Ruderman et al., 2002; Volman et al., 2013). Engaging in activities in multiple life domains offers you more opportunities and resources, which can be used to promote growth and performance in all life domains (Marks, 1977). Moreover, spending time on enjoyable activities in a life domain outside work (for example engaging in sports or a dance class) can be energizing, satisfying, and offers a variety of other resources that can be used for your work (Ruderman et al., 2002; Ten Brummelhuis & Trougakos, 2013) causing a positive flow-on effect of these resources to the work domain

(Allis & O'Driscoll, 2008). This work underscores that it is important to define yourself based on the different roles that you have in your life and to actively engage in those multiple roles. There is a caveat though: one needs to consider how to manage the demands of the different roles.

Thankfully, researchers have thought about this as well. There is a body of research that examines the struggle of people to combine work and life demands while remaining motivated and energized to fulfill both roles (e.g. Allen et al., 2000; Byron, 2005; Grawitch et al., 2010; Greenhaus & Powell, 2006; Haar et al., 2014; McNall et al., 2010). The predominant focus in that area is on how demands from one domain interfere with demands from another domain. For example, working long hours because you need to finish a grant proposal will take away from time you can spend at home with your family. Luckily, there is also some research attention to the strategies people can use to balance their work and non-work roles. That research is important not least because work and non-work activities compete for the same finite amount of resources that a person has (Grawitch et al., 2010).

To enable yourself to have a life outside academia (and to have the time and energy for it) requires a strategic allocation of your resources such as time and energy during the work day (Grawitch et al., 2010). Sturges (2012) categorized various strategies people use in order to craft their work–life balance. Crafting the work–life balance means that people actively try to alter the boundary between work and life such that a balance will result. I will list and describe a few of the strategies Sturges (2012) documented which seem very applicable to academics. The first are temporal crafting strategies, which means that people make changes in work times (when work starts and ends) as well as how they structure their time during the working day (for example, cognitively demanding tasks such as writing a paper during mornings and less demanding tasks such as department meetings during afternoons). The latter also helps to figure out which tasks (demands) are more important than others and to prioritize your work accordingly (Grawitch et al., 2010). The second strategy is locational crafting, that is, working away from the office to blend work and non-work. For example, when I have the chance to work at home I can easily combine it with going to my local gym during down hours. That way I can actively engage in self-care by minding my physical well-being.

The last strategy I will mention is cognitive crafting. This entails defining or re-defining your work–life balance in such a way that it can actually be achieved and fits your situation. For example, a person can define a work–life balance when she/he has the weekends off, even though she/he works long hours during the week. By actively defining what a work–life balance means to you (don't forget to negotiate this with significant others in your life), you are likely to change the way you look at the demands of both domains (e.g. I really want to finish this paper tonight so I can attend the soccer match on Saturday with my brother). Do you notice how a job demand (writing a paper) becomes a preferred demand (I want to work on it tonight)? When that happens, research suggests (e.g. Van den Broeck et al., 2010), it drains our resource pool less.

Since I made the decision to have a life a few years ago, to have weekends off, to pay more attention to my family and my friends, to take care of myself by eating healthier, exercising regularly, and going to art exhibitions and concerts more often, I have become much happier. I have even made new friends since then, and I have become more productive as an academic. I have a better sense of what tasks are important for me, I carefully plan my work hours, and I can do things more efficiently. Thus, the best advice I can give is to get a life!

Conflicts with your Inner Critic

Have you ever felt a fraud? That it is only a matter of time before people in your institution find out you really should not have been awarded that PhD? Chances are you are experiencing the imposter syndrome or phenomenon which is a common feeling among academics (Clance & Imes, 1978). People who experience imposter tendencies more often feel their successes are undeserved and attribute successes to luck rather than ability (Imes, 1979; Topping & Kimmel, 1985). They are inclined to overestimate the abilities of others and to underestimate their own (Clance & O'Toole, 1988).

Many studies have been done to measure imposture cognition and to examine its antecedents (for an overview see Whitman & Shanine, 2012). Although there is not a lot of research examining the consequences of feeling like an imposter, the evidence that has been gathered paints a bleak picture. People who feel like an imposter generally experience higher levels of exhaustion, psychological distress, anxiety, and lower levels of job satisfaction, self-esteem, and self-efficacy and engage less in organizational citizenship behaviors (i.e. engaging in discretionary behaviors that are not in employees' formal job requirements but help effective functioning of the organization; Vergauwe et al., 2015; Whitman & Shanine, 2012). It is worth pointing out that those who experience imposter tendencies do not differ in performance from those without such experience (Cozzarelli & Major, 1990; Want & Kleitman, 2006) and it can be concluded that imposters hold incorrect negative self-views.

Whitman and Shanine (2012) suggest using active coping strategies to deal with the stress and anxiety caused by feeling like an imposter. These strategies are: (1) positive thinking, (2) direct action, and (3) help seeking. Positive thinking means reappraising the situation by searching for the brighter side of it, which helps you to find a solution. Direct action is engaging in certain behavior (such as working harder, longer hours, more efficiently) meant to overcome the problem or situation. Help seeking is quite straightforward and means seeking advice and support from friends and colleagues. There is empirical evidence that support from colleagues indeed buffers the negative consequences of imposter tendencies (Vergauwe et al., 2015).

I can relate to feeling like an imposter. I long felt I did not quite belong and was full of self-doubt which gave rise to my "inner critic". I developed a very loud inner critic (in fact, it sometimes felt like a full stadium of critics) which would refute the things I did by saying I was never up to par. For me several things helped to put things into a more realistic perspective and to engage in a constructive conflict with my inner critic. One, as a reviewer and associate editor, I was fortunate to read many interesting and high-quality papers. That experience helped me tremendously to assess the quality of papers, and I could use this experience for my own writing. It also meant I read many papers that were not publishable (yet). Reading those latter papers really helped to turn down the volume of my inner critic and I realized, among other things, that I could submit my papers to journals sooner than I used to do.

A second strategy that worked for me is to cognitively reappraise feedback. Instead of reading "You need to find a different occupation" into it, I was able to see the feedback for what it really was, namely a suggestion on how to improve my work ("It would be advisable to use a different data analysis technique"). Again the experience of writing constructive reviews myself was helpful in this cognitive endeavor. Nowadays, when my inner critic yells that I am no good, I just ask her to be more specific (no good at what? Define "good") and to give me suggestions on how to improve. Third, instead of worrying at length about something I do not know or cannot do, I tried seeking help. There are always people who are better at things than I am, and asking them for help is not a sign of weakness but, based on the collaboration literature I discussed earlier, it is actually a pretty smart move.

TO CONCLUDE

At this point of my life, I am a happy academic in a tenured position at Eindhoven University of Technology. As a social scientist I am a weird duck in this STEM (Science, Technology, Engineering, and Mathematics) pond but I am embracing my different-ness. I recently started to get engaged in exciting interdisciplinary research projects with colleagues from different academic disciplines (e.g. philosophy, mechanical engineering, industrial design, human–computer interaction). I am sure we will have our fair share of disagreements but I am ready to face and work through those and really look forward to the things we will learn. I have faced my own battles regarding the work–life balance and my inner critic, which in hindsight were good for me to re-discover my worth both as a private person and as an academic researcher.

I can only hope that my reflection here on the perks and perils of (collaborative) work in academia is useful to some of you.

REFERENCES

Akhavan, P., Ebrahim, N. A., Fetrati, M. A., & Pezeshkan, A. (2016). Major trends in knowledge management research: A bibliometric study. *Scientometrics, 107*(3), 1249–1264.

Allen, T. D., Herst, D. E. L., Bruck, C. S., & Sutton, M. (2000). Consequences associated with work-to-family conflict: A review and agenda for future research. *Journal of Occupational Health Psychology, 5*(2), 278–308.

Allis, P., & O'Driscoll, M. (2008). Positive effects of nonwork-to-work facilitation on well-being in work, family and personal domains. *Journal of Managerial Psychology, 23*(3), 273–291.

Ankrah, S., & Al-Tabbaa, O. (2015). Universities–industry collaboration: A systematic review. *Scandinavian Journal of Management, 31*(3), 387–408.

Baker, M. (2016). 1,500 scientists lift the lid on reproducibility. *Nature: International Weekly Journal of Science, 533*(7604), 452–455.

Barnett, R. C., & Hyde, J. S. (2001). Women, men, work, and family: An expansionist theory. *American Psychologist, 56*(10), 781–796.

Barnett, R. C., Marshall, N. L., & Pleck, J. H. (1992). Men's multiple roles and their relationship to men's psychological distress. *Journal of Marriage and the Family, 54*(2), 358–367.

Bennett, L. M., & Gadlin, H. (2012). Collaboration and team science: From theory to practice. *Journal of Investigative Medicine, 60*(5), 768–775.

Brett, J. M. (1984). Managing organizational conflict. *Professional Psychology: Research and Practice, 15*(5), 664–678.

Byron, K. (2005). A meta-analytic review of work–family conflict and its antecedents. *Journal of Vocational Behavior, 67*(2), 169–198.

Clance, P. R., & Imes, S. A. (1978). The imposter phenomenon in high achieving women: Dynamics and therapeutic intervention. *Psychotherapy: Theory, Research & Practice, 15*(3), 241–247.

Clance, P. R., & O'Toole, M. A. (1988). *The Imposter Phenomenon: An Internal Barrier to Empowerment and Achievement.* Philadelphia, PA: Haworth Press.

Cozzarelli, C., & Major, B. (1990). Exploring the validity of the impostor phenomenon. *Journal of Social and Clinical Psychology, 9*(4), 401–417.

De Clerq, D., Rahman, Z. M., & Belausteguigoitia, I. (2017). Task conflict and employee creativity: The critical roles of learning orientation and goal congruence. *Human Resource Management, 56*(1), 93–109.

De Dreu, C. K. W. (2006). When Too Little or Too Much Hurts: Evidence for a Curvilinear Relationship Between Task Conflict and Innovation in Teams. *Journal of Management, 32*(1), 83–107.

De Dreu, C. K. W., & Beersma, B. (2005). Conflict in organizations: Beyond effectiveness and performance. *European Journal of Work and Organizational Psychology, 14*(2), 105–117.

De Raeve, L., Jansen, N. W. H., Van den Brandt, P. A., Vasse, R., & Kant, I. J. (2009). Interpersonal conflicts at work as a predictor of self-reported health outcomes and occupational mobility. *Occupational and Environmental Medicine, 66*(1), 16–22.

De Wit, F. R. C., Greer, L. L., & Jehn, K. A. (2012). The paradox of intragroup conflict: A meta-analysis. *Journal of Applied Psychology, 97*(2), 360–390.

De Wit, F. R. C., Jehn, K. A., & Scheepers, D. (2013). Task conflict, information processing, and decision-making: The damaging effect of relationship conflict. *Organizational Behavior and Human Decision Processes, 122*(2), 177–189.

Demerouti, E., Bakker, A. B., & Voydanoff, P. (2010). Does home life interfere with or facilitate job performance? *European Journal of Work and Organizational Psychology, 19*(2), 128–149.

Dijkstra, M. T., van Dierendonck, D., & Evers, A. (2005). Responding to conflict at work and individual well-being: The mediating role of flight behaviour and feelings of helplessness. *European Journal of Work and Organizational Psychology, 14*(2), 119–135.

Donohue, W. A., & Kolt, R. (1992). *Managing interpersonal conflict*. Newbury Park, CA: Sage Publications.

Dubbelt, L., Rispens, S., & Demerouti, E. (2016). Gender discrimination and job characteristics. *Career Development International, 21*(3), 230–245.

Eva, K. W. (2009). The reviewer is always right: Peer reviewing of research in Medical Education. *Medical Education, 43*(1), 2–4.

Fanelli, D. (2018). Is science really facing a reproducibility crisis, and do we need it to? *Proceedings of the National Academy of Sciences, 115*(11), 2628–2631.

Grawitch, M. J., Barber, L. K., & Justice, L. (2010). Rethinking the work–life interface: It's not about balance, it's about resource allocation. *Applied Psychology: Health and Well-Being, 2*(2), 127–159.

Greenhaus, J. H., & Powell, G. N. (2006). When work and family are allies: A theory of work–family enrichment. *Academy of Management Review, 31*(1), 72–92.

Greer, L. L., & Jehn, K. A. (2007). The pivotal role of emotion in intragroup process conflict. *Research on Managing Groups and Teams, 10*, 23–45.

Greer, L. L., Jehn, K. A., & Mannix, E. A. (2008). Conflict transformation: A longitudinal investigation of the relationships between different types of intragroup conflict and the moderating role of conflict resolution. *Small Group Research, 39*(3), 278–302.

Haar, J. M., Russo, M., Suñe, A., & Ollier-Malaterre, A. (2014). Outcomes of work–life balance on job satisfaction, life satisfaction and mental health: A study across seven cultures. *Journal of Vocational Behavior, 85*(3), 361–373.

Imes, S. A. (1979). The impostor phenomenon as a function of attribution patterns and internalized femininity/masculinity in high-achieving women and men. (Doctoral dissertation, Georgia State University, 1979). *Dissertation Abstracts International, 40*, 5868B.

Jehn, K. A. (1994). Enhancing effectiveness: An investigation of advantages and disadvantages of value-based intragroup conflict. *International Journal of Conflict Management, 5*(3), 223–238.

Jehn, K. A. (1995). A multimethod examination of the benefits and detriments of intragroup conflict. *Administrative Science Quarterly, 40*(2), 256–282.

Jehn, K. A., & Bendersky, C. (2003). Intragroup conflict in organizations: A contingency perspective on the conflict–outcome relationship. *Research in Organizational Behavior, 25*, 187–242.

Jehn, K. A., & Mannix, E. A. (2001). The dynamic nature of conflict: A longitudinal study of intragroup conflict and group performance. *Academy of Management Journal, 44*(2), 238–251.

Jehn, K. A., Greer, L., Levine, S., & Szulanski, G. (2008). The effects of conflict types, dimensions, and emergent states on group outcomes. *Group Decision and Negotiation, 17*(6), 465–495.

Klein, R. A., Ratliff, K. A., Vianello, M., Adams Jr, R. B., Bahník, Š., Bernstein, M. J., ... & Cemalcilar, Z. (2014). Investigation Variation in Replicability: A "Many Labs" Replication Project. *Social Psychology, 45*, 142–152.

Marks, M. (1977). Organizational adjustment to uncertainty. *Journal of Management Studies, 14*(1), 1–7.

McNall, L. A., Nicklin, J. M., & Masuda, A. D. (2010). A meta-analytic review of the consequences associated with work–family enrichment. *Journal of Business and Psychology, 25*(3), 381–396.

Nabout, J. C., Parreira, M. R., Teresa, F. B., Carneiro, F. M., da Cunha, H. F., de Souza Ondei, L., ... & Soares, T. N. (2015). Publish (in a group) or perish (alone): The trend from single-to multi-authorship in biological papers. *Scientometrics, 102*(1), 357–364.

Perry-Jenkins, M., Repetti, R. L., & Crouter, A. C. (2000). Work and family in the 1990s. *Journal of Marriage and the Family, 62*(4), 981–998.

Peterson, R. S., & Ferguson, A. J. (2014). Strategies for developing trust through constructive conflict resolution in teams. In O. B. Ayoko, N. M. Ashkanasy, & K. A. Jehn (eds.), *Handbook of Conflict Management Research* (pp. 193–204). Cheltenham, UK and Northampton, MA, USA: Edward Elgar Publishing.

Rispens, S. (2014). Beneficial and detrimental effects of conflict. In C. B. Ayoko, N. M. Ashkanasy, & K. A. Jehn (eds.), *Handbook of Conflict Management Research* (pp. 19–32). Cheltenham, UK and Northampton, MA, USA: Edward Elgar Publishing.

Römer, M., Rispens, S., Giebels, E., & Euwema, M. (2012). A helping hand? The moderating role of leaders' conflict management behavior on the conflict-stress relationship of employees. *Negotiation Journal, 28*(3), 253–277.

Ruderman, M. N., Ohlott, P. J., Panzer, K., & King, S. N. (2002). Benefits of multiple roles for managerial women. *Academy of Management Journal, 45*(2), 369–386.

Schooler, J. W. (2014). Turning the lens of science on itself: Verbal overshadowing, replication, and metascience. *Perspectives on Psychological Science, 9*(5), 579–584.

Simonton, D. K. (2013). Scientific genius is extinct. *Nature, 493*, 602.

Steinel, W., Van Kleef, G. A., & Harinck, F. (2008). Are you talking to me?! Separating the people from the problem when expressing emotions in negotiation. *Journal of Experimental Social Psychology, 44*(2), 362–369.

Sturges, J. (2012). Crafting a balance between work and home. *Human Relations, 65*(12), 1539–1559.

Ten Brummelhuis, L. L. & Trougakos, J. P. (2013). The recovery potential of intrinsically versus extrinsically motivated off-job activities. *Journal of Occupational and Organizational Psychology, 87*(1), 177–199.

Tjosvold, D., Wong, A. S. H., & Feng Chen, N. Y. (2014). Constructively managing conflicts in organizations. *Annual Review of Organizational Psychology and Organizational Behavior, 1*, 545–568.

Topping, M. E., & Kimmel, E. B. (1985). The imposter phenomenon: Feeling phony. *Academic Psychology Bulletin, 7*(2), 213–226.

Van den Broeck, A., De Cuyper, N., De Witte, H., & Vansteenkiste, M. (2010). Not all job demands are equal: Differentiating job hindrances and job challenges in the Job Demands–Resources model. *European Journal of Work and Organizational Psychology, 19*(6), 735–759.

Vergauwe, J., Wille, B., Feys, M., De Fruyt, F., & Anseel, F. (2015). Fear of being exposed: The trait-relatedness of the impostor phenomenon and its relevance in the work context. *Journal of Business and Psychology, 30*(3), 565–581.

Volman, F. E, Bakker, A. B., & Xanthopoulou, D. (2013). Recovery at home and performance at work: A diary study on self-family facilitation. *European Journal of Work and Organizational Psychology, 22*(2), 218–234.

Want, J., & Kleitman, S. (2006). Imposter phenomenon and self-handicapping: Links with parenting styles and self-confidence. *Personality and Individual Differences, 40*(5), 961–971.

Whitman, M. V., & Shanine, K. K. (2012). Revisiting the impostor phenomenon: How individuals cope with feelings of being in over their heads. In P. L. Perrewé, J. R. B. Halbesleben, & C. C. Rosen (eds.), *The Role of the Economic Crisis on Occupational Stress and Well Being* (Vol. 10, pp. 177–212). London, UK: Emerald Group Publishing Limited.

PART V

Personal style within academia

13. The road taken: my personal odyssey in academia

Kristina Potočnik

Estimated reading time: **24 minutes and 11 seconds**.

CHAPTER HIGHLIGHTS

- Being humble in relation to your own potential and abilities is a far more effective characteristic for academic success than being arrogant.
- Doing 'service' to your discipline is eventually going to result in unexpected yet beneficial outcomes for your career.
- Focus on a few excellent projects that have the potential to become highly impactful in your field of interest rather than undertaking many different projects which are interesting but might not contribute significantly to the literature you hope to engage with.
- In order to maximize the success of collaborative projects, look for collaborators with compatible personalities, who are highly productive, are able to meet work commitments, have effective communication skills, and above all, can be trusted to work effectively and ethically.
- We tend to think we can do more than we actually can and the consequences of taking on too many commitments range from feelings of your own guilt to disappointment with you on behalf of your colleagues whom you let down.

> *Two roads diverged in a yellow wood,*
> *And sorry I could not travel both*
> *And be one traveler, long I stood*
> *And looked down one as far as I could*
> *To where it bent in the undergrowth.*
> Robert Frost

INTRODUCTION

Making a career decision is a complex and, for many individuals, strenuous process (Gati et al., 1996). There are many difficulties related to making career decisions, ranging from the lack of information about the process of how to choose a specific occupation to inherent indecisiveness or lack of readiness to choose a specific career path (Gati et al., 1996). Making a future career choice is arguably one of our most important life decisions, as it will, to a large extent, determine our lifestyle (Milot-Lapointe et al., 2018). It will structure our work and leisure time, it will provide us with financial rewards and benefits; determine our professional identity and sense of contribution to society and shape our social network. Therefore, when standing at the crossroads of career options, one has to really understand the implications of each and decide on one that one thinks would best fulfill the above-mentioned aspects.

Thinking of my beginnings in academia takes me back to the spring of 2003 when I started brainstorming about different topics for my bachelor's thesis research. I remember how passionate I felt about work and organizational psychology and how much more I wanted to understand about this specific field. This drive for further learning around the most recent advancements in the field is what motivated me to attend the European Conference of Work and Organizational Psychology in Lisbon in 2003. This was rather unusual, as back then it was not common to attend scientific conferences if you were not a doctoral student or a scholar. I am convinced that attending this conference has greatly shaped my preferred career choice, as, a year later, I decided to pursue my doctoral studies in the same field.

In this chapter, I will take you through my personal odyssey in academia starting from the very beginning of how I went about choosing my doctoral program to how I survived five intense years of doctoral studies, leading up to the desperation of looking for my first full-time academic job. As you will see, this has not only been a journey of many ups and downs, of occasional melt-downs, but also full of inspiring and gratifying moments. As I go through the different phases of my academic journey, I will refer to two overarching and recurring themes that have significantly shaped my career to date: serendipity and resilience.

For those who are interested in the ending before the story even begins – the road to becoming an academic that I set off on almost 15 years ago was the best choice I could have made and it is one I have never regretted taking.

I AM GRADUATING SOON BUT I WOULD LIKE TO LEARN MORE!

When I think back to my university years, I can still remember how scared I was of the idea of graduating from my bachelor's and having to find a job. All I could think about at that point in my life was that I really should learn a bit more if I was to excel as a practitioner psychologist. According to the career self-management perspective (Greenhaus et al., 2000), I was engaging in setting my career goals and developing the strategies of achieving these goals. Learning and improving personal skills and knowledge can be categorized as an intrinsic career goal and research has found that individuals with this type of goal are more inclined to look for further education (Seibert et al., 2013). Also, the fact that I really liked the idea of doing more research meant that I was naturally more inclined to look for postgraduate options in order to not only fulfill my research interests but also, much to my parents' dismay, to prolong my studies.

As I knew that work and organizational psychology was my field of interest, I decided to look for a postgraduate program that would specialize in this area. In the first place, the language barriers limited my options, as back then I could only work proficiently in either Slovenian or English. In Slovenia, we had no specialized postgraduate programs in this field (this is often called "the curse of small countries") and therefore of necessity I had to look for my options abroad. This brings me to a second barrier – the financial aspect. I had a small scholarship, which in some countries, such as the UK, would probably not even cover my monthly coffee intake. Therefore, I had to look for opportunities in more affordable places. As I was keen to learn Spanish for a while alongside furthering my knowledge of work and organizational psychology, I decided to explore opportunities in Spain. After evaluating different options, I decided to go for a doctoral program at the University of Valencia. This decision was, to a large extent, based on a serendipitous encounter with several members of staff who were teaching on this program during the European Conference of Work and Organizational Psychology I attended in Lisbon.

Serendipity, defined as the "accidental discovery of something valuable" (Cunha et al., 2010, p. 319), has played a key role in determining my academic journey. Applying for the doctoral program was largely based on luck and coincidence. If I had not attended quite an expensive academic conference as an undergraduate student who was about to embark on her final year at the university, I would most likely not have considered this program. It is important to highlight this, as deciding on a doctoral program is the first major factor in shaping your academic career.

Another factor that makes a difference is a person's resilience or the ability to successfully deal with, and recover from, stressful situations (Luthans, 2002). Although this was not my case, it is very likely you will have to apply to a number of programs in order to either secure a place on at least one of them or, hopefully, get onto more than just one and then have the luxury of choosing the one that fits your interests and goals best. Shortlisting the programs, contacting potential supervisors, crafting your research proposal, submitting it and waiting to hear back from the universities can be very stressful for an aspiring doctoral student. If you are going abroad like I did, you also need to factor in sworn translations of your transcripts and degrees, not to mention the mind-numbing visa applications. These processes require a lot of work and can be very lengthy, often with unpredictable outcomes – in other words, they can be a significant cause of stress. More resilient people are likely to appraise such stressful situations as less threatening and hence are able to cope with them more effectively compared to those who are less resilient (Lazarus, 1993). Taking into account that pursuing an academic career is a journey ripe with stressful events, ranging from high rejection rates for publications and grant submissions to continuous and often highly critical scrutiny of your teaching and research by your students and peers (Baruch & Hall, 2004), it is necessary to start highlighting the importance of resilience for a successful academic journey from the very begining.

I AM IN – BUT CAN I DO THIS?

Not surprisingly, receiving an offer from the university of your choice (and in my case, from the only program I had applied for) is a source of incredible relief and reassurance. *Yes, I can do this!* But, can I? Unfortunately, the self-doubt and worry of failing is very common when you embark on any new career opportunity (Andrews et al., 2014) and pursuing a doctorate and ultimately an academic career are not exempt from this. I would dare to say that it is this constant interrogation of your own capabilities of completing a doctoral program successfully that ultimately determines your academic success. When we question how much we know of a certain theory or how good we are at conducting a specific data analysis, we are either in fact identifying our knowledge gaps, striving to better ourselves or, preferably, reassuring ourselves that we actually know this stuff already. Therefore, being humble in relation to your own potential and abilities is a far more effective characteristic for academic success than being arrogant (de Vries, de Vries, & Born, 2011; Rowatt et al., 2006). I will come to this point later on again, but I do think it is important to highlight this here, as many doctoral students fall into a trap of feeling self-important and seeing themselves as masters of their universe just because they got onto a doctoral program. Do not do that!

As a doctoral student, you will soon realize how cruel the academic world can be. You will be subjected to incessant scrutiny and critique and you will just have to get on with it. If you are humble, you will be able to deal with all this much better and in a more constructive way than if you have an arrogant, I-know-it-all attitude. Also, resilience can help deal with situations of intense scrutiny. You need to be able to cope with negative feedback and act upon it in order to improve the quality of your work.

These feelings of self-doubt will likely persist all the way up to your Viva[1] but you will have many opportunities of getting the reassurance that you are on the right track. The obvious advice is to start attending academic conferences as soon as you can. These offer many serendipitous encounters that can shape your career (for the better!) as I explained earlier was the case for me. They are not only instrumental in showcasing your research, but also in starting to build your network. To stand any chance at all of getting research funding nowadays you have to apply with an international collaborative team of colleagues from your field. Presenting your findings at an academic conference is a great opportunity to start building such teams. Also, you might be lucky that the leading experts from your field are in the audience when you present, in which case you are likely going to get more rigorous, spot-on, but also possibly more negative than positive feedback about your project. So, remember – humility and resilience are the keys to leveraging on rather than dwelling on feedback! Finally, participating at conferences can open up other career-enhancing opportunities for you, such as getting invitations from guest editors to contribute to their special issues in journals in your field of interest.

Apart from conferences, do not be shy in actively soliciting feedback from your peers on the doctoral program and of course your supervisors. The saying "There is no such thing as too much feedback" fully applies when it comes to your doctoral research. You may not always agree with the feedback you get, you may not always be able to act upon it, but, at the very least, learning about what others think of your research will make you think in critical or alternative ways about your own work.

One last point about feedback. You would be surprised at how much you learn about your own research strengths and flaws from reading and commenting on other people's work. Reviewing manuscripts for journals and conferences as a doctoral student was a revelation for me in this respect. I know some think of reviewing as a chore but it is a necessary chore for ensuring that only the best and most rigorous studies get published. Therefore, you should always carry out reviews for journals, not only for the sake of collegiality and doing a service to your discipline but also for slightly less altruistic reasons. Reviewing and commenting on other people's work will give you the opportunity to learn about what others in your field are doing well ahead of their work being published. This can give you more (and timely) ideas about how to improve your own research. You might even find out that someone has already conducted a very similar study to yours, in which case you will have an opportunity to amend your initial idea in order to improve the novelty of your research and increase its publication potential. You might also learn about some very useful references, which you need for the justification of, for instance, the specific methodological choice in your research. Therefore, my last advice to you as doctoral students is to engage in reviewing as much as you can.

Getting through the doctoral program is tough. It is a journey with countless up and downs, constant self-doubt, and reflexivity about whether this was the right choice and whether you will ever get to the end of it at all. Trust me, perseverance is key as well as resilience (yes, it really is important) and, to some extent, serendipitous encounters along the way. For instance, getting an invitation to write a particular book chapter just because I happened to be at the social hour of such and such division at a particular conference is what I am referring to here.

I DID IT – WHAT NEXT?

As you have probably gathered, the title of my chapter is inspired by Robert Frost and his poem "The Road Not Taken" in which he tried to suggest that he regretted his decision of taking "the road less traveled by" (Frost & Untermeyer, 2002). I do not know much about American literature nor can I pretend to be a literary critic, but I interpret this poem from the opposite angle. For me, this poem is about a crossroads offering different options and the one that will eventually be chosen will largely determine the life of an individual. The road I took 15 years ago was the one that has made all the difference to not just my career but also my life. Getting a doctorate meant that the obvious career choice for me would be in academia. Other options such as consultancy or working in industry were far less appealing to me because I felt the research skills and networks that I had developed during my studies were better suited to academic work. Although I knew that it was not going to be easy, I really did not expect job hunting in academia to be that hard. After all, I had successfully survived five years of doctoral studies – what can be harder than that, right?

Well, let me tell you. My funding finished 10 days after my Viva and I officially became an unemployed person. Claiming unemployment benefits after having studied for 22 years of my life was quite soul-destroying for me. There is extensive research highlighting the detrimental effects of unemployment on individual mental health and well-being (McKee-Ryan et al., 2005; Paul & Moser, 2009). Applying a concept of "déformation professionnelle", defined as the psychological tendency to see and interpret situations from the perspective of one's professional knowledge and experience (Henriksen, 2018), I could tell how all the premises of one of the key theories that helps explain the effects of unemployment on individuals could be applied to my own case.

The theory of latent deprivation (Jahoda, 1981, 1982) suggests that work not only provides individuals with manifest benefits, such as salary, but also with a set of latent benefits which are also important for achieving well-being. These latent benefits are: (1) having social contact, which refers to the opportunity of establishing relationships with individuals other than family members; (2) having status, which refers to the social identity that work on its own or working for a specific organization provides; (3) a clear time structure, which refers to the division of time across multiple tasks in a day; (4) enhanced activity, which refers to individual physical and psychological activation as a result of one's work; and (5) having a sense of collective purpose, which refers to one's perception of how much one is contributing to a cause that transcends oneself and represents a greater good. Those who are unemployed are lacking these latent benefits of work, which in turn has implications on a range of unemployed individuals' outcomes, including their well-being (Muller & Waters, 2012; Paul & Batinic, 2010; Selenko et al., 2011).

Apart from having social contact (because I had managed to build a strong social network during my studies), I was lacking all these latent benefits derived from work. I would particularly highlight the lack of social status, which was especially hard to accept. I felt I was an unproductive member of society who, in addition, was an immigrant on benefits. As you can guess, and what the latent deprivation theory so aptly predicts, I was not feeling good about myself and my life and, therefore, my main priority was to find a job as soon as possible.

My job hunting included submissions of a number of applications to different Spanish and British universities. Eventually, after six months of calvary, I was successful in applying for a postdoc position at Brunel University London, UK. Interestingly, I came across this job ad while I was editing a newsletter for the Division of Organisational Psychology of the IAAP (International Association of Applied Psychology) and my future line manager, a fellow of the IAAP, sent the ad over to us to include in our newsletter! So, serendipity kicked in again – if I had not been editing the ad to be included in the newsletter, I would most likely have missed out on this opportunity as I would often just skim through any electronic newsletters at best. The lesson here is that as doctoral students you should not turn away opportunities for getting involved in all sorts of professional and collegiate activities. Although these types of jobs are voluntary in nature and, most of the time, provide no financial incentive, doing 'service' to your discipline is eventually going to result in unexpected yet beneficial outcomes for your career.[2] Going back to the importance of reviewing for journals mentioned earlier, my advice for you is to consider being a successful giver (Grant, 2013) – have a concern for your own self-interests while at the same time give your time to your academic community.

I am convinced I survived these first six post-PhD months of uncertainty, countless rejections, and increased anxiety about what was going to happen once my unemployment benefits ended only because by that point I had built up sufficient amounts of resilience to be able to cope. Similar to dealing with demands of all sorts while doing a doctorate, resilience was a key resource I leveraged while looking for a job. There is evidence to suggest that resilient unemployed individuals are more likely to believe in their skills and their employability and hence persevere more in looking for a job than those who are less resilient (Chen & Lim, 2012). This was evident again later on when my two-year postdoc position was ending and I had to look for yet another job. This time I was much better prepared for the rejections and, in fact, I felt like I was a "professional" job hunter by that point. I got my permanent full-time job at the University of Edinburgh, where I still work, within the first three years of having completed my doctorate.

THE AFTERMATH

Academic life is undoubtedly tough. I am not aiming for this chapter to be about my survival story as I am not sure I have survived just yet. In the beginning of my postdoc career, I started working on one particular project, which resulted in a top publication[3] and opened the door for me to one of the best universities in the world. Since then, I have always tried to focus on fewer rather than many different projects with the aim of producing highly impactful pieces, albeit with varying degrees of success. I know this will vary from country to country but based on a recent study by Podsakoff et al. (2018) and my own experience, my general advice for you is to focus on a few excellent projects that have the potential to become highly impactful in your field of interest rather than undertaking many different projects which are interesting but might not contribute significantly to the literature you hope to engage with. Establishing a well-designed program of research at the beginning of your career will help you with this focus and enable you to position yourself within your chosen scholarly network. Getting other colleagues involved in your research program is also important, not only for gaining another perspective on your ideas but also for sharing the load involved in conducting research and writing it all up. To maximize the success of collaborative projects, for instance in terms of successful funding applications, you are advised to at least work alongside a "partner" or a co-investigator who will help you with the actual proposal writing as well as an esteemed colleague or "the sage" who will mainly be instrumental in shaping the research idea and crucially adding credibility to the project (Galdas, 2016).

Collaborative research nowadays seems to be taken as given across different disciplines and only slight gender differences have been observed in relation to research collaborations, with women apparently having slightly more collaborators than men (Bozeman & Gaughan, 2011). However, there are many factors to consider when choosing colleagues for effective research collaboration (Bozeman et al., 2016). In order to maximize the success of collaborative projects, one should look for collaborators with compatible personalities, who are highly productive, are able to meet work commitments, have effective communication skills, and, above all, can be trusted to work effectively and ethically (Bozeman et al., 2016). When thinking of collaborative research from this perspective, I am sure we can all think of examples when we were not set up for success. According to Bozeman et al. (2016), factors that are detrimental to effective collaboration most often relate to issues of not delivering the agreed portion of the project on time, crediting disputes and so-called ghost authorship, which occurs when you work with people who claim credit for work they have not done or insist on co-authoring your work despite not having contributed to it at all.

I am sure we all have at least some experience of such "bad" collaborations, and the lesson here is to be able to recognize when the collaborative project can go wrong and withdraw sooner rather than later. I have worked on projects that were not set up for success and although I could see early signs that the project was doomed to fail, I persisted. This irrational behavior on my behalf can best be explained with the so-called sunk cost bias or our tendency "to pursue a course of action even after it has proved to be suboptimal, because resources have been invested in that course of action" (Braverman & Blumenthal-Barby, 2012, p. 187). Upon reflection, this has most likely been my biggest mistake to date – not giving up on collaborations when it was quite clear that they would not result in any successful outcomes.

Furthermore, working on collaborative projects, which might not be strictly aligned with your research program, is also worth considering. Since the very beginning of my career, I have been extremely fortunate in establishing collaborations with a diverse group of people, ranging from my fellow PhD colleagues to my PhD supervisors and other staff involved in my doctoral program. This has taught me about research trends in other areas and has helped me diversify my interests and expand my publication record, but, more importantly, I managed to achieve this without losing sight of my own primary research interests. This takes me back to my point about establishing a well-designed program of research – in order to be a credible scholar, you have to be able to construct a narrative of your contribution and research trajectory for the medium- to long-term. If you diversify in your research too much, you might find it difficult to achieve this. Only a few people are smart enough to make a significant contribution and change the conversations about specific phenomena in more than one or two areas.

In summary, the complexity of the phenomena that we are studying across the social sciences, with an increasing focus on multidisciplinary research that requires ever more complex methodology and research designs, will dictate collaborative research in the future (Bozeman et al., 2016). Working in a collaborative team requires a great deal of patience and resilience, as many things can go wrong at different stages of the project. More importantly, if you think the problems cannot be solved, be prepared to abandon the project and move on to greener pastures.

Another lesson I would like to share with you is the importance of learning the art of saying "no". This is still a work in progress for me, but, for the past few years, I have turned down some offers of collaborative projects. I have learned that we always think we can do more than we actually can and the consequences of taking on too many commitments range from feelings of your own guilt to disappointment with you from the colleagues you let down. There is always space for collaborating with your colleagues, but make sure you commit to it when the time is right.

One final lesson I could share with you is about the importance of writing. Try to write every day, even if only for one hour. Although the quality of your writing is obviously important for publishing your work, establishing a writing habit is crucial to becoming a successful academic (Pollock & Bono, 2013; Silvia, 2007). Therefore, establishing such a habit should be your main priority at the beginning of your career. As with any habit, once in place, you will get used to it!

MY FINAL THOUGHTS

The aim of this book is to share our idiosyncratic experience of doing academic business with you and therefore, by default, we are each telling a different story. I have never written such a personal reflection of my own academic odyssey. Now at the end, I feel it has been a proper cathartic experience – I had never even realized I had so many repressed emotions in relation to my doctoral studies and early postdoc years. My last piece of advice for you, therefore, is that you keep a journal or a diary in order to vent your frustrations as you go through your studies. Anecdotally speaking, I am sure that this is better for your well-being than holding it in or denying that it has been a tough journey.

And the very final advice to you (the last one, I promise), which truly is important to highlight when telling a story such as this one, refers to keeping a work–life balance. Some of the habits that you must establish in order to be a successful scholar, such as a writing habit, can quickly swirl into a non-stop activity, but you need to know when to stop and make time for leisure. You need to enjoy your doctoral studies and have fun while you are doing it because at the end of the day all work and no play makes people very miserable.

NOTES

1. Viva stands for viva voce or "the examination conducted by speech" (Hartley & Fox, 2004, p. 727). In the context of doctoral studies, it refers to the last step before getting a degree. The way in which the Viva is conducted varies across countries, ranging from a completely public defense with an audience in Scandinavia and Spain to a mail examination in Australia and a private event in which a doctoral student sits in front of a committee of two to three examiners in the UK (Hartley & Fox, 2004).
2. Doing service to your discipline in terms of reviewing for journals and supporting academic associations might eventually lead to more important and visible roles, such as editorships of all sorts at the journals in your field of interest. Most universities highly value such roles when considering applications for promotion.
3. The publication I am referring to here is Anderson et al. (2014). This paper has been cited more than 2 000 times and has won the Emerald Citation of Excellence Award and Journal of Management Scholarly Impact Award.

REFERENCES

Anderson, N., Potočnik, K., & Zhou, J. (2014). Innovation and creativity in organizations: A state-of-the-science review and prospective commentary. *Journal of Management*, *40*(5), 1297–1333.

Andrews, L. M., Bullock-Yowell, E., Dahlen, E. R., & Nicholson, B. C. (2014). Can perfectionism affect career development? Exploring career thoughts and self-efficacy. *Journal of Counseling & Development*, *92*(3), 270–279.

Baruch, Y., & Hall, D. T. (2004). The academic career: A model for future careers in other sectors? *Journal of Vocational Behavior*, *64*(2), 241–262.

Bozeman, B., & Gaughan, M. (2011). How do men and women differ in research collaborations? An analysis of the collaborative motives and strategies of academic researchers. *Research Policy*, *40*(10), 1393–1402. doi:10.1016/j.respol.2011.07.002.

Bozeman, B., Gaughan, M., Youtie, J., Slade, C. P., & Rimes, H. (2016). Research collaboration experiences, good and bad. Dispatches from the front lines. *Science and Public Policy*, *43*(2), 226–244.

Braverman, J. A., & Blumenthal-Barby, J. S. (2012). Assessment of the sunk-cost effect in clinical decision-making. *Social Science & Medicine*, *75*(1), 186–192.

Chen, D., & Lim, V. (2012). Strength in adversity: The influence of psychological capital on job search. *Journal of Organizational Behavior*, *33*(6), 811–839.

Cunha, M. P. e., Clegg, S. R., & Mendonça, S. (2010). On serendipity and organizing. *European Management Journal*, *28*(5), 319–330.

de Vries, A., de Vries, R. E., & Born, M. P. (2011). Broad versus narrow traits: Conscientiousness and Honesty–Humility as predictors of academic criteria. *European Journal of Personality*, *25*(5), 336–348.

Frost, R., & Untermeyer, L. (2002). *The Road Not Taken: A Selection of Robert Frost's Poems*. New York, NY: Henry Holt and Company.

Galdas, P. M. (2016). Who is writing what? A proposed taxonomy of roles and responsibilities when collaboratively writing a research proposal. *International Journal of Qualitative Methods*, *15*(1), 1–3.

Gati, I., Krausz, M., & Osipow, S. H. (1996). A taxonomy of difficulties in career decision making. *Journal of Counseling Psychology*, *43*(4), 510–526.

Grant, A. (2013). *Give and Take: A Revolutionary Approach to Success*. New York, NY: Hachette.

Greenhaus, J. H., Callanan, G. A., & Godshalk, V. M. (2000). *Career Management (3rd ed.)*. Fort Worth, TX: Harcourt.

Hartley, J., & Fox, C. (2004). Assessing the mock viva: The experiences of British doctoral students. *Studies in Higher Education*, *29*(6), 727–738.

Henriksen, D. (2018). *The 7 Transdisciplinary Cognitive Skills for Creative Education*. Cham: Springer International Publishing.

Jahoda, M. (1981). Work, employment, and unemployment: Values, theories, and approaches in social research. *American Psychologist*, *36*(2), 184–191.

Jahoda, M. (1982). *Employment and Unemployment: A Social–Psychological Analysis*. Cambridge, MA: Cambridge University Press.

Lazarus, R. S. (1993). From psychological stress to the emotions: A history of changing outlooks. *Annual Review of Psychololgy*, *44*(1), 1–22.

Luthans, F. (2002). The need for and meaning of positive organizational behavior. *Journal of Organizational Behavior*, *23*(6), 695–706.

McKee-Ryan, F. M., Song, Z., Wanberg, C. R., & Kinicki, A. J. (2005). Psychological and physical well-being during unemployment: A meta-analytic study. *Journal of Applied Psychology*, *90*(1), 53–76.

Milot-Lapointe, F., Savard, R., & Le Corff, Y. (2018). Intervention components and working alliance as predictors of individual career counseling effect on career decision-making difficulties. *Journal of Vocational Behavior*, *107*, 15–24.

Muller, J., & Waters, L. (2012). A review of the Latent and Manifest Benefits (LAMB) scale. *Australian Journal of Career Development*, *21*(1), 31–37.

Paul, K. I., & Batinic, B. (2010). The need for work: Jahoda's latent functions of employment in a representative sample of the German population. *Journal of Organizational Behavior*, *31*(1), 45–64.

Paul, K. I., & Moser, K. (2009). Unemployment impairs mental health: Meta-analyses. *Journal of Vocational Behavior*, *74*(3), 264–282.

Podsakoff, P., Podsakoff, N., Mishra, P., & Escue, C. (2018). Can early-career scholars conduct impactful research? Playing "small ball" versus "swinging for the fences". *Academy of Management Learning & Education*, *17*(4), 496–531.

Pollock, T. G., & Bono, J. E. (2013). From the Editors: Being Scheherazade: The importance of storytelling in academic writing. (Editorial). *Academy of Management Journal*, *56*(3), 629–634.

Rowatt, W. C., Powers, C., Targhetta, V., Comer, J., Kennedy, S., & Labouff, J. (2006). Development and initial validation of an implicit measure of humility relative to arrogance. *The Journal of Positive Psychology*, *1*(4), 198–211.

Seibert, S. E., Kraimer, M. L., Holtom, B. C., & Pierotti, A. J. (2013). Even the best laid plans sometimes go askew: Career self-management processes, career shocks, and the decision to pursue graduate education. *Journal of Applied Psychology*, *98*(1), 169–182.

Selenko, E., Batinic, B., & Paul, K. (2011). Does latent deprivation lead to psychological distress? Investigating Jahoda's model in a four-wave study. *Journal of Occupational and Organizational Psychology*, *84*(4), 723–740.

Silvia, P. J. (2007). *How to Write a Lot: A Practical Guide to Productive Academic Writing* (1st ed.). Washington, DC: American Psychological Association.

14. Changing the tunes: an academic career story

Joana Story

Estimated reading time: **22 minutes and 23 seconds**.

CHAPTER HIGHLIGHTS

- By doing a good job, showing up, and making yourself available, people start to trust you, and, with that, you gain your reputation and develop more credibility.
- Do not stay away from political fights, but pick the right ones: the ones that truly make a difference.
- Do not ignore internal politics; understand that you should develop political skills to be successful.
- Consider cultural fit when making career decisions.
- Have a strategic approach to connections, relationships, and appointments.

If we are going to live with our deepest differences
then we must learn about one another.
Deborah J. Levine

INTRODUCTION

Reflecting on a professional journey is an exercise many should engage in. I learned a lot from the process. However, I must confess that writing this book chapter has been a challenge. As an academic, I am used to writing, but very infrequently use the first person while doing it (an exception is an essay from an early career; see Story, 2013). As an individual, I feel that while some of my experiences may be interesting and relevant to share with others, it feels very self-indulgent. As a woman, I am concerned about voicing some of my experiences, as they can be seen as "political" or "having an agenda".

So, as I describe my journey, I wanted to make one thing clear: this is my experience, my voice, and my career. I moved to three different countries in three different continents. I made career moves that are probably not perceived as strategic or don't make sense to some people. I put more value on my personal preferences than career ones. I don't have any regrets. It didn't always feel that way and it doesn't discount the fear and anxieties that I still have. I like what I do. I like my research. I like my life. So, any perceived tips or advice you may take from this, keep in mind the different contexts, expectations, and values we may have. You will hear about music, tunes, and rhythm in this chapter. Full disclosure: I know very little about music, I am completely out of tune, and I am a horrible dancer. I *do* enjoy a good metaphor though …

CHANGING THE TUNES

My academic journey started over ten years ago when I entered a master's program. I never wanted to become an academic, never thought I would actually enjoy it, and most importantly, I had no idea what an academic life would entail. But I enjoyed the dance. It made sense to me, I studied, worked hard, and received feedback. I had a wonderful mentor and advisor who believed in me and pushed me to become better. I was this young Brazilian woman in the United States with a strong accent and he encouraged me to teach, write, and present my work at conferences. The academic life I never envisioned had just become a reality. I decided to continue on with my PhD at the University of Nebraska-Lincoln. These years were very challenging and they helped me find my own rhythm. They helped clarify my research priorities, what type of academic I wanted to become, and, more importantly, *how* I wanted to become that academic.

One of the most challenging experiences as a young scholar is to find that first job. How to make the selection? Where to work? How to behave in an interview? How do you negotiate your salary? There are too many questions, many unknowns, and a lot of competition. Having experienced recruiting and selection of academics in search committees now, I look frequently at the CV of PhD candidates and see that year after year their CVs are stronger and they are more strategic. When I was about to finish my PhD, I was neither. I had a decent CV and letters of recommendation, and was very open to a global search mostly because I like new experiences and new challenges. I was looking for fit and quality of life. I was not looking for a specific university. I selected where I wanted to live, and then I looked for the school. Therefore, I explored the areas of the United States that I liked the most, Europe, and Brazil. It felt extremely risky and challenging making that decision: what is going to happen with my career? I heard one piece of good advice: "Just because they want you, it doesn't mean you need to say yes. Don't confuse flattery with fit." I took this to heart and made a decision that was both strategic and personal.

I ended up in a school in Portugal (Nova School of Business and Economics) that had a position that truly matched my interests; it was in a great city, in a great country, and in a reputable school. Furthermore, since I spoke the language, it seemed "easier" in terms of adaptation. While I investigated the university further, I really liked what I learned. The school is extremely international, has quality academics, and prioritizes research. After 8 years and getting tenure, I am back in Brazil. I spent 17 years away and now that I am home it feels very foreign to me.

It has been a little over eight years since I finished my PhD. Thus far, it has been an interesting journey full of exciting and fascinating learning experiences and I have taken many things away from it. In order to tell my story in the form of a chapter, I will draw on four different types of music/dance as metaphors: *fado*, *samba*, *capoeira*, and *choro* (Figure 14.1). Within each of these phases four themes have emerged and carried over and are still relevant: *being a woman*, *dealing with politics*, what it means to work in countries that are *less well known* in academia, and, finally, the impact of *community* (Figure 14.2). "Being a woman" highlights the impact that gender roles play in academia. "Dealing with politics" highlights how you handle/deal with organizational politics plays a role in your success. "Less well known" highlights the perceptions of working in environments that are not "famous". "Community" highlights the impact that surrounding yourself with a good support group is key. This construct emerged as a key theme, as it related to all the others.

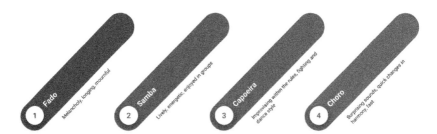

Figure 14.1   *Phases of my academic career*

FADO

Fado is music of longing; it is a little mournful and melancholic with a sense of longing. It is considered the soul of Portuguese music and it is beautiful. Well, when I arrived in Portugal that was my general feeling. My ideas about academia came from a very US-centric perspective and as soon as I arrived at

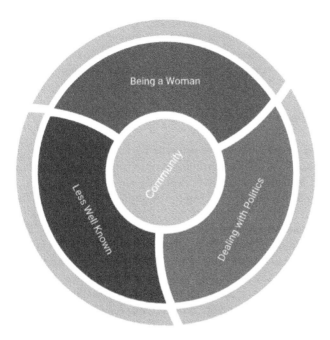

Figure 14.2   Common themes through the phases

the school I realized that, while the model is applied there, the experiences/
challenges are different. Thus, I was lost and missed the comfort of what
I knew. Even though I knew that the Portuguese system was going to be
different, I was anticipating that the commonalities would be larger. I made
a mistake that a scholar of cross-cultural management should not have made:
I minimized the differences. And there were many differences: My students
were mostly foreign; the teaching faculty was quite diverse; due to the Bologna
agreement, students popped in and out; the undergraduate degree was only
three years; and there was a pre-experience master's program (non-academic);
the academic master's and PhD were also less structured, which made it harder
to have access to students, which meant less access to research assistants
(unless you got a grant from the government).

These differences were so challenging but so interesting that it took me
about two years to get a small understanding of the new system, my new
students, and colleagues. It is also important to highlight that there were many
adaptations, that should not be undermined: adaptation to not only a new
institution (university) and a new environment (country) but also a new job
(position) – I was no longer a graduate student who could rely on an advisor

and a support system. I was responsible for my career, the opportunities, and the consequences of my decision-making. It was terrifying. Not unlike many people that move to a different country, I wanted to leave. In fact, a couple of colleagues that arrived with me left after a year. I stayed. But I was still looking around and got a couple of job offers. In addition to these adaptations, some themes made this journey richer and complicated and they bear a discussion.

Being a Woman

I cannot discuss the first few years as an academic without talking about gender roles. In a business school environment, it is not uncommon to be dominated by males. In my first couple of years at the new school, while I did not have to deal with overt sexism ("A post-doc who persisted", 2017; Hardy, 2018; Suggs, 2018) from any of my colleagues, there was a general lack of awareness that gender roles and support for woman academics was necessary. I only had one female colleague that did research in a field close to mine and she was more senior. I was also the only foreign woman hired, therefore, I felt often left out of many discussions as I was not Portuguese (even though I spoke Portuguese) and did not understand many of the cultural references and jokes, but also I didn't have a support system. I also remember being very defensive teaching in the beginning as students wanted to "test" me in the classroom and I had to earn their respect in many ways that my male colleagues did not (I checked this). I learned how to deal with it by calling out these behaviors when appropriate and discussing them with powerful allies, and it became less of a concern.

Dealing with Internal Politics

As a graduate student, you are more or less aware of the political environment in your school, or department (at least I was). As a young academic I was very naïve and self-righteous about not wanting to deal with it and dismissing the impact that politics could have on your career. Therefore, I easily accepted many things that perhaps I shouldn't have when it came to some procedures, classes, or even sharing an office. I was frustrated by it and I internalized it, but reflecting on it, I am glad that I did not address *some* of these issues. They were not that important, and because I did not make a big deal out of it, I was not seen as a difficult person, which made my life easier in the following years.

"Less Well Known"

I also did not realize that there was so much academic "snobbery" when you decide to go to a less well-known school. Many people in the United States assumed that I did not get a job there and that's why I went abroad. I was just shocked to be all the sudden perceived as a "second rate" academic by some of my acquaintances. I remember going to the Academy of Management Meeting in my second year at Nova SBE, and many people that appeared eager to talk to me, looked directly at my name tag, and decided that I wasn't worth talking to. It was kind of funny and annoying at the same time. It is paradoxical that academics could be so close minded about the world.

Community

The slow-forming, trusting relationships that I began to form with colleagues made a big difference in my adaptation, and in my success in the first years. The school hired more people and more women, and I started working with some colleagues there. This improved my connections, my understanding of the system, and my relationships with students. I had people to talk and to complain to. I had people that helped to keep my expectations in check.

Slowly, I began to understand my new role and its expectations. Once I realized how the music was played, things became clearer and I was able to change the tune. One that, as a Brazilian, I was most familiar with.

SAMBA

Samba is energetic and lively. It is enjoyed in groups. After the isolation and melancholy of fado, I learned what steps to take and who to talk to or partner up with to make sure the "dance" would succeed. Thus, in this phase, partnerships with Portuguese colleagues were formed and a rhythm was clear.

I became more open and asked to be more involved in projects. I started developing relationships with master's students who wanted to do their thesis project with me and learned more about the Portuguese environment, their organizations. I learned ways to overcome some of the main challenges such as data collection through involvement with students and partnerships. I also began to be more involved with other programs in the school, such as executive education classes, and to overall engage more with the school. The school also continued to hire more foreign professors and we developed relationships that made life in and out of the school more pleasant.

Being a Woman

Studying the importance of diversity in organizations was always a topic of interest of mine.[1] However, it was only in this phase of my life that I could truly recognize the importance of having people like you in the workplace. The school hired two women that had a big impact on my career. One was a foreign professor like me – she and I got along great. She was from another department, but we became close friends. We could make sense of our feelings and environment together; we could share some of our concerns about being a woman in the school, primarily how to deal with students that would treat us differently or complain about things that we knew none of our other colleagues had to deal with. This brought a great sense of community, a sense of belonging (Morrison, 2002). The other was a Portuguese woman who studied similar things and understood the Portuguese culture. She helped me make sense of potential cross-cultural misunderstandings and gave me support. I relied on them heavily. In a male-dominant school, this was very important.

Dealing with Politics

In this phase, dealing with politics became easier, as I was more or less familiar with the rules and the "game". I also developed more power, as more people knew me. This was such an important phase and learning experience for me. I learned that by doing a good job, showing up, and making yourself available, people start to trust you and, with that, you gain your reputation and develop more credibility. I also learned not to stay away from "fights" but to pick the right ones: the ones that truly make a difference. I now know that taking your time and not jumping through people or "hoops" was a more effective strategy for me in that specific context.

"Less Well Known"

I started to look at the opportunities that come from being in a less well-known school versus its perceived shortcomings. I learned from my foreign students, conducted cross-cultural research, and learned about the impact that having access to certain environments has. For example, in this phase, I had the incredible and unique experience of teaching executives in Angola. It was an environment that was new, less researched, difficult, and I had some access to it.

Community

In the Samba phase, mentorship and friendship marked the community aspect. With the many incoming young foreign scholars, the school started to organize itself differently, and we were assigned a mentor. My mentor, Miguel Pina e Cunha, is a top scholar in the field, Portuguese, and extremely open to helping. He helped me navigate the service, teaching, and research aspects of academia. He also helped to keep me grounded. My friendships made the experience joyous, exciting, and energetic. With more involvement and engagement, the more I learned about this new environment and new context, the more new interests started to emerge, and soon the music changed its tune to capoeira.

CAPOEIRA

Capoeira is quick, complex, and is a mixture of dance and martial arts. Capoeira also has its origins in Africa. While there are clear steps (i.e. jinga) it is also improvised as you do not know "who" you will be "playing" against. The idea is that you enter an environment in which you understand the most important rules and know the game but you still have to make sense of it and work with others. Capoeira lets you improvise within rules but it is also a fighting style. In this phase I was more confident, I took more risks, I picked more "fights" and started to exert a little more of my influence. I took on more executive education, master's and PhD students, and research-centered work. I was also going for tenure/promotion.

Being a Woman

Not surprisingly, within my role in the school, this was no longer a concern. I had already developed a reputation and students knew how I was. However, at this stage I started teaching executive education much more frequently and had very good evaluations, but not infrequently I encountered some comments/ concerns from students about my experience. I received some comments in my evaluations that I was "too feminist", that I was biased (even though I made a point of only presenting studies) towards women, etc. While this in the past probably would have been seen as negative to me, in the capoeira phase, I felt that I was doing my job and was completely comfortable with the feedback. Another concern also presented itself with the more executive classes I taught: some male students would comment on how I looked, dressed, and one was even winking at me as I was teaching a class. Navigating through this was interesting and I made a point of correcting some behaviors and pointing out how they were inappropriate. This was tiring.

Dealing with Politics

In this phase, politically, my main concern was dealing with the tenure clock, submitting my papers for promotion, making sure that certain accomplishments were not undervalued, but at the same time "being nice". The balance of strongly selling yourself and at the same time not "being pushy" was quite complicated and related to my gender. Because the school had by then established more or less clear processes, this insecurity and uncertainty about the tenure process was less of a concern. In fact, I got unanimously voted for tenure and it was not a surprise because of all of the processes that the school had put into place such as mentorship and clear objective rules.

"Less Well Known"

This also became less of a concern, as the school became more and more well known in Europe. The school was climbing up the rankings, I relied less and less on the North American environment, and Portugal was becoming a key and attractive place to live and work. In conferences, my colleagues and I started to be recognized: people wanted to talk to us. I often received emails from people asking how it was to work at the school, etc. Interesting changes were occurring, and by no means as a result of something that I was responsible for.

Community

In this phase, the community, while expanded, was also closely tied. The number of people I trusted and worked with increased a bit but I was also very protected to my relationships. The community expanded to many other individuals such as administrators, employees, students, organizations, and media. I was known there. I was invited to many occasions and events. The challenge in this phase was to say no to the things that did not add value or to which I felt I couldn't contribute. So juggling these roles of not being a junior faculty anymore was challenging and my universe expanded. My close relationships were key in order for me to be confident enough to say no while not hurting potential opportunities.

I was confident, comfortable, and enjoying my life and experiences. However, as many individuals who live outside their own country and away from family understand, you start to question and wonder if that's where you want to spend the rest of your life. After 17 years of living abroad, and after eight years in Portugal, I received a phone call from a colleague in a school in Brazil wondering if I was interested in applying for a position. Many personal reasons but also great timing made me sing a different tune: choro.

CHORO

Choro is a Brazilian style of music that approaches European classical music and in many ways it is also similar to jazz, even though it pre-dates it. Choro is known for the large leaps in its melody and its dizzying speeds, surprising changes of harmony and improvised sound. This best describes my decision and experience of moving back to Brazil. While Brazil is my home country, São Paulo is not my home city. I was less familiar with the educational system than I care to admit. I moved to a school that is very large and traditional, so I was completely unfamiliar with the culture of academia, the school, and my department. Many rules and norms that are completely obvious to many were not obvious to me. The faculty is less international, and it was assumed that because I am Brazilian I would know most of it. I am learning to navigate this as a choro player: naturally and spontaneously. I just finished my first semester and it is a comfort that many things stay the same: classes, students, and university procedures. It is more or less relevant as well that the four themes from the past also emerged in this environment.

Being a Woman

The importance of having key women in leadership positions has become even more relevant here. While the top management of the school currently is male, there have been female deans before. In fact, they are professors at the school and exert power. Thus far, I have not perceived any issues with gender differences. Not unlike other business school environments, there are more senior male professors but the department head is female. In the classroom, I have not felt or perceived any testing as I did in the past, or comments that could be perceived as problematic from my undergraduates and executives alike. I am not naïve enough to think that my age and experience is irrelevant to this. I believe that it makes a big difference to how others perceive me now. Gender, perhaps because of the culture and experience of the school and because of my own experience and age now, has become less important. However, because of where I am in my academic career, having female leadership is very important to me.

Dealing with Politics

How to navigate through new waters? How to understand the political environment? I am in the learning phase here, but with one key challenge: I am an Associate Professor. While I have an advantage of being able to take my time in dealing with potential concerns, I feel that I need to exert some more influence. I was singled out in a meeting because people had "concerns" about my hiring. I also had to more or less deal with the perceived idea that I was "taking" from people versus "adding" to them. I often times feel that I am treated with the same processes as an Assistant Professor with no experience and that I need to prove myself despite having eight years of experience. This is a bit annoying but not surprising. I am still learning based on behavioral observation how to adequately present my arguments and myself. I feel that in this environment, differently from in my previous school in Portugal, I need to exert a bit more of my power and influence early on.

"Less Well Known"

The world just became larger. However, much like the United States, Brazil is a world on its own. The city of São Paulo is larger than Portugal in terms of population. Therefore, while globally the school is less well known, in the world in which I am currently living, the school is widely known. The new systems, the new procedures, Brazilian academia, all of it is different. I am now the "less well known" academic. I feel very foreign in my own country and in my own school. My strategy is to continue with my international career but slowly learn the Brazilian environment. I hope that, with the help of my colleagues and master's and PhD students, in a couple of years this will feel very different.

Community

My community keeps getting larger and larger. I continue with my contacts in the United States and Portugal, but now, I am making new ones in Brazil. In fact, the transition feels a bit easier because of it. While foreign to me, this is my country. I have friends here. I have family. I more or less know how to work, but at the school this is a bit harder. One key colleague has been instrumental in bringing me into the fold; we talk frequently, he checks up on me, goes into battle for me, and overall has been a model colleague that brought me into his group, now my group. We go out frequently to each other's houses, I feel supported by them and, without them, I would really question my decision to move back. I am making more contacts and getting to know more people.

CONCLUSION

While I decided to tell my journey from a linear perspective, much of my experience shaped by my academic career was not very clear. I now can look at it through more objective lenses. I also separated the phases into four distinct ones but often they overlapped. Many times I felt that I was learning and growing and then one event took me back to the start. From a development perspective, this makes sense; however, it is harder to tell a story going back and forth.

The four themes that have emerged are related to each other. For example, the sense of community probably provided a support and helped me deal with each of the other themes better. Therefore, I would highlight it as the most important aspect of my academic journey and development. It is hard to provide takeaways from one experience, but if I were to select them, I would focus on: (1) Upon selecting a place to work, see if there is a cultural fit, if you have role models and people who can be your community. This is very important and will facilitate your adjustment. (2) Do not ignore internal politics; understand that you should develop political skills to be successful. (3) Keep singing, keep dancing! Even though you may be out of tune. You may find that it is just as joyous and fun. I did.

NOTE

1. See https://medium.com/national-center-for-institutional-diversity/the-power -of-academic-role-models-like-me-7f4f2c59279d; https://www.chronicle.com/ article/Role-ModelsMentors/44794 (accessed September 3, 2018).

REFERENCES

A post-doc who persisted (2017). *Science, 357*(6347), 222. Retrieved September 3, 2018 from http://science.sciencemag.org/content/357/6347/222/tab-pdf.
Hardy, K. (2018, February 4). #MeTooPhD reveals shocking examples of academic sexism. *The Guardian*. Retrieved October 3, 2018 from https://www.theguardian .com/commentisfree/2018/feb/04/metoophd-reveals-shocking-examples-of-academic -sexism.
Morrison, E. (2002). Newcomers' relationships: The role of social network ties during socialization. *The Academy of Management Journal, 45*(6), 1149–1160.
Story, J. S. P. (2013). Essay from an early career: to each his/her "own tune". *Management Research: The Journal of the Iberoamerican Academy of Management, 11*(1), 100–107.
Suggs, L. (2018, August 22). Combating Sexism in academia. *Psychology Today*. Retrieved September 10, 2018 from https://www.psychologytoday.com/us/blog/the -fundamentals/201808/combating-sexism-in-academia.

15. Everything is a process, even an academic career[1]

Jan Mendling

Estimated reading time: **22 minutes and 4 seconds**.

CHAPTER HIGHLIGHTS

* Collaborations are great, but they make less sense before you have developed your own little area of expertise.
* Embrace challenge, even if it is something new to you.
* There are no shortcuts and no substitutes for good research.
* You can only protect your research interests if you say "no" quite often.
* You should do research because it makes you happy. Nothing more and nothing less.

> *Life is a lively process of becoming.*
> Douglas MacArthur

MY CASE OF GROWING UP AS AN ACADEMIC

My research focuses on business process management (Dumas et al., 2018), which is an area of research at the intersection of computer science, information systems, operations management and organization science. In business process management, we are interested in various types of business processes and the way in which they can be managed. We believe in the mantra that "everything is a process", and indeed also career paths have been researched from a process perspective (Abbott & Hrycak, 1990). A specific research area called process mining focuses on the analysis of business processes based on event log data recorded by information systems (van der Aalst, 2016). Process mining of career paths would look at the question how academic careers unfold by analyzing an event log file that represents a big number of such careers, and it would try to identify common patterns of e.g. promotions. The book in which this chapter is published can be seen as an event log file – though not in a structured format – with each author's history representing one entry in this event log (with the case "Jan Mendling" and its related event sequence being one of them). As this is not a process mining book, it is left to the reader to identify common paths and recurring patterns. Still, it is useful to present a sequence of events first before discussing learnings and recommendations.

WHAT I BELIEVE WERE DECISIVE EVENTS FOR ME

When I started my studies, I was already 21 years old. Many of my fellow students were two years younger, because they had not conducted an apprenticeship in banking as I had. I had chosen to study business administration at the University of Trier, Germany, not too far away from my home town Andernach. Indeed, I enrolled in economics first, because business administration had restricted access. Moving to Trier was a conservative choice, less driven by ambition, but more by the desire to be a student together with friends from school and from my bank days. The studies of business administration only mildly challenged me, partially because I knew some of the technical details from working at the bank. I was one of the best students in my cohort and happy that the studies left me enough time to read in other areas. So it happened that I additionally enrolled in business computer science, a degree program that was newly established in Trier in 1998.

Finding my Research Area

With hindsight, it was lucky that this new study program was set up, because it continues to be my major area of interest. We started with a cohort of some 15 students, a small elite group that Professor Hans Czap fostered with dedication. It was shortly before the millennium. The Internet, electronic commerce and the dot-com start-ups were on the rise, and we felt like pioneers studying these phenomena. In 1999, I went to the University of Antwerp (back then still UFSIA – St. Ignatius University Centre, Antwerp) in Belgium as an exchange student, where I enjoyed the outstanding classes of Professor Carlos de Backer. At that time, I started to become more international in thinking, which is an important aspect in academia. Shortly after being back in Trier is the first time that I recall having the idea of pursuing an academic career (though my mother recently proved me wrong, as Figure 15.1 demonstrates). I joined the selection committee for a new position of professor of information systems as a student delegate. During the selection process, I learned which criteria were important for being short-listed and to what degree the candidates met these criteria.

There were strong differences in the quality and quantity of the publications of the candidates. This was an important lesson. I had always enjoyed reading

Note: This figure has been rediscovered recently by my mother. It seems that I had the idea of becoming a professor already as a teenager. I must emphasize though that I had no idea back then what a professor really is or does.

Figure 15.1   The back cover of a notebook from school days

research articles and writing seminar papers. So, before I finished my studies, I knew that my publication record would be important. I put this into action right away. With the support of my supervisor Professor Markus Nüttgens, we submitted my first papers that built on my diploma work (Mendling & Müller, 2003; Mendling & Nüttgens, 2002).

Finding my Mentors

In 2003, I moved to Vienna with the ambition of pursuing my doctoral studies. I was optimistic about finding a position, because there were several professors working in my areas of interest. I decided to start at Wirtschaftsuniversität Wien (Vienna University of Economics and Business) under the supervision of Professor Gustaf Neumann, one of the co-authors of the famous German text-book *Wirtschaftsinformatik* (English: *Business Information Systems*). He gave me lots of freedom to continue with my research on process exchange formats and inspired work in role-based access control (Mendling et al., 2004) and transformation between different process standards (Mendling et al., 2006a).

In 2005, many pieces of my PhD were already there, but I did not see the big picture. Michael Moser was a student who was interested in writing his master's thesis on XML transformations. Our discussion led to the idea of trans-forming process models into a format that formal verification tools like the Woflan analyzer could read.[2] And then I had my eureka moment: I would take the process models from the SAP Reference Model, replace the transformation to Woflan with an own verification approach, calculate structural metrics for the process models, and use these as predictors of error probability in a logistic regression model, which I was familiar with from my studies in Trier. It was at this point in time that I met Professor Wil van der Aalst for the first time in person at the International Conference on Business Process Management (BPM 2005).[3] The initial publication out of this collaboration was my first full paper accepted at the BPM conference (Mendling et al., 2006b). With hindsight, I am very happy about the way my topic emerged. It integrated formal research and engineering of prototypes with empirical analysis. Both my PhD thesis and the corresponding book published by Springer are well cited.[4] Even though articles and conference papers are important, I still believe it is equally important to have a monograph in your publication list.

Establishing my Collaborations

During my PhD, I pursued some side projects. In 2005, I met Jan Recker, then PhD student at QUT (Queensland University of Technology) Brisbane, now professor at the University of Cologne. We teamed up to work on configurable process models. Again, Wil van der Aalst was on board, and now also Professor Michael Rosemann. This collaboration resulted in my first paper accepted at the International Conference on Advanced Information Systems Engineering (CAiSE) (Recker et al., 2006). Rosemann offered me a position at QUT Brisbane which I happily accepted. I started in June 2007 and became office mates with the authors of the workflow patterns and the book on process-aware information systems.[5] In Brisbane, we often had visitors from all around the world. I got to know many researchers who I only knew by name from articles that I had read. Also my first article in an A+ journal stems from that time.[6] In the end, it was only one year, but a very fruitful one. There were personal reasons that brought me back to Europe.

In summer 2008, I joined Professor Oliver Günther's team at Humboldt University (HU) in Berlin as a junior professor (German equivalent to assistant professor). It was a team working on a diverse set of topics, which broadened my horizon. I was now a senior team member and had the opportunity to set up my own mini specialization in Business Process Management and Enterprise Systems in the master's program. Thanks to the courses on this specialization, I got many talented students excited about business process management. Several papers resulted from their seminar papers and theses.[7] As a junior professor, I obtained the right to supervise PhD students. In 2012, Matthias Lange became my first "academic son" with a thesis on enterprise architecture management, summarized in an article published in the *European Journal of*

Information Systems (Lange et al., 2016), followed by Henrik Leopold (2013), and others.

Being back in Europe offered me the opportunity to collaborate more closely with Professor Hajo Reijers and Professor Barbara Weber, both back then assistants at their respective *alma mater*. My PhD thesis had raised various empirical questions on what makes process models understandable (Mendling et al., 2007). It was for me the starting point of conducting research using controlled experimental designs. Soon, these empirical works, most prominently Mendling et al. (2010), started to inspire engineering research such as the stream on natural language processing for process models. This stream was fully developed by Henrik Leopold and Fabian Pittke in their doctoral theses.[8] A key benefit of Berlin is the proximity of various strong research institutions. For me, the collaboration with Professor Mathias Weske's team turned out to be especially fruitful. First ideas on calculating similarity of process models had already been outlined in Mendling et al. (2007) and van Dongen et al. (2008), but the behavioral abstraction we used was not fully effective.[9] An elegant solution based on behavioral profiles emerged out of the collaboration with Hasso-Plattner-Institute (HPI) in Potsdam, resulting in an article published in *IEEE Transactions on Software Engineering* (Weidlich et al., 2011) and several further excellent papers.[10] Even though I did not have enough funding for a PhD position under my supervision, these collaborations allowed me to contribute to many more publications than I could have developed alone.

Around that time, I joined the newly established ski seminar for doctoral students on information systems.[11] In this circle of faculty, I contributed expertise in the area of information systems engineering. The idea of this winter event is to bring together PhD students from the different involved institutions and discuss research quality. Students present seminal papers and own research and get intensive feedback from peers and faculty. A good share of my understanding of the information systems field stems from the discussions at this seminar.

Building Up my Research Team

By the end of 2010, I had published 99 papers and 19 articles, which had attracted some 3 000 citations. Most of these works were engineering papers with a few experiments. At that time, I applied for a full professor position at Vienna University of Economics and Business and I knew that these quantitative figures would be important. I looked good on many indicators, I demonstrated enthusiasm at the hearing and gave competent answers. My application was successful and I was happy (compare Figure 15.2[12]). In August 2011, I started working in Vienna again.

------------ Forwarded Message ------------

Subject:	RE: [WI] Ausschreibung: Professur aus Wirtschaftsinformatik an der Wirtschaftsuniversität Wien
Date:	FRI, 21 Mar 2008 21:03:00 +1000
From:	Jan Mendling <j.mendling@qut.edu.au>
To:	Gustaf Neumann <neumann@wu-wien.ac.at>

Schade, dass ich dafuer noch zu "junior" bin. Irgendwann will ich auch Professor in Wien sein :-)

Frohe Ostern,

Jan

Note: In March 2008, a new full professor position was opened at Vienna University of Economics and Business. It seems that I had it already in the back of my mind to return to Vienna as a full professor. At that time, I wrote Gustaf Neumann that, sadly, I was still too junior to apply.

Figure 15.2   Email correspondence with Gustaf Neumann

A true asset of my new position were the two PhD positions that I could staff, and later another two additional ones. I hired Monika Malinova and Johannes Prescher, who had both been students at HU Berlin. Soon, Cristina Cabanillas and Claudio Di Ciccio followed as postdoctoral research fellows, both funded by the European Union (EU) project GET Service. It is now nine years since I started as a full professor and many things have changed. Our team has grown to ten researchers and I have management duties at the department level. In the research community, my ambition is to foster business process management as a discipline and build bridges to the neighboring communities of information systems, operations management and organizational routines.

Both the textbooks that I co-authored – Hansen et al. (2019) and Dumas et al. (2018) – aim to integrate the diverse and quickly developing topics of business process management and information systems into a coherent whole that is easy to digest for undergraduate students.

WHAT I MIGHT HAVE DONE RIGHT

Sense-making with hindsight can never be fully trusted. Still, I dare to imagine that the fact that things turned out fine for me is not fully a matter of luck. By looking at the course of my career, I want to highlight several observations. When I try to formulate them as recommendations, I have to emphasize that they should not be seen as a magic potion. They might be better suited as devices for self-reflection.

I Took Initiative and Collaborated

The first observation that I find striking when reading the previous section is the number of people that are listed. I'm not sure whether I am such a humble person as to highlight the contributions of others, but the point that I am sure of is the fact that research is a social process. I always enjoyed meeting, discussing, analyzing and writing together with people who knew certain things better than I did. I learned a lot in this way. But I also first did my homework and developed my own ideas. If you want to collaborate, it is good to bring something more to the table than just pure interest.

If put as a recommendation, I would say: find a balance between collaboration and your own work. Do your own studies and write your own papers first. In this way, you learn all the steps involved in conducting a research project. Your supervisor is there to help you, but it's best to be proactive and try to work largely independently. Collaborations are great, but they make less sense before you have developed your own little area of expertise. If you are not an expert, how can colleagues possibly benefit from working with you? You have to be the very expert on your topic and you have to know all the details of your studies.

While support is a great help, you should never make yourself dependent on others in the core areas of your research. There is just no way to outsource this research work. Be a researcher. When you are older, you can become a research manager. Be independent. Collaborations also depend on the amount of effort that you put into them: the more you contribute, the higher the chance that it will pay off double. However, there is no guarantee for success. Some initiatives flourish, others do not. Collaborations hardly offer quick and easy returns, but they will help you in the long run in a way that you cannot anticipate. For these reasons, it is, first, good to be open to collaborations and, second, to take collaborations seriously. Collaboration is great, when you make it great.

I Accepted New Challenges

The second observation is that I have never been shy to accept the next challenge. When I wrote my first research proposal, served as a program committee chair for the first time or submitted for the first time to a top journal, I had respect, but I was not afraid. Chances are high that submitted manuscripts will be rejected. The sheer percentages might look frightening, but do not forget that the quality of other submissions is a long-tail distribution. The acceptance rates of good submissions are much higher than the numbers you typically read about. And even when submissions were rejected, I knew that it would be less effort when I submitted the next time and that the learning experience would be worth it.

This one is quite easy to put as a recommendation. My friend Professor Marta Indulska often says: "You've got to be in it, to win it" and she is completely right. By jumping into the cold water, I learned to swim. I give one example. When collaborating with Matthias Weidlich on behavioral profiles, I got so excited about the concept that I pushed for submitting the work to *IEEE Transactions on Software Engineering*, arguably the by far best journal in the field. I did not know anyone who had published in that journal, but I believed that our work was good enough for it. The first review round already had generally supportive reviews and, eventually, the manuscript was accepted. How could we have had a paper accepted, if we had not submitted it there?

I Focused on Positive Things

The third observation is that, in the end, it is the research that matters. I have met lots of people who tried to be overly strategic with their career development. I am not sure if they fared better than me. I tend to believe that, if you focus on your research topics, pursue them with passion and try to shape them in a way that other researchers can build on, then this is the most sustainable path to follow. In the end, it is the research that matters, and not the fact that you chatted with important persons during the coffee break. Do not trust the gossip that there are gains to be made from being a friend to this or that person. A less envious interpretation is that a senior person might have given very valuable feedback to a promising idea. Approach networking from this angle. Talking with an experienced expert is a great learning experience. The great majority of researchers have integrity and are genuinely interested in the progress of the field. There are no shortcuts and no substitutes for good research.

If you wanted to put this as a recommendation: be kind, be a friend. You will meet people in academia that do things that you do not like, as much as you have met people you do not like earlier at school or in everyday life. Be forgiving and reassure yourself that many of them will still act with good intentions. And if they do strange things, it is typically because they are or feel under pressure and stress. Do not listen to negative emotions that this observation might trigger in you and stay constructive. Everybody is contributing something to the progress of a field in this or that way. It is good to appreciate this. Marcus Aurelius' *Meditations* is a good read.[13] Be forgiving.

I Read for Inspiration

The fourth observation is that I found it often exciting to integrate ideas from other domains into business process management. In order to accomplish this,

I found it helpful to read more broadly rather than just within my narrow field of research focus. If you have only focused on one topic, go and find a second one. Reading is very important for a scholar. You need to know how your work relates to the recent developments of your field and you can use contributions from neighboring fields as inspiration. To give you some idea of the extent of my reading, I refer to those papers that I read for self-education. I keep the respective PDFs in a separate folder, which makes it easy to trace when I read what. This folder contains 219 documents for 2018. Most of them are articles. The number does not include manuscripts I read for review.

As a recommendation, this could mean: try out new things, read broadly. Sure, the next incremental study on XYZ might get you published, but I find it much more satisfactory to throw a new idea into a discourse. Critical thinking is instrumental for spotting the weak points of established arguments. Reading helps to develop this skill and to improve as a researcher. I find it very important to read seminal papers and papers that reflect upon research methods and practices. Biographies of great minds are also inspiring and, personally, I like history.

Now you can try out your own critical thinking. Do not follow these recommendations by the book. These recommendations alone do not necessarily lead you in a good direction. They only operate on the surface. There is something underneath them that helps you to find the way. I strongly believe that it is a state of mind and not the next tactical move here or there that helps you to succeed. Take risks and develop your own way. There is equifinality: many roads lead to Rome. As much as Feyerabend (1977) argues against methods in research, I would argue against a method for pursuing an academic career.

WHAT I AM STILL DOING WRONG

Since I started, I have given around 100 faculty talks, tutorials and keynotes at events outside my university, supported various committees and editorial boards, served as a reviewer for funding agencies and journals, taken part in around 60 PhD committees and offered around 100 university courses, partially alone, partially together with colleagues. Even though Von Foerster (2003) says that one should always increase the number of choices, it is good to do less and allow yourself some rest at various stages. I am not very good at that.

A good way to assess yourself without too much coaching or other form of external feedback is to analyze the status of the most important tools that we use as academics: the electronic mailbox and the electronic calendar. Each of these two little helpers quite accurately reflects the current backlog of things to do and the commitments of the near future. Some people use more sophisticated tools, but I usually do not.

I use my mailbox as a to-do list. Things stay in my inbox until they are done. If I need to take note of a to-do item, I write an email to myself. How would I like my mailbox to be? Sure, empty, but this is neither effective nor realistic. While I am writing this text, I have 35 emails in my mailbox. I am quite happy if I have less than 30, because then I can easily visualize what is still to be done and prioritize. In bad times, the size of my inbox grows towards 100. The mailbox also tells you how old the to-do items are. My oldest is three months old. Around half of the mails are two weeks old or younger. Analyzing my email communication, I find that I tend to communicate with too many people.

I manage my appointments using an electronic calendar. If I have to meet or call someone, if I have to do something at or before a particular point in time, it ends up in my calendar. For the week at the time of writing, I count 25 calendar entries. These include joining a PhD defense as a committee member, traveling to see a project partner, participating in the kick-off workshop and joining a guided tour at a partner's production site, various meetings and calls with colleagues, team members and a visiting researcher, submitting an abstract of a magazine article, chairing a jury for an award and hosting a half-day symposium accompanied by a social dinner. Earlier this year, I made the effort to analyze with which type of activities I fill my calendar. I found out that I simply do too much in all categories. More specifically, I felt that I take too many meeting requests and that I could reduce travel.

The observations of both these tools illustrate the broad and diverse range of tasks and communication partners that one runs into. As a young researcher on the journey towards a PhD degree, one can typically focus on a single specific research topic with little distraction from other duties. Each promotion towards finally becoming a full professor comes with additional duties and a broader spectrum of activities and interaction partners. This is nothing to complain about, but hopefully a richness of activities that the reader will enjoy. Still, the beauty of being a researcher is the freedom to work on research questions that we personally find interesting. However, this freedom also comes with the obligation to keep up the lonely fight for having enough time for these research questions – everyday. You can only protect your research interests if you say "no" quite often. And it is important that you not only become better at what you do, but also faster.

The range of two or three dozen activities of a usual work week can be overwhelming. What I have found useful for myself is to have a standardized scheme of an archetypical week that integrates all duties and leaves slack time. My ideal week starts on Monday with administrative meetings until noon followed by one or two meetings in the afternoon. An ideal Tuesday has no meetings and is completely left for research work. A typical Wednesday is completely filled with weekly research consultations with PhD students and postdocs. In the later afternoon, we have our team seminar with one or two research talks. Thursdays are filled with teaching and ideally there are no meetings on Fridays, leaving the whole day for research. In an ideal week, there is also no work in the evening or at the weekend except for occasional reading and writing. Unfortunately, we are not living in an ideal world and just as little in an ideal week.

WHAT I FIND REALLY IMPORTANT

In the end, I have to emphasize how difficult it is to give general advice. I wrote the recommendations above with some reluctance for several reasons. First, there are already many excellent books and articles that give good and detailed advice. Recker (2013) and Van de Ven (2007) are just two of them. Second, I do not believe that knowing simple rules could have a true impact on the success of an academic career. I believe that you should not look at your academic career as something that can be pursued by use of a method. And even if such simple rules existed, they might be valid today in a particular research domain, but likely be obsolete in the near future. Third, I dislike the idea of young researchers playing strategic games, instead of establishing confidence in their own research. I strongly agree with the phrase coined by great inventor Thomas A. Edison: "Genius is 1% inspiration, 99% perspiration!" (Dyer & Martin, 1910). In general, life has no shortcuts: success is achieved the hard way. So why should we make the effort to become an academic? Hard work can be of two different types, pain or passion, and maybe that is the key: to find the kind of work that is hard but does not feel like that, because it is a passion. I cite Professor Carlos de Backer. In his farewell address to the graduate students of UFSIA Antwerp in 2000, he asked "Why are you doing all this? What is the purpose of all these studies, business careers, and academic work?" His answer is so simple and powerful at the same time: "Omdat je gelukkig bent – It is for you to be happy." You should do research, because it makes you happy. Nothing more and nothing less.

NOTES

1. I am very grateful to all the fine academics that I have had the pleasure to collaborate with. Most prominently, I want to alphabetically mention my friends Wil van der Aalst, Cristina Cabanillas, Claudio Di Ciccio, Henrik Leopold, Monika Malinova Mandelburger, Jan Recker, Hajo A. Reijers, and Matthias Weidlich who provided comments on a draft of this chapter.
2. More specifically, we defined and implemented a transformation from process models that were defined as Event-driven Process Chains (EPCs) to the YAWL workflow exchange format that could be imported by Woflan (Verbeek et al., 2001). Woflan would then report problems such as deadlocks.

3. Wil van der Aalst is arguably the Pál Erdős of business process management with 109 046 Google Scholar citations (November 9, 2020). He invited me several times to Eindhoven, where we collaborated on papers in relation to my thesis. He played an important role for the verification part of my thesis and continued to be an important mentor for my career.
4. As of November 9, 2020 and according to Google Scholar, there have been 203 citations for the PhD thesis (Mendling, 2007) and 585 citations for the Springer book (Mendling, 2008). My PhD thesis was proposed by Wil van der Aalst for publication in Springer's Lecture Notes in Business Information Processing (LNBIP) Series.
5. The workflow patterns and the book on process-aware information systems (Dumas et al., 2005; van der Aalst et al., 2003) are seminal contributions. My colleagues were, among others, Arthur ter Hofstede, Marlon Dumas and Marcello La Rosa.
6. The article Ouyang et al. (2009) was published in *ACM Transactions on Software Engineering and Methodology*, which is an A+ journal in software engineering.
7. These students were, among others, Thomas Baier, Fabian Friedrich, Christopher Hahn, Henrik Leopold, Monika Malinova, Johannes Prescher, Matthias Schrepfer, and Johannes Wolf. Papers include: Friedrich et al. (2011); Recker et al. (2013); Schrepfer et al., 2009).
8. Several articles resulted from Henrik's and Fabian's work, including Leopold et al. (2012) and Pittke et al. (2015).
9. This had been one of my early collaborations with Professors Boudewijn van Dongen and Remco Dijkman.
10. Work with HPI Potsdam built on collaboration with Professor Mathias Weske and his then PhD students Matthias Weidlich, Artem Polyvyanyy and Sergey Smirnow.
11. The ski seminar was initiated by professors Roland Holten (University of Frankfurt), Jan Recker (then assistant at QUT, Brisbane), Stefan Seidel (then assistant at University of Liechtenstein) and Christoph Rosenkranz (then assistant at University of Frankfurt), and later extended with Professors Nick Berente, Jan vom Brocke, Aron Lindberg and Dr. Ed Weiss.
12. In March 2008, a new full professor position was opened at Vienna University of Economics and Business. It seems that I had it already in the back of my mind to return to Vienna as a full professor. At that time, I wrote Gustaf Neumann that, sadly, I was still too junior to apply.
13. There is, for instance, an edition by Oxford University Press published as Aurelius (2013). Do not be fooled by the publication year of the book: the text dates from the period of his reign as Roman emperor, i.e. 161–180.

REFERENCES

Abbott, A., & Hrycak, A. (1990). Measuring resemblance in sequence data: An optimal matching analysis of musicians' careers. *American Journal of Sociology, 96*(1), 144–185.
Aurelius, M. (2013). *Meditations*. Oxford, UK: Oxford University Press.
Dumas, M., La Rosa, M., Mendling, J., & Reijers, H. A. (2018). *Fundamentals of Business Process Management*. Berlin: Springer.

Dumas, M., van der Aalst, W. M. P., & ter Hofstede, A. H. M., eds. (2005). *Process-aware Information Systems: Bridging People and Software through Process Technology*. Hoboken, NJ: Wiley-Interscience.

Dyer, F. L., & Martin, T. C. (1910). *Edison: His Life and Inventions*. New York, NY: Harper Brothers.

Feyerabend, P. K. (1977). *Against Method: Outline of an Anarchist Theory of Knowledge*. London, UK: New Left Books.

Friedrich, F., Mendling, J., & Puhlmann, F. (2011). Process model generation from natural language text. In H. Mouratidis, & C. Rolland (eds.), *Advanced Information Systems Engineering: Proceedings of the 23rd International Conference CAiSE 2011* (Vol. 6741, pp. 482–496). Heidelberg: Springer-Verlag.

Hansen, H. R., Mendling, J., & Neumann, G. (2019). *Wirtschaftsinformatik* (12. Aufl.). Oldenbourg: de Gruyter.

Lange, M., Mendling, J., & Recker, J. (2016). An empirical analysis of the factors and measures of enterprise architecture management success. *European Journal of Information Systems*, *25*(5), 411–431.

Leopold, H. (2013). *Natural Language in Business Process Models: Theoretical Foundations, Techniques, and Applications* (Vol. 168). Berlin: Springer.

Leopold, H., Smirnov, S., & Mendling, J. (2012). On the refactoring of activity labels in business process models. *Information Systems*, *37*(5), 443–459.

Mendling, J. (2007). *Detection and Prediction of Errors in EPC Business Process Models* (Unpublished doctoral dissertation). Wirtschaftsuniversität Wien.

Mendling, J. (2008). *Metrics for Process Models: Empirical Foundations of Verification, Error Prediction, and Guidelines for Correctness* (Vol. 6). Berlin: Springer.

Mendling, J., & Müller, M. (2003). A comparison of BPML and BPEL4WS. In R. Tolksdorf, & R. Eckstein (eds.), *Berliner XML tage 2003* (pp. 305–316). Berlin: XML-Clearinghouse.

Mendling, J., & Nüttgens, M. (2002). Event-driven-process-chain-markup-language (EPML): anforderungen zur definition eines xml-schemas für ereignisgesteuerte prozessketten (EPK). In M. Nüttgens, & F. J. Rump (eds.), *EPK 2002 – geschäftsprozessmanagement mit ereignisgesteuerten prozessketten, proceedings des gi-workshops und arbeitskreistreffens* (pp. 87–93). Trier: GI-Arbeitskreis Geschäftsprozessmanagement mit Ereignisgesteuerten Prozessketten.

Mendling, J., Moser, M., & Neumann, G. (2006a). Transformation of yepc business process models to YAWL. In H. Haddad (ed.), *Proceedings of the 2006 ACM symposium on applied computing* (SAC). Dijon: ACM.

Mendling, J., Moser, M., Neumann, G., Verbeek, H. M. W., van Dongen, B. F., & van der Aalst, W. M. P. (2006b). Faulty EPCS in the SAP Reference Model. In S. Dustdar, J. L. Fiadeiro, & A. P. Sheth (eds.), *Business Process Management: Proceedings of the 4th International BPM Conference* (Vol. 4102, pp. 451–457). Berlin: Springer.

Mendling, J., Reijers, H. A., & Cardoso, J. S. (2007). What makes process models understandable? In G. Alonso, P. Dadam, & M. Rosemann (eds.), *Business Process Management: Proceedings of the 5th International BPM Conference* (Vol. 4714, pp. 48–63). Berlin: Springer.

Mendling, J., Reijers, H. A., & Recker, J. (2010). Activity labeling in process modeling: Empirical insights and recommendations. *Information Systems*, *35*(4), 467–482.

Mendling, J., Strembeck, M., Stermsek, G., & Neumann, G. (2004). An approach to extract RBAC models from BPEL4WS processes. In *13th IEEE International*

Workshops on Enabling Technologies (WETICE 2004), Infrastructure for Collaborative Enterprises (pp. 81–86). Modena: IEEE Computer Society.

Mendling, J., van Dongen, B. F., & van der Aalst, W. M. P. (2007). On the degree of behavioral similarity between business process models. In M. Nüttgens, F. J. Rump, & A. Gadatsch (eds.), *6. workshop der gesellschaft für informatik e.v. (GI) und treffen ihres arbeitskreises "geschäftsprozessmanagement mit ereignisgesteuerten prozessketten (wi-epk)"* (Vol. 303, pp. 39–58). St. Augustion: CEUR-WS.org.

Ouyang, C., Dumas, M., van der Aalst, W. M. P., ter Hofstede, A. H. M., & Mendling, J. (2009). From business process models to process-oriented software systems. *ACM Transactions on Software Engineering and Methodology*, *19*(1), 2:1–2:37.

Pittke, F., Leopold, H., & Mendling, J. (2015). Automatic detection and resolution of lexical ambiguity in process models. *IEEE Transactions on Software Engineering*, *41*(6), 526–544.

Recker, J. (2013). *Scientific Research in Information Systems: A Beginner's Guide.* Berlin-Heidelberg: Springer.

Recker, J., Mendling, J., & Hahn, C. (2013). How collaborative technology supports cognitive processes in collaborative process modeling: A capabilities-gains outcome model. *Information Systems*, *38*(8), 1031–1045.

Recker, J., Mendling, J., van der Aalst, W. M. P., & Rosemann, M. (2006). Model-driven enterprise systems configuration. In *Advanced information systems engineering: Proceedings of the 18th international CAiSE conference* (pp. 369–383). Berlin: Springer.

Schrepfer, M., Wolf, J., Mendling, J., & Reijers, H. A. (2009). The impact of secondary notation on process model understanding. In A. Persson, & J. Stirna (eds.), *The Practice of Enterprise Modeling: Proceedings of the 2nd IFIP WG 8.1 Working Conference* (Vol. 39, pp. 161–175). Berling: Springer.

Van de Ven, A. H. (2007). *Engaged Scholarship: A Guide for Organizational and Social Research.* Oxford, UK: Oxford University Press.

van der Aalst, W. M. P. (2016). *Process Mining: Data Science in Action.* Berlin: Springer.

van der Aalst, W. M. P., ter Hofstede, A. H. M., Kiepuszewski, B., & Barros, A. P. (2003). Workflow Patterns. *Distributed and Parallel Databases*, *14*(1), 5–51.

van Dongen, B., Dijkman, R., & Mendling, J. (2008). Measuring similarity between business process models. In *Proceedings of the International CAiSE conference on advanced information systems engineering* (pp. 450–464). Berlin: Springer.

Verbeek, H. M. W. F., Basten, T., & van der Aalst, W. M. P. (2001). Diagnosing Workflow Processes using Woflan. *The Computer Journal*, *44*(4), 246–279.

Von Foerster, H. (2003). *Understanding Understanding: Essays On Cybernetics and Cognition.* New York, NY: Springer-Verlag.

Weidlich, M., Mendling, J., & Weske, M. (2011). Efficient consistency measurement based on behavioral profiles of process models. *IEEE Transactions on Software Engineering*, *37*(3), 410–429.

16. Doing things differently: turning the game of academia upside down

Markus Hällgren

Estimated reading time: **19 minutes and 7 seconds**.

CHAPTER HIGHLIGHTS

- Research is too important to be limited to what is popular. To survive and thrive one needs to be passionate about the topic and pursue research for the beauty of it, whatever that topic may be.
- Publications are important but participating in scholarly debates is as important, if not more so.
- Be different and attract attention.
- Surround yourself with like-minded (but functionally heterogeneous) and passionate people – better than yourself.
- Most projects reach a point of no return, where the best option is to continue. In such circumstances, you should break down the end-goal into sub (partial) goals and turn necessary activities into a plan.

Embrace your uniqueness.
Time is much too short to be living someone else's life.
Kobi Yamada

INTRODUCTION

Academia is a reflection of society at large. It should be no surprise to find that some research themes are more popular than others, at any given time. For example, in Management and Organization Studies "new public management" has been, and to a large extent still is, influential. The theme of the day when I defended my dissertation 15 years ago was "innovation". Everyone was pursuing it. In fact, we received some funding for a four-year project[1] in this area of study. Fifteen years later "innovation" is still popular but it shares the attention space with concepts such as "sustainability" and "digitalization". The focus on these phenomena is natural, as they represent significant challenges and opportunities to society as most of us know. However, they fail to appeal to me because so many researchers are drawn to them. My general feeling was then, and still is, that "everyone" pursues similar ideas.[2] More importantly, I felt that it creates what has been called a "red ocean" (Kim & Mauborgne, 2005); that is, a place of fierce competition with scarce resources and attention. I wanted to find something outside the mainstream. The consequences of the red ocean are that popular themes attract high-profile researchers who often – but not always – directly or indirectly block the path of younger researchers. They do this, theoretically by having a great influence on the discourse, and practically through arranging workshops, conference tracks and special issues by virtue of being a "given name". As a consequence, you often get the impression that aspiring academics compete on the margins with less interesting phenomena.

Oscar Wilde is claimed to have said that "Everything popular is wrong". This book chapter is concerned with my experiences in challenging academically popular themes. My intention is not to diminish any contribution in any theoretical or empirical area, critique any junior or senior researcher, or provide pointers to aspiring academics. And it would be presumptuous to claim that my experiences should be turned into advice that works for every aspiring academic without a critical examination or critical eye. At the end of the day I do, however, hope that potential readers find my text useful and perhaps even encouraging. The aim is to reflect on my experiences trying to create an academic "blue ocean" and on what some of the benefits have been. The key message is that research is too important to be limited to what is popular. To survive and thrive one needs to be passionate about the topic and pursue research for the beauty of it, whatever that topic may be.

MY STORY

My academic story started off similar to others, I suspect. At the School of Business & Economics in Umeå University, Sweden I wrote my dissertation about the management of deviations in the construction of diesel power plants. The dissertation had some elements that were new to the community; it was the practice-based approach and the concept of "deviations" rather than "crises" or "risks" that were interesting to me.

Parallel to my dissertation (a monograph) I pursued free-standing articles. The main reason was to try out ideas related to the empirical material, and to travel, meet people and participate in the academic conversation at numerous conferences. I was also very fortunate to have two supervisors (Professor Anders Söderholm and Professor Tomas Blomquist) who believed in me, encouraged me, and provided some of the funding. On the back of that process my colleagues and I outlined the "Projects-as-Practice" approach, outlined in my most-cited article (Blomquist et al., 2010; Hällgren & Söderholm, 2011).

From Diesel Power Plants to Climbing Expeditions

Within a few years, after having presented my material and been published in the typical project studies outlets, I needed a new challenge. In 2007 there was a EURAM (European Academy of Management) conference in Oslo, Norway that I wanted to attend. I could not, however, bring myself to write another article about power plants. At this point in time, a friend suggested that I watch the movie *Touching the Void* and read the book with the same title (Simpson, 1997).

Touching the Void is the true story of two alpine mountaineers, Joe Simpson and Simon Yates, who attempted to climb the unclimbed face of Siula Grande in the Peruvian Andes. During their ascent they realized that they were committed to the undertaking and that the snow conditions made it impossible to descend the way they came. There was no option but to continue. The problem was that they did not have enough fuel to melt snow to make water (the lack of which at altitude contributes to altitude sickness), and at the same time, the climb was taking more time and energy than they had calculated. They finally reached the top of the mountain and started their descent soon after down another part of the mountain. Struggling with the conditions on the mountain, Joe descended a cliff and fell, pushing his lower leg through his kneecap. When Simon arrived they both realized that they were in a very dire situation where there was no help available. Selflessly, Simon decided to take the significant personal risk of lowering Joe down the mountain side rather than continuing himself. At this point a snowstorm was upon them. The snowstorm obscured their sight as Simon lowered Joe, who fell over the side of the mountain. Poised in a position where they cannot see or hear each other, Joe was unable to release his weight from the tightened rope. The snow started to give way. Simon realized that he must cut the rope and send his climbing partner to certain death. Joe fell ten meters, crashed through a snow-covered crevasse and fell another ten meters to a ledge. However, there was no way for Joe to let Simon know that he was still alive.

At this point Simon started the journey back to the camp, and Joe found himself trying to find a way out of the crevasse. To make a long and exciting story short, Joe miraculously made it out of the crevasse onto the glacier they had passed on their way to the mountain. The glacier was, however, interspersed with crevasses, both hidden and visible, creating a maze that was very difficult to navigate, and that under normal conditions would require careful scouting. The snowstorm had also covered all signs of their previous hike up the mountain. Without losing his fighting spirit, Joe started crawling and falling with his broken leg over rocks and slopes towards the camp that was a good 10 kilometers away.

The key to Joe's survival was attributed to the fact that he broke down the process of getting out of the crevasse onto the glacier and to the camp into partial goals. When he did not make a certain stretch in the time that he had set he would break down in tears in disappointment.

The point I want to make by telling this story is that the movie and the book made me realize that climbing expeditions are examples of temporary organizations. Climbing expeditions and construction projects, such as those for diesel power plant projects, are both defined in terms of time, cost and scope; they include planning, risk management and logistics. Perhaps more importantly, the story made me realize that most projects reach a point of no return, where the best option is to continue. The way to continue is to break down the end-goal into sub (partial) goals, and then by means of a Work Breakdown Structure, turn necessary activities into a plan.

From Lone Researcher to Research Program

I started developing a paper based on this insight but could not find much research on the topic. To try my idea, I took the initiative and presented the paper at a research seminar for my colleagues in order to receive some friendly and constructive feedback. Based on the feedback I later submitted the paper that was accepted at the EURAM conference. After some re-work the paper (Hällgren, 2007) was accepted for publication in the *International Journal of Project Management*, one of the major journals for project studies. I believe that this and similar papers are very important in revitalizing research by offering a fresh perspective on common phenomena (Hällgren, 2007). The experience was also very influential for me personally: it proved that it was possible to do something that was not expected, and it whetted my appetite for the topic. In the next few years I developed this interest in my free time, published a few articles and book chapters and attended some topic-related conferences (Aegerter Alvarez et al., 2011; Hällgren, 2009, 2010, 2011; Hällgren et al., 2013; Jacobsson & Hällgren, 2016; Kutsch et al., 2016). The more attention I paid to the topic the more I realized how interesting it was.

In 2010, I was fortunate enough to receive a three-year postdoc scholarship from the Swedish provider "Handelsbankens forskningsstiftelser". It was a "Wallander" stipend[3] that allowed me to pursue my interests full time. There was, however, a problem. Being officially a "project studies researcher", gatekeepers and established patterns might hinder me from shaping the field. To challenge the *status quo*, I would have to do something different, in addition to my quirky research interest.

If a movie and a non-fiction book had been important for my first step, a popular-style academic book and another popular non-fiction book were important for the next. A friend of mine suggested that I read *Blue Ocean Strategy* (Kim & Mauborgne, 2005) to develop a business idea that we had. The simple message and toolbox in the book resonated with me. The message is essentially that what is popular is perhaps not necessarily wrong (contrary to Wilde's aphorism) but fierce competition follows in its wake. In industry, organizations fight for customers' money with price, quality and/or speed of innovation. The result is a market where everybody is watching everybody and where results come from competing at the margin. The competition is so fierce that the ocean (the industry) is colored red from the blood of all the organizations that are chewed by the meat grinder. Instead, the authors argued, organizations should consider creating "blue oceans" by not competing with others. These organizations define the ocean themselves and hence their possible competition. Famous examples include Cirque de Soleil and Apple, through its development of products like "iTunes". Cirque de Soleil invented a new and artistic form of circus, catering to a more mature audience; Apple's iTunes redefined how we procure and enjoy music. I realized that the message would be transferable to an academic context.

The questions I was forced to ask myself were: If "everyone" is pursuing "innovation", what could I do differently? If "everyone" is working locally, what could I do differently? If "everyone" is pursuing publications, what could I do differently? I decided to research the researchers and asked 30 of my accomplished, well-known and experienced colleagues a simple question: "What should I do next? What does it take to become a senior scholar?" The answers ranged from five sentences to two pages, and analyzing them gave the result that, since most people want to do research, there is no point in emphasizing it. Instead, when applying for positions, it is better to discuss the importance of education and administration. I also realized that I should probably continue to focus on extreme contexts and how they could be useful in understanding Management and Organization Studies; that there are tools to work virtually; that there are other things to being a scholar than merely publications.

Publications are important but participating in scholarly debates is as important, if not more so, particularly if one wants to build a research environment. The answers to my question inspired me to edit a book on the topic, similar to this one (Hällgren, 2014). In it I asked nine senior scholars of Management and Organization Studies to reflect upon their journey and provide whatever advice they had for others. Their advice still guides my work in academia: write on a daily basis; maintain a work–life balance; have fun and be relevant; seize chances, be a leader and act as one; stay passionate and curious.

The other book that influenced me is the distinctly non-academic *The Four Hour Work Week* (Ferriss, 2007), which was also suggested by a friend enthralled with its even simpler message: what is popular is indeed wrong and one should reconsider things to live a more fulfilling life, with less work (if one will). The acronym "DEAL" sets out the core of the book: *Define* and prioritize among goals; *Eliminate* activities that do not help you achieve your goals; *Automate* essential activities that can be done by someone else, or that can be done in a batch to save time; *Liberate* yourself by not always being available, for example at the office or on social media. The book may be criticized as being more of an argument for personal branding and as part of the self-referential "lifestyle movement".[4] Nevertheless, it made a strong impression on my younger self. It was not so much that I wanted to work only four hours a day (although perhaps I wanted to work a little less than I was doing) but rather that I realized I should define what I wanted from my professional and personal life. To achieve this I had to make some tough choices, and the process is what I took from the book.

Today, after a few attempts, and more than a year, I still keep an electronic journal in the Evernote software in which I break down my five-year goals (e.g., "to be a good father and husband", "be a good teacher with novel pedagogy", or "do research for 80 per cent of my time") to three things that I want to accomplish within specific time periods – within a year, six months, one month, one week, and one day. On a daily basis that may translate to reading with the kids, creating a video podcast episode to complement passionate lectures, and applying for external funding. True to the axiom that no plan survives the first contact with the enemy, I often fail to achieve my tasks. Over the years, though, I have realized that it is not the goal *per se* that is important – the goal has to change with changing conditions – but defining the goal helps with the process. In addition to the goals, I also make a note of "what have I learned today", "what can I do differently" and "what am I grateful for". These insights I aggregate into the higher-level notes and goals. Over time the process has allowed me to identify trends in my personal and my professional life. And to appreciate what I have.

Moreover, having a scholarship can be quite lonely, as most of the work is not shared. These books, my past adventures and the wisdom of one of my supervisors, Professor Anders Söderholm, have taught me two important lessons: the importance of working with similar-minded, passionate people, and the importance of challenging assumptions that are taken for granted. While people at my current workplace were and still are very accomplished, I realized that it was unlikely that everyone who is theoretically and practically passionate about climbing expeditions and other extreme contexts would be based in Umeå. Nor would it be possible to attract them to start working here. The only way to gain access to such people would therefore be to bring Umeå to them. Hence, we started the research program: "Extreme Environments – Everyday Decisions" (www.TripleEd.com). It is now well established at the School of Business and Economics in Umeå University.

Extreme Environments: Everyday Decisions (TripleEd)

The idea behind TripleEd is that it should be an international interdisciplinary research program with a local core that investigates organizing and decision-making in extreme contexts. The program has grown and today includes researchers and collaborators from all over the globe, involved in different projects pursuing different ideas that interest them. While the program is loosely held together, it is a platform that allows us to pursue common interests, as well as arranging workshops, seminars, conferences and conference tracks; writing joint research applications, articles and book chapters; and to some extent being involved in teaching and developing teaching materials. Today, seven years after the first funding, and 11 years after my first conference presentation about extreme contexts, we have been fortunate enough to have some major publications related to research on "extreme contexts" (Hällgren & Rouleau, 2018; Hällgren et al., 2018) and we have together with other international actors developed a research network that comprises some of the most accomplished scholars within Management and Organization Studies (www.organizingextremecontexts.org). Many of these scholars are also willing to travel to Umeå to give seminars and be involved in different research activities. This is where I am at the moment. The future will bring what the future will bring.

SOME REFLECTIONS RELATED TO SHAPING ONE'S OWN DESTINY

There is so much I could and should have done differently over the years, and while *learning* from the past is important, I do not think that there are necessarily any benefits to be had of *living/staying* in the past. Therefore, I choose to look forward. The reason for telling my story is to reflect on my own process, and to, hopefully, make it useful to you as well.

Being Different and Attracting Attention

If we are all pursuing the same ideas we will become academics dressed in similar theoretical, methodological and empirical attire. Ultimately if only a few control everything, the scholarly debate will become stale. I would prefer to be one who stands out; the one who does things differently; the one who attracts attention with different ideas.[5] One way of doing this that was helpful for me was to become involved in research out of curiosity and look for inspiration outside academia. As others have done, I found fiction and indeed non-fiction were good sources of inspiration. For example, together with David Buchanan at Cranfield University I now do research on teamwork and leadership based on zombie movies (Buchanan & Hällgren, 2019). It has nothing to do with establishing myself at the top of some imagined ladder, but rather it is my way of feeling that I can influence my own destiny.

Strive to Work with People Better than Yourself

Throughout my career, whatever that is and has been, I have been fortunate in having the opportunity to work with people much smarter and more accomplished than myself. There is always something that can be learned from others regardless of position and experience, including how to write, how to collect data and how to develop a research environment.

Of course, one could argue that working with smart people is a natural part of working at an Ivy League university such as Stanford, Harvard or Cambridge. These universities naturally attract high-profile scholars. It is certainly a matter of prestige to be invited to give a research seminar there and perhaps people at these universities are better off compared to those working at less well-known institutions. However, there are benefits to be had from being affiliated with a university such as Umeå in the northern part of Sweden, which is an hour's flight from Stockholm, and where winter brings a meter of snow and the thermometer plummets to below -30 degrees Celsius. The benefits include a certain sense of exoticism (what about petting a live moose?); a friendly and open discussion climate where people work together; regional funding for collaboration; shared curiosity; and the pursuit of an idea rather than the constant pressure for A-level publications.

Build an Interdisciplinary Team

Reflecting on my past I notice that there are reasons to look beyond the immediate surface, and turn weaknesses into strengths. For example, as part of the blue ocean strategic thinking, my intention is to work with a strong local interdisciplinary core at Umeå University, rather than working, as traditionally, only with faculty at the same department. The benefit is greater freedom to choose work partners and a sense of common mission. In turn this has proven successful in attracting funding from the departments involved. A group of international collaborators has been allocated to the local core; besides being good company and possessing excellent, top-notch knowledge, our collaborators allow for new perspectives and open up new avenues for collaboration.

Be Passionate

The life of a scholar is hopefully too long to be spent on trivial things. My third reflection relates to the importance of pursuing a research agenda that excites, makes a difference and that you can live with even when the going gets tough. I have had the good fortune to spend two years as a visiting professor at Stanford University; the first year at a center (Scandinavian Consortium for Organizational Research, www.scancor.org) started by the late James G.

March (1928–2018) and the second year at the department of Sociology under his mentoring. These years were incredibly formative for me and I owe all of it to Jim. He taught me important lessons as a person and as a scholar. The most important is "Yo sé quien soy" (I know who I am) (March, 2011).

BECOMING A SCHOLAR

The aim of this book is to provide "stories of becoming an organizational scholar". This has been my story. My narrative. My reflections. If you find them useful I am happy. Writing these last sentences I can honestly say I feel that I have been in charge of my own destiny, but with a tremendous amount of help from the true scholars with whom I have had the great privilege and honor to work.

Finally, a scholar is "a person who attends a school or studies under a teacher; a person who has done advanced study in a special field; a learned person; a holder of a scholarship".[6] Personally, I associate being a "true scholar" with the inspiration of Anders Söderholm and the legacy of James G. March. People who know about some things; people who are passionate about discussing ideas for the sake of their beauty; and people who are playful and forever curious. Finally, to me a scholar is also a person who shapes conversations and tries to make a difference, rather than playing it safe.

Jim, thank you for everything. You are missed. Rest in peace.

NOTES

1. The project, "Innovation networks and systems integration for improved competitiveness" was funded by Vinnova – Sweden's Innovation Agency.
2. This is certainly not to argue that "red ocean research" is unimportant or not worthwhile pursuing. It is merely an observation that it attracts interest from many researchers.
3. As a side note, because I received other funding and became full professor in 2013, before the end of those three years, I eventually had to pay back a year of the granted scholarship. The lesson could probably be, on one hand, "use the money" and do not tell (as I know others have done). On the other hand, I can sleep well at night and I am happy and proud that I was honest. At the end of the day, all we have is our honesty.
4. See https://medium.com/thinking-askew/personal-branding-a-critique-dbab42510be0 (accessed November 23, 2018).
5. True to the axiom that "there is no rule without exceptions", I have just submitted three applications for a grand total of about US$5 million about artificial intelligence in very traditional industries.
6. Merriam-Webster online dictionary.

REFERENCES

Aegerter Alvarez, J. F., Pustina, A., & Hällgren, M. (2011). Escalating commitment in the death zone: New insights from the 1996 Mount Everest disaster. *International Journal of Project Management*, *29*(8), 971–985.

Blomquist, T., Hällgren, M., Nilsson, A., & Söderholm, A. (2010). Project as Practice: Making project research matter. *Project Management Journal*, *41*(1), 5–16.

Buchanan, D., & Hällgren, M. (2019). Surviving a zombie apocalypse: Leadership configurations in extreme contexts. *Management Learning*, *50*(2), 152–170.

Ferriss, T. (2007). *The Four Hour Work Week*. New York, NY: Random House.

Hällgren, M. (2007). Beyond the point of no return: On the management of deviations. *International Journal of Project Management*, *25*(8), 773–780.

Hällgren, M. (2009). Groupthink in the Death Zone: Failure of temporary organizations. Paper presented at the *European Academy of Management Conference*, Liverpool, UK.

Hällgren, M. (2010). Groupthink in temporary organizations. *International Journal of Managing Projects in Business*, *3*(1), 94–110.

Hällgren, M. (2011). Situated teams: Dropping the tools on Everest. In P. Lièvre, & M. Aubry (eds.), *Gestion de projet et expéditions polaires: Que pouvons-nous apprendre?* Grenoble: Presses de l'Université de Grenoble.

Hällgren, M. (ed.). (2014). *Reflections on a Scientific Career: Behind the professor's CV*. Stockholm/Copenhagen: Liber/Copenhagen Business Press.

Hällgren, M., Lindahl, M., & Rehn, A. (2013). The ghosts of shared leadership: On decision-making and subconscious followership in the Death Zone of K2. In C. M. Giannantonio, & A. E. Hurley-Hanson (eds.), *Extreme Leadership: Leaders, Teams and Situations Outside the Norm* (pp. 83–95). Cheltenham, UK and Northampton, MA, USA: Edward Elgar Publishing.

Hällgren, M., & Rouleau, L. (2018). Researching risk, emergency and crisis: Taking stock of research methods on extreme contexts and moving forward. In R. P. Gephart, C. Miller, & K. Svedberg Helgesson (eds.), *Routledge Companion to Risk, Crisis and Emergency Management* (pp. 146–161). London, UK: Routledge.

Hällgren, M., Rouleau, L., & De Rond, M. (2018). A matter of life or death: How extreme context research matters for Management and Organization Studies. *Academy of Management Annals*, *12*(1), 111–153.

Hällgren, M., & Söderholm, A. (2011). Projects-as-practice: New approach, new insights. In J. Pinto, P. Morris, & J. Söderlund (eds.), *Handbook of Project Management* (pp. 500–518). Oxford, UK: Oxford University Press.

Jacobsson, M., & Hällgren, M. (2016). Impromptu teams in a temporary organization: On their nature and role. *International Journal of Project Management*, *34*(4), 584–596.

Kim, W. C., & Mauborgne, R. A. (2005). *Blue Ocean Strategy: How to Create Uncontested Market Space and Make the Competition Irrelevant*. Boston, MA: Harvard Business Review Press.

Kutsch, E., Hällgren, M., & Turner, N. (2016). The internalization of attention at 28,000 feet: Revisiting the K2 2008 disaster. In B. C-N, A. Purnus, M. Huemann, & M. Hajdu (eds.), *Managing Project Risks for Competitive Advantage in Changing Business Environments* (pp. 196–215). Hershey, PA: Business Science Reference.

March, J. G. (2011). A scholar's quest. *Journal of Management Inquiry*, *20*(4), 355–357.

Simpson, J. (1997). *Touching the Void*. London, UK: Vintage.

17. What happens when your kids draw your career?

Spencer Harrison

Estimated reading time: **22 minutes and 16 seconds**.

CHAPTER HIGHLIGHTS

- The effort that it takes to do research has an "opportunity cost" for the people around us, that love us, and that might not understand fully what we do.
- Our work will seep into other parts of our lives, and into the lives of those around us.
- It is important to connect your work to bigger scientific ideas that your target audience understands.
- Make sure your work can allow people around you to smile *with you* more often.
- Science might allow you to produce "words about wisdom" but it can also be "scary stuff."

> *The chief enemy of creativity is good sense.*
> Pablo Picasso

INTRODUCTION

Science is hard.

There are lots of journals. Only a few "count".

Science also takes a long time. Most of my projects take four years from idea inception to completion. A lot of my projects have taken longer. Four years is a long time. It is long enough for a career to completely change trajectory. For an individual to completely change a career. Here I'm interested in the span of human experience during that time period. Four years is long enough for a child to be born, learn how to talk, learn how to walk, learn how to potty. Basically they become a fully functioning miniature human whose mistakes are still wonderful, adorable, and admirable. I bring up the notion of children because the children of researchers often have little impact on their parents' research (although I've thought of adding my kids as co-authors just to build their CVs so that they have a better shot at getting into PhD programs – by the time they are old enough it will take "five A's") and yet the research may have an impact on them.

That is, anything, that takes four years + passion + sacrifice + collaboration + travel + data + analysis + writing + re-writing ... well, anything that looks like that will have an impact on the people that are supporting the people doing the work.

(Yes, the above was my favorite paragraph to write! ~~I wrote.~~ Copy and pasted "re-writing" 23 times! A month ago my son was complaining that I asked him to write a draft of a story and then create a final draft based on the prior draft. This led to a lot of pouting and posturing. The basic question was, "Why do something twice when I can do it right the first time?" I was mildly excited at this point. I pulled out my computer and opened up a file folder for a recently accepted publication. I then pointed at the files. *All the glorious files!* I thought. And I counted them. Out loud. 67 drafts. "Look, it took me 67 drafts to get this published." He begrudgingly went back to a desk and re-wrote his story. I don't think he was inspired. I don't think I've counted from one to 67 out loud since.)

The point is, that our research has an impact. But I'm not talking about evidence-based management, citation count, translation to the classroom, translation to practitioner articles, or providing some sort of veneer of scientific legitimacy to business schools. I'm simply suggesting that the effort that it takes to do research has an opportunity cost on the people around us, that love us, and that might not understand fully what we do. Often these people are our friends ("So you get paid to write text books?" or "Research means you do ... what again?"). But we can typically explain what we do well enough that they might understand. Very often these people are our children. They see our furrowed brows. They feel our needful hugs. They hear our strained voices. They know our energy is going somewhere. But where? What work do we really do in their eyes? What is a productive business professor to a business professor's child?

LITERATURE REVIEW

Science is a greedy profession. It is like "The Nothing" from the film *The Never Ending Story* or "The Black Thing" from *A Wrinkle in Time* or "The Smoke Monster" from *Lost*. Greedy professions are shapeless smoke that seems to seep into any crack in your mind, your schedule, or your dedicated energy, and re-direct it toward the questions you are pursuing. That is both the power of science and the danger of science. That might sound overly dour. Let me try re-writing that, since I have already established how important re-writing is. Science is a giving profession. It is like the main character in the film *Star Man* or the Wisps in *Brave* or the final scene of *Raiders of the Lost Ark* when everyone's face melts (okay, it might seem like I'm dour again – give me a chance). In each case, large flashes of light eventually solve problems. And the light, well, it follows the physics of light – it seeps into everything. So good or bad, science captures us, propels us, helps us.

Precisely because science can be so shapeless it has been tempered. The game it plays with nature turned back on itself so that we can count the evolutionary necessity of bends in a duck's penis the same way we can count the impact of a scientist. Science has been tamed. Gamified. A's. Tenure. Publication score weighted by author order and citation count. This weight can be so taxing that Newton cajoled Flamstead's research assistant into stealing Flamstead's data about comet trajectories. Notably, all this counting that adds up our careers is made possible by anonymity.

Most of what we write is stripped of our names and then sent to people that have similar ideas. These other people – reviewers, referees, peers – are working in similar areas. Reading our ideas "for free". With deadlines they did not expect to incorporate into a busy schedule. At the same time, they also want to publish in the same journals about similar ideas. The incentives are misaligned. Or maybe it is a form of enlightened "aligned misalignment": by putting people in the worst psychological position to evaluate novelty only the best ideas get through? (What would happen if we created a system to put reviewers in the most developmentally oriented psychological state? What if they had to look at photographs of cute kittens for 30 minutes before reviewing, or, even simpler, if we had cute kitten photos all over the review portal, or, even simpler, if we had nudges that encouraged reviewers to "find the gold in the paper" or "locate the surprise in this paper and describe it to the author in the most compelling way possible".)

I just know it is hard. Reviewing yes. But the review process. The writing. The re-writing. It all takes a long time. And is fraught with pitfalls.

It all reminds me of weeklong backpacking trips. You have to plan ahead and choose a set of limited supplies. Methods, data collection, sample selection

– these are the tents, water filters, and sleeping pads we choose for our journey. Any added weight means more that we have to carry. We start with fresh legs and optimism. Any new idea seems imminently publishable. "There is no way this new idea will take as long to get submitted as the current set of papers I'm already working on!" And then, as the miles build up, and the harnesses and padding on backpack's suspension system begin to dig in, the questions start to build up: Did I bring too many socks? Should I carry less water to save weight, but filter it more often, thereby costing time? Should I have packed a rainfly? The problem with science is that your mind is on like 20 different backpacking trips at the same time! Hence the analogies to "smoke monsters" or benevolent creatures/weapons of light: the work we do can easily pervade.

What this literature reveals is that I am weird. You were warned in the first sentence. But mostly my rambling collection of pop references gets at the idea that we do a lot of work. Hard work. And our work will seep into other parts of our lives. We know this. We know some people are integrators, others are segregators (I'm more of the latter, I wear my office key on a separate lanyard from my house keyring). What I think our literature says less about (cue the angelic tuba that triumphantly announces the need for induction and theory building!) is what our children think about how we spend our time.

METHOD

So I asked my kids: Emerson, 11; Lincoln, 9; Bridger, 7; Mary Alice, 5. But before our interviews, I had them draw my office. I asked them to "draw where daddy works and what helps him do his work".

I'm not going to claim to have done much else. I didn't code the data. I didn't try to develop a model. This is raw. To be honest, to incentivize my kids I said: "Would you like to see your artwork printed in a book?" In some ways this chapter is a cheap concession to them. At a deeper level, it was an opportunity for me to see my world from their perspective. You can see we didn't have long conversations. About 15 minutes each. After each drawing + dialogue I offer a short reflection.

FINDINGS

Case Study 1: Conversation with Emerson (11 Years Old)

Note: S = Spencer; E = Emerson.

S: What helps me do my work?
E: The notes.
S: Why do you think the notes help?

E: Ah, so you can look at the notes and put them altogether and make them into something amazing.

S: What sort of amazing things do you think I make at work?

E: You can write books that would give inspiration to other people.

S: What do think is the most important thing in my office?

E: You. The computer.

S: Why?

E: Because you can do all sorts of stuff on there and it holds loads of information.

S: What are other things you think are important in my office?

E: Your "stuffies".[1]

S: Why?

E: Because they can remind you of your family.

S: What is the $MC = E^2$ in the upper corner?

E: It is Einstein's equation. He was a famous scientist and it was an amazing discovery that he made. It made everything in science a little easier so people can take that equation and say "if this equals this, then this must equal that".

S: If I create something amazing at work, what do you think it helps people do?

E: It could change the world, making it a better place.

S: How?

E: You could take a piece of junk and write a paper on it and show the ways it could turn into something useful.

S: Have you heard me talking about that?

E: Yes.

S: What have you understood from me talking about that?

E: That everything has its own uses and you don't have to waste everything.

S: Are there any other details in the drawing you made that are important to you?

E: I like the Tinker Toys.

S: Say more.

E: I also like playing with the stuffies and looking at the old photos and rewards. [Translation: the diplomas on the wall.]

S: Why do you like looking at those?

E: It makes me feel proud to have a dad that is so successful.

S: Why did you draw the cricket bars?

E: Because you like to eat them.

S: What do you remember about the project I did with crickets?

E: That people can mix crickets into a nice healthy snack. That people are making more food out of crickets.

S: Is that important?

E: Yes because we can eat the crickets.

Figure 17.1   Emerson's drawing of dad's office

Reflection

First, I am amazed at the detail in the drawing (Figure 17.1). There is no "E = MC²" on the glass wall, but there is a drawing of a character Emerson made up called Super Eyeball who is saying "We love U dad!" There are also canisters of Tinker Toys in the office. Not on the bottom shelf. You can see the packet of "crickit bars" – which I do not have – but I do have a packet of cricket chocolate chip cookies next to a can of fried crickets. The nature of the drawing gives the office a messy feel, which is very true to reality. And the aforementioned glass wall always has boxes and arrows: proto-prototypes of theory.

I am struck by how central the notion of inspiration is to Emerson. He does not really know what E = MC² means but he knows it is important. He also doesn't fully know what I research but he understands enough. At the time of the interview I had been revising a paper about companies making food for human consumption out of insects. He understands that the idea is important, at least to me. But it makes me happy to see it as something important for others. It also makes me happy that he sees my office as a fun place. I think I would rather have my kids feel immediately welcome in my office and a visiting executive wonder "why does this guy have so much kids' stuff here?" rather than the reverse.

Notice his comment about the computer: "You can do all sorts of stuff on there and it holds loads of information." That will come up again later (so, I sort of coded it).

Case Study 2: Conversation with Lincoln (9 Years Old)

Note: S = Spencer; L = Lincoln.

S: Can you tell me about the picture?

L: These four guys are executives listening to you. You are standing on a stage. And there is a little poster and big screen behind you with the stuff you are talking about.

S: Is this an important part of my work?

L: Yes. Teaching.

S: Why?

L: Well you need to teach the executives what to do so that when they're like you they'll know what to do.

S: How old are the executives?

L: We could say maybe in their early 20s.

S: What do executives do?

L: They usually get taught by the INSEAD teachers and sometimes they get to do fun activities.

S: You've got a lot of things going on in this picture. Which do you think are most important for me to do my work?

L: The podium.

S: Why is the podium important?

L: So you can teach things and they can hear you from far. So if you're in a huge room with loads of executives there are speakers so they can hear you.

S: What are the things you think I teach to executives?

L: How to be a better professor. And how to work with people correctly. They could be making people feel down and they would stop working with them.

S: What else do you think is important?

L: The screen. It could have interesting information you forgot to explain. And they could read that and get inspired by it. And also the pictures are important because if an executive does not get what you are saying you have got the pictures to explain what is going on.

S: I noticed some sharks in the pictures, what made you think about those?

L: I drew them because I thought sometimes you might teach about endangered creatures.

S: What made you think that might be something I teach about?

L: I do not know. Sharks were the first thing that popped into my head.
S: Tell me about my outfit.
L: You are wearing a suit and a tie so you look like a professional business man.
S: Do you think the outfit is important?
L: Yes, er no, not really, you could go in any outfit to a teaching session.
S: What helps me do my work?
L: I do not know. When you're planning for a lesson and you forget about it you can look at the drawings and say, "Now I know what he is thinking about".

Figure 17.2   Lincoln's drawing of dad's office

Reflection

Hah! I love his definition of executives. Twenty must seem so old to a 9 year old. (As an aside, for my kids right now, teenagers are "the devil". Ask them who did something wrong or who created turmoil at school and it is always "the teenagers". It is like my kids are trapped in a 1950s movie surrounded by older kids with combs and switchblades in their back pockets and greasy, wavy hair that looks like it was extruded from a Play Doh mold.) I also love the sharks (Figure 17.2). I do not think I have ever used a shark image in any of my presentations. But there is a deeper truth he's getting at: I love putting big, vibrant images in my presentations.

I think part of what he is drawing is a specific moment. Before my first lecture at INSEAD, I actually brought my entire family to a case room on a Saturday. I loaded up some slides and I went through the first 15 minutes of my lecture. I was dressed in a suit. There was a podium (with an INSEAD logo) and a huge screen. The four executives almost equal the five members of the family there that day.

Also notice that this is very teaching focused. So in Lincoln's mind, teaching is a key aspect of my work. You can also see him trying to make sense of why teaching is important. While sharks might be a really good metaphor for some of my students, he connects them to "endangered creatures". There is a bit of a similarity here with Emerson's reference to $E = MC^2$. In both cases, they are connecting my work to bigger scientific ideas that they understand to be important.

Case Study 3: Conversation with Bridger (7 Years Old)

Note: S = Spencer; B = Bridger.

B: There is your turkey, there is your hot chocolate. Do you have an Apple Computer? You do!

S: Can you tell me about the picture?

B: You have a telephone. You have some baskets with things that can help you work. I wonder what that is? [Points to the squiggle in the lower left corner.] Oh, it is a wire! And you're looking up your new thing you're going to teach your students. I think. Yes.

S: Why?

B: Because it helps other people learn?

S: What do I help other people learn?

B: Things that they don't know.

S: Like …?

B: Like, I do not know what businessmen would do. Maybe … they could learn a new thing they did not know and that they could have that for homework.

S: What sort of homework do you think I give people?

B: Researching on things like stuff that people need to know if they want to grow up big.

S: Is there anything else in my office that is important for helping me do my work?

B: A light.

S: Okay. You mentioned me teaching and you mentioned me asking people to do research. Tell me more about what I do in terms of research and teaching.

B: You show them easy ways for how to do research if they do not understand it.

S: How do I do that?

B: You make it easy for them.

S: What sort of things do I research?

B: I do not know.

S: Really, you have never heard me talk about it?

B: Yes, I have, but I do not remember anything. Finding out new things? Like the discovery of a new Orca whale [we discussed this this morning at breakfast].

S: Am I a scientist?

B: No.

S: What am I?

B: You are a professor.

S: What does a professor do?

B: Um. Let us see. They look up things and they learn and stuff.

S: Anything else you want to tell me about your drawing or my work?

B: No.

Reflection

Bridger's drawing (Figure 17.3) is the same setting as Emerson's. He has rotated the perspective 90 degrees. Now we are looking directly at me. His version of my office is cleaner (notice that even Lincoln's slides looked a little cluttered) but there is a nifty little swirl in the lower left corner that I take as a symbol of my general messiness.

You can see that the point of my work is teaching – "And you are looking up your new thing you're going to teach your students. I think. Yes." But he is also introducing the notion of research while also making a distinction between a professor and scientist. I am the former, not the latter. Also notice that both

Figure 17.3   Bridger's drawing of dad's office

Lincoln and Bridger have introduced large marine animals (Note: they did not draw their pictures at the same time, nor did they hear each other's interviews so this is really interesting. Someone should write a book titled *We All Wanted to be Marine Biologists: Why We Loved the Sea Until We Didn't*).

A central theme here is learning. I think it's interesting that he has connected my learning as a precursor to my students' learning. It's also nice that he drew me next to a perfect cartoon turkey.

Case Study 4: Conversation with Mary Alice (5 Years Old)

Note: S = Spencer; MA = Mary Alice.

S: Tell me about your picture.
MA: This [top image] is you typing on your computer and you drawing a radish.
S: What else can you tell me?
MA: You are typing.
S: Why am I typing?

MA: Because you are working. You're playing on the computer and working on it.

S: Why do I type?

MA: Because you are at work.

S: Is typing what you do at work?

MA: Yes.

S: What do I type about?

MA: You type about radishes and other stuff that is fruits and vegetables.

S: What is going on this picture [middle]?

MA: You are not there. The cross on you [shows you are not there] because you are at work so long.

S: What's going on next to it?

MA: That is you eating at the table at INSEAD. Remember you eating at the table? And then you're typing again and looking at the computer.

S: What is the green building [bottom left]?

MA: That is work.

S: What is this building [to the right]?

MA: That is home. And you're not there. So you are all in work still.

S: Why do you think work is drawn really big and home is drawn small?

MA: Because that page was filled so I had to draw home really small.

S: What is this [above the house]?

MA: That is mommy waiting for you and she is saying, "Where is your daddy?"

S: What helps me do my work?

MA: Working on your computer and not playing on it.

S: What does my computer allow me to do?

MA: To put words on it and read on it. And it allows you to draw pictures.

S: What does daddy put words about?

MA: He puts words about wisdom but not scary stuff?

S: What kind of wisdom?

MA: You get Legos and toys and you have friends and "do-do's"[2] there.

S: Why do you think I have those things in my office?

MA: Because you are going to give those to us. And you have books at work that we can play with if we visit work.

S: Anything else you want to say about my work?

MA: I do not know anything else.

S: What about the other picture [below]?

MA: Mom is waiting long and long. She is sad. Because you are not there and because she really wants you at home.

S: What should I learn from your drawings about my work?

MA: To be nice. And to be kind and do nice things to other people.

Figure 17.4   *Mary Alice's drawing of dad's office*

Reflection

Apart from large marine animals and the toys I have in my office … (Note: I do enjoy having the toys and I keep them more as symbols of creativity and fun than anything else, but I do have them for experiential exercises too! I swear) … computers figure heavily in these drawings. So my kids know that the computer is a really important tool for me. Mary Alice uses the computer as a way to link me to even more fundamental thinking tools: words and drawings (Figure 17.4). What do I use these tools for? "Words about wisdom but not scary stuff?"

This one is the most heartbreaking. I don't have to do much interpretation:

Home is smaller than work.

Mommy waiting for you.

The cross on you [shows you're not there] because you're at work so long.

Mom is sad.

Be nice.

I can soften this by seeing that she sees my office as a fun place to be and that I'm doing something about radishes and vegetables. That seems healthy. But it would be far healthier if home was twice the size of work. And mom was not sad. And there was not a "cross that shows you're not there".

DISCUSSION

Yes, our work seeps into the lives of those around us. Even those that don't understand it. Perhaps especially those that don't understand the substance of the work, but see the substance of the costs because then they can't use it to rationalize how important the work must be. Notice how Emerson and Lincoln are already beginning to rationalize why my work must be important without understanding it whereas Mary Alice sees the absence more clearly even though she has been alive to see it for a smaller period of time.

Science is a monster of darkness and light. We give it existence through our curiosity. It obtains structure from the structures that have grown up around it. I can fill my office with toys, use beautiful large photographs of sharks to teach and inspire, and surround my office with nascent theories but at the same time science is growing to twice the size of my house, crossing me out, and leaving people waiting for me.

Whatever success I have deserves reflection. Science might allow me to produce "words about wisdom" but it can also be "scary stuff".

LIMITATIONS

This is just my career.

PRACTICAL APPLICATIONS

I would suggest doing the same activity. Ask your child to draw a picture of your work and then talk to them about it. Personally, I think the decorating in my office is working out just fine. I should probably just spend less time there.

CODA

I was really affected by going through this exercise. It was meant to be playful and fun. In many ways it was. But it was also painful and meaningful. Which of the details are most important? I'm still not sure. I appreciate that they see my job as having some sort of impact, even if they are not quite sure for whom or how. I also take solace that my kids see me as happy – they generally drew me smiling – and surrounded by reminders of them (drawings on the walls).

My goal now is to make sure my work can allow them to smile *with me* more often.

NOTES

1. "Stuffies" are plush animals I have in my office. I have a Beaker doll I was given for visiting the Google PiLab. I also have Zoidberg, because I liked his character on Futurama. And I have Rigby and Mordecai from *The Regular Show* – watch it! It's awesome!
2. "Do-do's" is phonetic for a French word my children have picked up that means a loved stuffed animal.

PART VI

Seizing the horizon

18. The day after tomorrow: academic career dilemmas and choices

Matej Černe and Tomislav Hernaus

Estimated reading time: **20 minutes and 17 seconds**.

CHAPTER HIGHLIGHTS

- Be authentic and unique; do not be afraid to stand out. However, acknowledge that universally recognized individual characteristics predicting academic success are proactivity, self-efficacy, and persistence.
- Helping behavior and humility go a long way.
- Embracing and learning from cultural differences, and surrounding yourself with a (professional and personal) support network, help in overcoming culturally-based misunderstandings and sources of frustration.
- Doing what you love and having passion for what you do helps you overcome many difficulties in academia that you are almost definitely going to be faced with.
- Being able to quickly switch between different tasks and accept the necessity of exhibiting task variety enables successful academics to develop mastery and self-progress.

> *Your power to choose your direction of your life*
> *allows you to reinvent yourself, to change your future,*
> *and to powerfully influence the rest of creation.*
> Stephen R. Covey

INTRODUCTION

After reading all the fascinating academic career development stories and unique occurrences in our contributors' paths, one must wonder – what can we learn, and what is in it for me? Where and how do we go from here? The final chapter in this volume attempts to summarize key themes discussed by the contributors and integrate takeaways stemming from their personal reflections. To foresee how we will do this, let us borrow what one of the contributors, Ante Glavaš, wrote in his chapter: "Read what is written here, then disregard it, and only use [it] as a starting point to think more deeply about [your] own unique path and learning" (Chapter 9, this volume). Key takeaways that we have identified might have worked for our contributors, but they might not work for you. The uniqueness of each individual has to be emphasized, leading us not to a universal or average academic that we should all strive to be, but an authentic, original, unique one, finding his/her own place in the academic sphere not only because of unique personality traits, individual characteristics and personal strengths but also weaknesses, which determine who we are.

Therefore, we have to stress that the chapters included in this volume are intentionally different! This is something the reader might have been wondering when reading them. They attempt to capture individual paths corresponding also with different writing styles (see Harrison's technique of reflecting upon one's own career through children drawings and interpretations [Chapter 17]), metaphors (see Galanaki's Odyssey epos or Story's dance in Chapters 3 and 14) that serve to support contributors' points and uniqueness. The importance of being authentic and original is well recognized in the literature on authenticity (see Cha et al., 2019; Van den Bosch et al., 2019) and creativity (see Klijn & Tomic, 2010); this volume highlights the importance of standing out in the context of academia as well. As Story (Chapter 14, this volume) puts it: "Keep singing, keep dancing! Even though you may be out of tune."

BEING AUTHENTIC BY NOT UNDERESTIMATING A TYPICAL "ACADEMIC PERSONA"

Despite the importance of being authentic and different, there are recurring key success factors and behavioral patterns of academics related to individual traits and characteristics throughout the chapters. While the academic context frequently forces us to be "supermen or superwomen" (see our take on a variety of job demands pertaining to an academic job, career or calling in Chapter 2 of this volume), certain individual features help. It has to be underlined that these individual characteristics are not related to personality traits (e.g. Big Five), and they are not much different from those delineating between successful or unsuccessful working professionals in general (Rosenbusch et al., 2013; Stajkovic & Luthans, 1998).

One of these is proactivity (Černe, Chapter 7, Mendling, Chapter 15, and Strauss, Chapter 8, this volume), which is related to anticipatory, change-oriented and self-initiated behavior (Grant & Ashford, 2008). In practical terms, as emphasized by our contributors, it means jumping upon opportunities and taking them head-on. To illustrate such behavior, Glavaš (Chapter 9, this volume) mentions the concept of "Kairos" – an Ancient Greek word meaning the right, critical, or opportune moment, which he uses as a metaphor for being ready for coincidences and opportunities that academic (or non-academic) life throws at you. Another, but related individual characteristic that tends to delineate successful from not so successful academics (or individuals in general) is self-efficacy, that is, one's belief in personal ability to succeed in specific situations or accomplish a task (Bandura, 1982). This characteristic has been highlighted in literature on work and academia (Zajacova et al., 2005) as well as recognized by our contributors (Černe, Chapter 7, this volume); it helps academics to be prepared for events and openings in an academic career.

Both proactivity and self-efficacy should be supplemented with persistence, perseverance and resilience. Zikic (Chapter 6, this volume) rightly claims that "one's persistence leads to a unique career opportunity". Along the same lines, Černe (Chapter 7, this volume) pinpoints persistence and hard work as key academic success factors. Likewise, Potočnik (Chapter 13, this volume) finds perseverance as well as resilience to be really important qualities for academic career development. To introduce some neuroscience thinking, we may add that "the brain is just like a muscle – use it or lose it" (Kirby et al., 1999). If you do not challenge your mind regularly, at best the status quo will remain, although there is a great chance of experiencing a decrease in cognitive abilities. Even more, on the other hand, significant or finest intellectual achievements are obtained only when we are challenged enough, that is, slightly pushed beyond our limits.

SERENDIPITY AND ACADEMIC CAREERS

Many of our contributors emphasize that, while they were ready to embrace changes, opportunities came to them in a relatively serendipitous, random manner; based on unpredictability (Galanaki, Chapter 3, Milanov, Chapter 4, Potočnik, Chapter 13, Zikic, Chapter 6, this volume). Serendipity is defined as the "accidental discovery of something valuable" (e Cunha et al., 2010, p. 319). Such an unplanned approach is well documented in the literature on careers and relates to chaos theory of career planning (Pryor & Bright, 2012). "Planned happenstance" (Mitchell et al., 1999) is a term Zikic (Chapter 6, this volume) uses to illustrate these occurrences. And while one might expect such an occurrence in careers of academic nomads (more on that later), chapters by academics that stayed put in their careers (Černe, Chapter 7, Galanaki, Chapter 3, Hällgren, Chapter 16, Hernaus, Chapter 10, Van Looy, Chapter 5, this volume) also highlight this theme.

On a related note, in addition to being unplanned, many contributors emphasize the role of luck, especially in terms of "being in the right place at the right time" (for instance, Glavaš, Chapter 9, Van Looy, Chapter 5, Zikic, Chapter 6, this volume). This is a clear indication of modesty in terms of evaluating one's own achievements, even in cases of academics who are extremely successful in terms of scholarly influence/citations or recognition. There is surprisingly a lot of convergence on this theme across chapters. Perhaps this notion is cultural, as the majority of our contributors come from Europe (it might be different in the case of scholars in the US, where, generally, emphasizing one's achievements might be more culturally expected; Nelson & Shavitt, 2002).

An alternative explanation for this theme might be related to professional culture: is it possible that successful academics are just being modest? This logic could make sense, as "academics should exhibit an inherent drive to help others and transfer knowledge, thereby being helpers" (cf., Grant, 2013) by definition, and, as such, not strive to over-emphasize their achievements. Humility has also been shown by recent meta-analytic evidence (Lee et al., 2019) to contribute to individual performance, outside the academia setting. Nonetheless, as highlighted in the literature on knowledge management, despite knowledge transfer, helping and service being embedded in expectations of academic careers, scholars also tend to hide knowledge (Demirkasimoglu, 2016; Hernaus et al., 2019). Our group of contributors just might be on the positive side, and since this is a rather successful group, we should all learn from them that helping and humility go a long way.

TAKING ADVANTAGE OF CAREER SHOCKS

Career shocks – positive impactful events (although we can also experience negative ones) in an academic's life, which may alter one's work motivation and behaviors, and facilitate the achievement of career goals (Seibert et al., 2013) – should be emphasized as another, highly relevant trigger for career development and eventually career success in modern academia. For instance, receiving a research or teaching award, winning a research grant, being invited to serve on a journal editorial board, or being promoted to a higher rank or appointed as a department chair sooner than expected are just few of such fortunate yet often well-earned career enhancers. We may add to the list and highlight specifically the importance of publishing a paper in a top-tier journal (such as the *Academy of Management Journal*, *Journal of Management*, *Administrative Science Quarterly*, and similar four-star or A+ publication outlets). As acknowledged by Černe, Glavaš and Mendling (Chapters 7, 9 and 15 respectively, this volume), such an achievement is really what makes a career difference. Nevertheless, we should mention that good timing of career shocks (relative to the developmental stage of an academic career) is almost equally as important as experiencing a positive shock in the first place (Kraimer et al., 2019; Morgeson et al., 2015).

SHOULD I STAY OR SHOULD I GO? CAREER NOMADS OR HOME-GROWN ACADEMICS

Contributors' paths have naturally been very much influenced by key decisions/choices in their careers, whether they came in a planned or shocking/ serendipitous manner. One of such key exemplary decisions that tends to turn one's career and life upside down is whether to leave one's originating country in search of better (or different) academic opportunities. Across different chapters, many pros and cons of either of the two approaches can be identified. While moving enables obtaining a variety of experiences, expands one's network of collaborators, and contributes to heterogeneous ideas breeding one's creativity (see early-career reflections by Mendling, Chapter 15, Milanov, Chapter 4, Story, Chapter 14, Zikic, Chapter 6, this volume), it is also associated with cross-cultural misunderstandings and issues related to being in a new environment, learning new languages and (working) habits, potential lack of support, or even psychological challenges, such as dealing with loneliness or, in extreme cases, depression. Not less important to note is that one can expect a temporary reduction in one's research productivity while switching between academic settings (e.g. Billsberry et al., 2019; Milanov, Chapter 4, this volume).

On the other hand, growing up in a stable academic setting and being appointed as a faculty member by your *alma mater* (i.e. academic inbreeding) has already been widely recognized as a problematic and deleterious practice (Altbach et al., 2015; Yudkevich et al., 2015) that is associated with lower scholarly output (Horta et al., 2010). While we do not intend to go against the mainstream thinking, pragmatic system-wide reasons why inbreeding may occur (and the practical difficulties associated with "undoing" this approach to faculty hiring) should, however, be considered. For instance, such scholarly recruitment "malpractice" is a sound approach in small- and medium-sized countries as "there are not that many alternatives in national academia for one to move to" (Horta & Yudkevich, 2016). Moreover, from our own early-career examples (Černe, Chapter 7, Hernaus, Chapter 10, this volume), we may say that it could still work but with an important add-on: maybe an individual does not need to be formally enrolled in doctoral studies, hold a postdoc position or be employed by an institution other than his or her PhD awarding university, yet he or she should be flexible enough to travel and accumulate experiences from other business schools and organizational scholars.

With reference to career moves, contributors expressed some ignorance (actually, lack of emphasis) of cultural differences (Milanov, Chapter 4, Zikic,

Chapter 6, Potočnik, Chapter 13, Story, Chapter 14, this volume). When one moves to a different country, one tends to underestimate the effect of "the little things": small contextual differences and cultural characteristics that make a person feel at home in a particular place. While these differences can also be a source of fascination, learning and personal development, especially if they are embraced, they can also lead to frustration and many misunderstandings in terms of what is expected (and important) in particular social situations.

If we take a slightly different turn to interpreting career changes and refer to literature and practice on organizational socialization (Bauer et al., 2007), we can conclude that, despite its clear benefits, almost no-one reports on formal on-boarding processes. It seems that academic institutions frequently do not practice what they preach, and socialization processes are frequently left for individuals to deal with, and the extent to which they are able to mobilize their support network is important. Such a network is crucial for academics (or individuals, generally) to feel included, and higher education institutions should strive to do more to make newcomers feel welcome and "part of the family".

TENSION BETWEEN INTRINSIC MOTIVATION, ACHIEVEMENT EVALUATION AND SOCIETAL IMPACT

The previous point also leads us to another recurring theme of how achievement is evaluated and recognized in various contexts. There were quite some reflections upon the "publish or perish" mantra in academia, where achievement is evaluated based on the number of published papers, research grants won and similar measures. In Chapter 2, the editors of this volume also write about this misalignment in terms of value placed on the different "stools" that constitute an academic job. Despite these external criteria of evaluation that unfortunately shape much of what we end up doing, a key success factor seems to be related to "doing what you love", that is, having passion for what you do (Glavaš, Chapter 9, Hällgren, Chapter 16, Harrison, Chapter 17, Milanov, Chapter 4, Zikic, Chapter 6, this volume).

Finding an intrinsic drive and meaningfulness in one's work (Amabile, 1993) clearly enables individuals to overcome the pressures and pitfalls of academia, or at least makes them less susceptible to its perils. Some contributors have had this gut feeling since the very beginning or early years, even well before being introduced to academia (Černe, Chapter 7, Mendling, Chapter 15, this volume) while some learned to focus on the positives, grow into it, and find sources of internal drive in one (or more) of the activities that are part of what academics do, either simultaneously or at different points in their careers (Glavaš, Chapter 9, Hernaus, Chapter 10, Van Looy, Chapter 5, this volume).

What moves us towards and through academia varies tremendously from one individual to the other. The vast majority of contributors seemingly have a strong focus on research and find internal drive in personal curiosity (Černe, Chapter 7, Hällgren, Chapter 16, this volume), examining something new, or in fact writing and publishing (Mendling, Chapter 15, Strauss, Chapter 8, this volume), with only a few (Hernaus, Chapter 10, Harrison, Chapter 17, this volume) going in-depth in their respective chapters on the teaching aspect of our job and calling. It appears that intrinsically, most of us [contributors] tend to like research more – or maybe it is just a result of bias coming out of an editorial decision to invite to this volume those academics who have already published respectively in leading publication outlets. However, one should not forget to care about a broader impact (see Hughes et al., 2019) that he or she should have on other people – students as well as academic colleagues – business community (Glavaš, Chapter 9, Rehn, Chapter 11, Van Looy, Chapter 5, this volume) and society in general (Glavaš, Chapter 9, Strauss, Chapter 8, this volume).

MULTIPLE ROLES OF ACADEMICS, TASK VARIETY AND TASK SWITCHING

Let us revert back to the notion of an "academic superhero" (Hay, 2017): a person not only good, but excellent in research, teaching, and other activities that comprise academics' (at least informal) job descriptions. We covered a lot of these topics in Chapter 2 on academic work design (activities were characterized as teaching- and student-related, research- and writing-related, or service- and administration-oriented ones), and upon reading the contributions to this volume, we are not surprised that our contributing academics highlighted or at least mentioned the issue of multimodal roles many times. There is no doubt that diverse academic roles often confront each other (Billsberry et al., 2019). While many of the contributors relate administrative work in particular to what they perceive as additional "annoying" activities that take away time from the core (teaching and/or research) (for example, Hernaus, Chapter 10, Strauss, Chapter 8, this volume), it is a constitutive part of the academic profession. Therefore, if we cannot escape then we must learn how to accept and embrace multiple roles to enjoy in a wide range of diverse responsibilities (Hernaus, Chapter 10, Milanov, Chapter 4, Rehn, Chapter 11, Van Looy, Chapter 5, this volume).

In addition to juggling between distinct roles, recognizing an "academic as manager/leader" (Hällgren, Chapter 16, Mendling, Chapter 15, Milanov, Chapter 4, Rehn, Chapter 11, Van Looy, Chapter 5, this volume) and embracing the need to exhibit planning, organizing, leading and supervising skills seems to be key – or at least unavoidable. Being able to quickly switch between different tasks and accept the necessity of exhibiting task variety enables successful academics to develop mastery and self-progress. In addition to administrative or academic leadership roles, contributors also emphasize connections to practice (Galanaki, Chapter 3, Glavaš, Chapter 9, Harrison, Chapter 17, Hernaus, Chapter 10, Van Looy, Chapter 5, this volume) and exposure in expert and popular media (Rehn, Chapter 11, Zikic, Chapter 6, this volume) as a way to touch people, exert influence, popularize science, and enable knowledge transfer flows across various domains. This constitutes not only a crucial element of our job or calling, but in fact becomes a responsibility of individuals that have the means (and expertise) to influence the development of young people, new generations entering the workforce of the future.

SOCIAL CONTEXT AS A KEY ENABLER OF ACADEMIC SUCCESS

A key recurring theme across chapters is a crucial role of the social system. On one hand, it is denoted by collaborations – networks leading to achievements (Galanaki, Chapter 3, Hällgren, Chapter 16, Mendling, Chapter 15, Rispens, Chapter 12, Zikic, Chapter 6, this volume). Contributors described different strategies of forming networks, but they were mostly in agreement that learning from people better than yourself and being included in international projects and collaborative networks is vital for academics entering this world. Events such as academic conferences, and especially informal parts of them (dinners, meet-ups, receptions) are critical in expanding personal linkages that might come in handy – not necessarily in terms of joint projects, but perhaps at some point in service, reviewing, editorial assignments, and so on – or just feeling more like you belong in an academic world. However, in order not to be disappointed, you should be very picky when it comes to choosing which conferences to attend. You should consider attending some of the largest and most prominent ones (such as the Academy of Management [AOM] Conference, the European Academy of Management [EURAM] Conference, the European Group for Organizational Studies [EGOS] Colloquium, the European Association of Work and Organizational Psychology [EAWOP] Congress, and the Strategic Management Society [SMS] Conference) as well as some more specific (small meeting) disciplinary or regional events.

Not saying "no" to collaborations and even friendly get-togethers seems to be critical at the beginning of academic careers. However, when such a career reaches maturity and the opportunities and possibilities become almost endless (especially for intrinsically-motivated individuals that find everything interesting), skipping conferences and saying "no" (see Černe, Chapter 7, Potočnik, Chapter 13, Zikic, Chapter 6, this volume) becomes quite an important preservation strategy that enables a healthy work–life balance (or work–life separation). You can very easily become overwhelmed with social interaction, especially when you become recognized for your achievements.

A clear guiding figure that can help in navigating the networks, which is heavily emphasized by contributors, is an academic role model. Selfless, supporting mentors and/or influential well-established scholars (Černe, Chapter 7, Hällgren, Chapter 16, Hernaus, Chapter 10, Story, Chapter 14, Strauss, Chapter 8, Zikic, Chapter 6, this volume) make a clear difference especially at the academic beginnings. To provide some evidence, we just need to take a look at mentor–mentee dyads (for instance, Matej Černe → Miha Škerlavaj; Jan Mendling → Wil van der Aalst; Karoline Strauss → Mark Griffin) or master–student collaborations (e.g. Ante Glavaš → Herman Aguinis; Markus Hällgren → James G. March; Kristina Potočnik → Neil R. Anderson; Sonja Rispens → Evangelia Demerouti; Karoline Strauss → Sharon K. Parker) of our contributors to get a feeling of how important the prestige of one's PhD or research advisor is (Kraimer et al., 2019). Certainly one of the clear tasks of mentors (i.e. senior and more experienced colleagues) is in fact related to connecting and including young academics in existing networks, personal linkages, and in fact tangible projects that have the potential to develop into "big things". At the same time, equally important is to "let go" of mentees for them to be able to develop their own careers, search for unique areas of study, as well as to establish unique networks of collaborators. Enabling young academics to "fly their wings" can also be challenging for mentors.

Yet another angle of social support emphasized by our contributors is that of family and friends (Černe, Chapter 7, Glavaš, Chapter 9, Harrison, Chapter 17, Hernaus, Chapter 10, Rispens, Chapter 12, Strauss, Chapter 8, Van Looy, Chapter 5, this volume). Virtually everyone mentions this aspect as an essential balance between work and having a life. While this is crucial in the case of moving careers, it is a differentiator in cases of contributors staying put as well. What is more, it seems to be a key factor in decisions not to move.

THE STRUGGLE OF FINDING A WORK–FAMILY (WORK–FREE TIME) BALANCE

Social context is not all roses in the cases of our contributors; since we love what we do, our families and friends constantly need to compete for our attention. Many contributors report on a struggle to obtain a work–life balance (Harrison, Chapter 17, Rispens, Chapter 12, Van Looy, Chapter 5, this volume), and many more experience the same yet decided not to pinpoint this issue explicitly. While it is difficult to offer practical suggestions on how to solve this when the editors clearly also struggle with this (Černe, Chapter 7, Hernaus, Chapter 10, this volume), having a professional life outside of academia (Glavaš, Chapter 9, Rehn, Chapter 11, Van Looy, Chapter 5, this volume), personal organizing and prioritizing (Hernaus, Chapter 10, Mendling, Chapter 15, this volume), fostering positive energizing relationships (Černe, Chapter 7, Mendling, Chapter 15, Zikic, Chapter 6, this volume), crafting work–life balance and strategic allocation of personal resources (Rispens, Chapter 12, Zikic, Chapter 6, this volume) and saying "no" (Černe, Chapter 7, Potočnik, Chapter 13, Zikic, Chapter 6, this volume) seem to be helpful.

In a way, academic jobs, since they are so autonomous and flexible, tend to penetrate every aspect of our lives. The intensified blurring of boundaries between work and personal life is furthered by advancements in information technology and digitalization, which *de facto* enable us to be constantly on-demand, connected 24/7 with our work. Absurdly, we love to do our work, and this emotional drive often leads us to workaholism and sometimes generates stress, burnout and health-related issues. Devising clear personal guidelines and policies for not even work–life balance, but in fact work–life separation (Kinman & Jones, 2008) or work–life integration (Harrington & Ladge, 2009) is likely a way forward – which in fact represents a way back to more clearly structured and delineated work schedules. In the end, this has to be done at a personal level where one needs to weigh the costs and benefits of different ways of working in academia.

GENDER BIAS IN ACADEMIA

We regret to confirm that gender inequality is still an issue in academia. Despite an increasing number of universities worldwide that have introduced gender equality measures (for an overview see Powell, 2018), both individual and institutional gender discrimination (or at least gender bias) persists (Lerchenmueller & Sorenson, 2018; Monroe et al., 2008; West et al., 2013). Both Strauss and Story (Chapters 8 and 14 respectively, this volume) importantly put the gender issue among faculty (and "being a woman") in the spotlight. The Gender Balance Scorecard for Business Schools (established a few years ago; see Wittenberg-Cox & Symons, 2015) gives an overview of the gender balance of MBAs and faculty at world-leading business schools (Financial Times ranking). Sadly, none of the Top 20 business schools have managed to break 30% female faculty, and only two B-schools have female deans (Global Business Schools Report, 2019). There is nothing more to be said. However, at least in this volume, we are happy to have a majority of female contributors (eight out of fifteen in total).

HAVE WE COME FULL CIRCLE?

To overview the key content put forth by our contributors, we have designed a word map[1] (Figure 18.1) that portrays key terms most frequently used in the chapter abstracts and highlights. To do so we used the abstracts and highlights (i.e. takeaways) of the chapters, which have a better content-to-connecting-words ratio than the full texts.

Figure 18.1　　Word map overviewing the book content

We produced another content word map (Figure 18.2) to create a valuable quick visual overview of the key issues, themes, and domains put forth by the volume contributors in their chapters. The map is based on semantic and content similarity, including the order of frequency being mentioned, that is, how many times each topic occurs across the contributions. Thus, we identified what they (we) find the most interesting, impactful, and crucial to discuss and describe within the world of academia. Interestingly, being "different" and "personal" were among the most commonly used words, followed by a similar weight given to "experience", "balance", and "success". Furthermore, "research" (as expected) and "book" (somewhat surprisingly) are mentioned more frequently than "teaching" and "service". Likewise, "individual" is mentioned four times more often than "group" and three times more than "network", indicating that academia is still a lonely place to be when starting the journey.

Many success factors and personal strategies to survive and thrive in the world of academia were shared throughout the volume. However, none of us (volume contributors) think that we are better than other academics. In our humble opinion, we are just brave and altruistic enough to share our career

Figure 18.2   Word map presenting key clusters of content in the book

success and pitfalls. Similar to Arthur Bedeian (1996) and his eye-opening essay in *Rhythms of Academic Life*, which still represents a highly relevant and inspirational piece of work, we offer personal experience and observations on academic beginnings. As such, we have followed in the footsteps of Hermes, Circe, and Athena (Homer, 1919), immortals who aided Odysseus in returning home. No, by *no* means do we feel like divine figures from Ancient Greek mythology. We have just used it as a good metaphor to get our reflective stories closer to the reader. Whether and to what extent we have succeeded is not up to us to judge. Ultimately, the test of time will do the work. Until then, we should not discard other useful advice about early-career success in academia. What immediately comes to mind are Bedeian's (1996, p. 5–9) suggestions for optimizing scholarly careers, which apparently are still more than relevant these days:

- Hit the ground running (get a quick start by making timely first-tier publications).
- Locate the best predictor of future performance (that could be the prestige of an individual's doctoral institution, a strong publication record, personality and ability, sole-authored publications).

- Location, location, location (career success is at least partially determined by the nature of social circumstances [e.g. a critical mass of colleagues involved in researching, writing, and publishing] people find themselves in).
- Publish, publish, publish (publication means visibility, esteem, and career mobility).
- Be proactive (if you cannot say "no", you should at least avoid saying "yes" to meaningless activities).
- Do different things (at different points in your career).
- Achieve academic credibility (by fostering scholarship and classroom learning instead of striving for power and status).
- Take quantum leaps (academic accomplishments are almost invariably honored more by others than the home institution).
- Balance work and family (try not to cheat your family and yourself of irretrievable time together).
- Continue your education (update and expand your knowledge base by working with other PhD students and younger colleagues).
- Become involved in the associations (interacting with others helps you to find points of reference for your career).
- Have fun! (Do not take your career too seriously.)

Let's see how you will make it. Good luck with your academic career odyssey[2] ahead.

NOTES

1. With the help of a free online tool WordClouds.com.
2. Symbolically enough, Career Odyssey is a board game specifically designed to help students explore careers that may be good matches for their talents and interests. Students develop insight into their own talents and interests and then try to match them to careers. The game is designed for individuals ages 12 through adult and is very helpful for individuals who are looking to make a career change, entering the workforce later in life, or just looking for ways to advance their careers.

REFERENCES

Altbach, P. G., Yudkevich, M., & Rumbley, L. (2015). Academic inbreeding: Local challenge, global problem. *Asia Pacific Education Review, 16*(3), 317–330.
Amabile, T. M. (1993). Motivational synergy: Toward new conceptualizations of intrinsic and extrinsic motivation in the workplace. *Human Resource Management Review, 3*(3), 185–201.
Bandura, A. (1982). Self-efficacy mechanism in human agency. *American Psychologist, 37*(2), 122–147.
Bauer, T. N., Bodner, T., Erdogan, B., Truxillo, D. M., & Tucker, J. S. (2007). Newcomer adjustment during organizational socialization: A meta-analytic review

of antecedents, outcomes, and methods. *Journal of Applied Psychology*, *92*(3), 707–721.

Bedeian, A. G. (1996). Lessons learned along the way: Twelve suggestions for optimizing career success. In P. J. Frost, & M. S. Taylor (eds.), *Rhythms of Academic Life: Personal Accounts of Careers in Academia* (pp. 3–10). Thousand Oaks, CA: Sage Publications.

Billsberry, J., Köhler, T., Stratton, M., Cohen, M., & Taylor, M. S. (2019). From the Editors: Introduction to the Special Issue on Rhythms of Academic Life. *Academy of Management Learning & Education*, *18*(2), 119–127.

Cha, S. E., Hewlin, P. F., Roberts, L. M., Buckman, B. R., Leroy, H., Steckler, E. L., ... & Cooper, D. (2019). Being your true self at work: Integrating the fragmented research on authenticity in organizations. *Academy of Management Annals*, *13*(2), 633–671.

Demirkasimoglu, N. (2016). Knowledge hiding in academia: Is personality a key factor? *International Journal of Higher Education*, *5*(1), 128–140.

e Cunha, M. P., Clegg, S. R., & Mendonça, S. (2010). On serendipity and organizing. *European Management Journal*, *28*(5), 319–330.

Global Business Schools Report (2019, March). 20-First. Retrieved May 22, 2019 from https://20-first.com/wp-content/uploads/2019/05/1905-2019-Business-Schools -Scorecard-PDF-FINAL.pdf.

Grant, A. M. (2013). *Give and Take: A Revolutionary Approach to Success*. New York, NY: Viking.

Grant, A. M., & Ashford, S. J. (2008). The dynamics of proactivity at work. *Research in Organizational Behavior*, *28*, 3–34.

Harrington, B., & Ladge, J. J. (2009). Work–life integration: Present dynamics and future directions for organizations. *Organizational Dynamics*, *38*(2), 148–157.

Hay, I. (2017). *How to Be an Academic Superhero: Establishing and Sustaining a Successful Career in the Social Sciences, Arts and Humanities*. Cheltenham, UK and Northampton, MA, USA: Edward Elgar Publishing.

Hernaus, T., Černe, M., Connelly, C., Poloski Vokic, N., & Škerlavaj, M. (2019). Evasive knowledge hiding in academia: When competitive individuals are asked to collaborate. *Journal of Knowledge Management*, *23*(4), 597–618.

Homer (1919). *The Odyssey*. London, UK and New York, NY: W. Heinemann; G. P. Putnam's sons.

Horta, H., Veloso, F. M., & Grediaga, R. (2010). Navel gazing: Academic inbreeding and scientific productivity. *Management Science*, *56*(3), 414–429.

Horta, H., & Yudkevich, M. (2016). The role of academic inbreeding in developing higher education systems: Challenges and possible solutions. *Technological Forecasting & Social Change*, *113*, 363–372.

Hughes, T., Webber, D., & O'Regan, N. (2019). Achieving wider impact in business and management: Analysing the case studies from REF 2014. *Studies in Higher Education*, *44*(4), 628–642.

Kinman, G., & Jones, F. (2008). Effort–reward imbalance, over-commitment and work–life conflict: testing an expanded model. *Journal of Managerial Psychology*, *23*(3), 236–251.

Kirby, G. R., Goodpaster, J. R., & Levine, M. (1999). *Critical Thinking*. Englewood Cliffs, NJ: Prentice Hall.

Klijn. M., & Tomic, W. (2010). A review of creativity within organizations from a psychological perspective. *Journal of Management Development*, *29*(4), 322–343.

Kraimer, M. L., Greco, L., Seibert, S. E., & Sargent, L. D. (2019). An investigation of academic career success: The new tempo of academic life. *Academy of Management Learning & Education, 18*(2), 128–152.

Lee, Y., Berry, C. M., & Gonzalez-Mulé, E. (2019). The importance of being humble: A meta-analysis and incremental validity analysis of the relationship between honesty–humility and job performance. *Journal of Applied Psychology, 104*(12), 1535–1546.

Lerchenmueller, M. J., & Sorenson, O. (2018). The gender gap in early career transitions in the life sciences. *Research Policy, 47*(6), 1007–1017.

Mitchell, K. E., Levin, S. A., & Krumboltz, J. D. (1999). Planned happenstance: Constructing unexpected career opportunities. *Journal of Counseling & Development, 77*(2), 115–124.

Monroe, K., Ozyurt, S., Wrigley, T., & Alexander, A. (2008). Gender equality in academia: Bad news from the trenches, and some possible solutions. *Perspectives on Politics, 6*(2), 215–233.

Morgeson, F. P., Mitchell, T. R., & Liu, D. (2015). Event system theory: An event-oriented approach to the organizaional sciences. *Academy of Management Review, 40*(4), 515–537.

Nelson, M. R., & Shavitt, S. (2002). Horizontal and vertical individualism and achievement values: A multimethod examination of Denmark and the United States. *Journal of Cross-Cultural Psychology, 33*(5), 439–458.

Powell, S. (2018). Gender equality in academia: Intentions and consequences. *The International Journal of Diversity in Organizations, Communities and Nations, 18*(1), 19–35.

Pryor, R. G., & Bright, J. E. (2012). The Chaos Theory of Careers (CTC): Ten years on and only just begun. *Australian Journal of Career Development, 23*(1), 4–12.

Rosenbusch, N., Rauch, A., & Bausch, A. (2013). The mediating role of entrepreneurial orientation in the task environment–performance relationship: A meta-analysis. *Journal of Management, 39*(3), 633–659.

Seibert, S. E., Kraimer, M. L., Holtom, B. C., & Pierotti, A. J. (2013). Even the best laid plans sometimes go askew: Career self-management processes, career shocks, and the decision to pursue graduate education. *Journal of Applied Psychology, 98*(1), 169–182.

Stajkovic, A. D., & Luthans, F. (1998). Self-efficacy and work-related performance: A meta-analysis. *Psychological Bulletin, 124*(2), 240–261.

Van den Bosch, R., Taris, T. W., Schaufeli, W. B., Peeters, M. C., & Reijseger, G. (2019). Authenticity at work: A matter of fit? *The Journal of Psychology, 153*(2), 247–266.

West, J. D., Jacquet, J., King, M. M., Correll, S. J., & Bergstrom, C. T. (2013). The role of gender in scholarly authorship. *PloS one, 8*(7), e66212.

Wittenberg-Cox, A., & Symons, L. (2015, April 27). How women are faring at business schools worldwide. *Harvard Business Review*. Retrieved May 25, 2019 from https://hbr.org/2015/04/how-women-are-faring-at-business-schools-worldwide.

Yudkevich, M., Altbach, P. G., & Rumley, L., eds. (2015). *Academic Inbreeding and Mobility in Higher Education: Global Perspectives*. Palgrave Studies in Global Higher Education. London, UK: Palgrave Macmillan.

Zajacova, A., Lynch, S. M., & Espenshade, T. J. (2005). Self-efficacy, stress, and academic success in college. *Research in Higher Education, 46*(6), 677–706.

Index